DK EYEWIT

P9-DOD-251

TOP 10
ROME

REID BRAMBLETT &
JEFFREY KENNEDY

Penguin
Random
House

Top 10 Rome Highlights

The Top 10 of Everything

CONTENTS

Rome Area by Area

Streetsmart

Within each Top 10 list in this book, no hierarchy of quality or popularity is implied. All 10 are, in the editor's opinion, of roughly equal merit.

Front cover and spine View across the Tiber River towards St Peter's Basilica
Back cover The Spanish Steps
Title page Trevi Fountain

The information in this DK Eyewitness Top 10 Travel Guide is checked annually. Every effort has been made to ensure that this book is as up-to-date as possible at the time of going to press. Some details, however, such as telephone numbers, opening hours, prices, gallery hanging arrangements and travel information are liable to change. The publishers cannot accept responsibility for any consequences arising from the use of this book, nor for any material on third party websites, and cannot guarantee that any website address in this book will be a suitable source of travel information. We value the views and suggestions of our readers very highly. Please write to: Publisher, DK Eyewitness Travel Guides, Dorling Kindersley, 80 Strand, London WC2R 0RL, Great Britain, or email travelguides@dk.com

Welcome to
Rome

Eternal city. Exuberant feast for the eyes, soul and stomach. Vespas parked by Baroque portals. Evocative ruins. Valentino models and Raphael madonnas. Strong espresso and delectable gelato. Visitors, artists and pilgrims have been flocking here since antiquity. With Eyewitness Top 10 Rome, it's yours to experience.

Once the most powerful city in the world, Rome has been 2,800 years in the making. Ancient Roman columns are embedded in Renaissance palazzo walls, Egyptian obelisks are recycled in Baroque fountains and Christian churches have been built over pagan temples. Experience the city purposefully by exploring the **Forum** or the **Vatican**, or sample it casually while pausing under the **Panthcon's** massive portico (providing shade since AD 125) or going for a spin around Bernini's fountains on **Piazza Navona**, once Emperor Domitian's racetrack.

Despite its heritage, Rome feels nothing like a dusty museum, mostly thanks to its flamboyant citizens who live much of their life outdoors in cafés and piazzas, negotiating cobbled alleyways, going for their *passeggiata* and always intent on *fare la bella figura* – that very Italian concept of looking fabulous and making an impression.

Whether you are coming for a weekend or a week, our Top 10 guide is organized to show you the best of everything that Rome has to offer: grand sights like the **Sistine Chapel** and **Colosseum**; tiny piazzas and views you will never forget; stupendous works by **Michelangelo** and **Caravaggio** hidden away in churches; and the best spots for *pizza al taglio* and hearty Roman cuisine. The guide gives you useful tips, from seeking out what's free to avoiding the crowds, and 11 easy-to-follow itineraries, designed to tie together a clutch of sights in a short space of time. Add inspiring photography and detailed maps and you've got the essential pocket-sized travel companion. **Enjoy the book and enjoy Rome.**

Clockwise from top: **Musei Capitolini; Fountain of Neptune (Piazza Navona); Spanish Steps; MAXXI; mosaic at Museo Nazionale Romano; Colosseum; Sistine Chapel fresco**

Exploring Rome

Rome is packed with magnificent piazzas, beautiful palazzi, ancient monuments and churches. There is a lot to see and do, and to help you make the most of your visit here are some ideas for a two- and four-day Roman holiday. Bear in mind that you can save time by reserving tickets beforehand, and that advance booking is obligatory at Galleria Borghese.

| 0 metres | 800 |
| 0 yards | 800 |

Key
— Two-day itinerary
— Four-day itinerary

St Peter's Basilica towers magnificently over Rome and is not only a beautiful church, but is also packed with works of art by the great masters.

Two Days in Rome

Day ❶
MORNING

See the **Colosseum** (see pp26–7), then walk past the **Roman Forum** (see pp20–21) and **Imperial Fora** (see pp26–7) to the virtually-recreated villa of a patrician family at **Palazzo Valentini** (see p49). Visit **Musei Capitolini** (see pp28–31), and don't miss the bird's-eye view of the Forum.

AFTERNOON

Stroll through the *centro storico* to **Piazza Navona** (see p60) and the **Pantheon** (see pp18–19) for atmosphere, ice cream and window shopping. Cross the Tiber by Ponte Sisto to lively Trastevere for a drink.

Day ❷
MORNING

Get up early to see **St Peter's** (see pp12–17) without the crowds when it opens at 7am – an unforgettable experience. Then visit the **Vatican Museums** (see p54), preferably having booked tickets in advance.

AFTERNOON

Spend some time at the lovely **Villa Borghese** park (see p117) followed by a visit to the Bernini sculptures at **Galleria Borghese** (see pp24–5) and the Etruscan finds at **Villa Giulia** (see pp40–41). Walk back through the park to **Piazza del Popolo** (see p116) to visit **Santa Maria del Popolo** (see pp38–9), before ending the day at **Piazza di Spagna** (see p115).

Four Days in Rome

Day ❶
MORNING

Begin with the **Pantheon** (see pp18–19), then wander over to **Piazza Navona** (see p60), stopping to admire Caravaggio's works in **San Luigi dei Francesi** (see p89) and **Sant'Agostino** (see p90). Marvel at the Bernini fountains and street performers, then browse the shops around the piazza.

AFTERNOON

Head to the fantastic **Museo Nazionale Romano's Palazzo Massimo alle Terme** (see pp34–7),

The Colosseum, built in the 1st century AD, has served as the prototype for all stadiums since.

The Pantheon, constructed in the 1st century BC, is the world's best preserved Roman temple.

which has an entire frescoed room from the Villa of Livia. Wind down with an evening in appealing Monti.

Day ❷
MORNING
Explore **Ostia Antica** (see pp42–3) and return in time for lunch in Testaccio.
AFTERNOON
Visit **Santa Maria del Popolo** (see pp38–9), then explore the **Piazza di Spagna** area (see p115). Climb the **Spanish Steps** (see p115) for a great city view. Walk back to the centre via the **Trevi Fountain** (see p115).

Day ❸
MORNING
Explore the **Colosseum** (see pp26–7), then visit **Palazzo Valentini** (see p49) and the **Musei Capitolini** (see pp28–31), stopping for lunch in the museum's roof terrace café.
AFTERNOON
See the evocative ruins of the **Roman Forum and Palatine Hill** (see pp20–23), then wander through the Jewish Ghetto and vibrant Campo de' Fiori.

Day ❹
MORNING
Start early to see **St Peter's** and the **Vatican** (see pp12–17) – the children's audio guide is highly recommended for adults too – then take the tram to the stop outside **Galleria Nazionale d'Arte Moderna** (see p55) for lunch.
AFTERNOON
Visit **Villa Giulia** (see pp40–41) before taking a stroll through the park to **Galleria Borghese** (see pp24–5) – make sure to book in advance.

Top 10 Rome Highlights

Theatrical mosaic masks of Comedy and Tragedy, Musei Capitolini

🔟 Rome Highlights

The unique appeal of Rome is that it is a 2,800-year-old indoor-outdoor museum, with ancient monuments, art treasures and timeless architecture. With religion at its heart and history in its soul, it dazzles and inspires visitors time and time again.

① Vatican City

This is home to the Pope, the world's largest church, and the most incredible work of art ever created – the Sistine ceiling (see pp12–17).

② The Pantheon

The most perfectly preserved of all ancient temples, this marvel of engineering has a giant oculus forever open to the sky (see pp18–19).

③ Roman Forum

Formerly at the heart of ancient power, the forum is now evocatively empty, broken by grand arches, solitary columns and carved rubble (see pp20–21).

④ Galleria Borghese

This stunning palace is filled with Graeco-Roman, Renaissance and Baroque works (see pp24–5).

⑤ Colosseum and Imperial Fora

Imperial Rome built many impressive monuments, including this splendid amphitheatre (see pp26–7).

6 Musei Capitolini

At the ancient centre of religious Rome are some of the world's greatest masterpieces, from 4th-century BC Greek sculptures to Caravaggio's revolutionary, even scandalous, paintings *(see pp28–31)*.

7 Museo Nazionale Romano

These collections, housed at five sites, feature some of the world's finest ancient art, including stunning frescoes and mosaics and Classical sculpture *(see pp34–5)*.

8 Santa Maria del Popolo

Built over emperors' tombs, this church offers a rich display of Renaissance and Baroque art, including masterpieces by Bernini, Raphael and Caravaggio *(see pp38–9)*.

9 Villa Giulia

This elegant 16th-century villa is home to the magnificent national collection of Etruscan antiquities *(see pp40–41)*.

10 Ostia Antica

Extending over several square kilometres, the remarkable ruins of ancient Rome's main port city hold many surprises and convey a powerful sense of everyday Imperial life *(see pp42–3)*.

TOP 10 ⭐ Vatican City

The Vatican is the world's smallest nation, covering just 50 ha (120 acres), and is a theocracy of just over 550 citizens, headed by the Pope, but its sightseeing complex is beyond compare. Within its wall are the ornate St Peter's Basilica, the astonishing Sistine Chapel, apartments frescoed by Fra Angelico, Raphael and Pinturicchio, and some 10 museums. The latter include collections of Egyptian, Greek, Etruscan and Roman antiquities; Paleochristian, Renaissance and modern art; and a world-class ethnographic collection.

Sistine Chapel ③
Michelangelo's ceiling **(right)** is one of the most spectacular works of art in the world (see pp14–15).

④ Etruscan Museum
Finds from the Regolini-Galassi tomb of a noble woman (7th century BC) are the highlights here, including a bronze bed and gold and amber jewellery **(left)**.

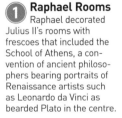

① Raphael Rooms
Raphael decorated Julius II's rooms with frescoes that included the School of Athens, a convention of ancient philosophers bearing portraits of Renaissance artists such as Leonardo da Vinci as bearded Plato in the centre.

⑤ Chapel of Nicholas V
The Vatican's hidden gem is this closet-sized chapel colourfully frescoed in 1447–50 with early martyrs by Fra Angelico.

⑥ Raphael's Transfiguration
Raphael was labouring on this gargantuan masterpiece (1517–20) when he died at 37, leaving students to finish the base. It shows Christ appearing to the Apostles in divine glory.

② Pio Clementino Museum
This museum has several famous Classical sculptures, including the contorted, Hellenistic Laocoön **(right)**, found in an Esquiline vineyard – Michelangelo saw the unearthing. There are also the Apollo Belvedere and Belvedere Torso, both huge influences on Renaissance artists.

Plan of the Vatican City

7 Egyptian Museum

The collection consists mostly of sculpture brought from Egypt for temples and private villas and gardens. There are also decorated mummy cases **(below)**, mummies and finds from a tomb that include a nit-comb.

8 Caravaggio's Deposition

Caravaggio's *chiaroscuro* technique accentuates a diagonal composition (1604) filled with peasant figures and grisly realism.

10 Borgia Apartments

Borgia pope Alexander VI had these beautiful rooms frescoed by Pinturicchio (Raphael was once his junior collaborator) between 1492 and 1495. The walls are now hung with lesser pieces from the Modern Art collection.

9 Leonardo da Vinci's St Jerome

Sketchy and unfinished – Leonardo was often a distracted genius – this 1482 painting is nevertheless an anatomical masterpiece.

NEED TO KNOW

MAP B2 ■ www.vatican.va

Museums and Sistine Chapel: Viale Vaticano 100 ■ 06 6988 3145

Open 9am–6pm Mon–Sat (last admission 4pm), 9am–2pm last Sun of the month (free); closed 1 & 6 Jan, 11 Feb, Easter, Easter Mon, 1 May, 29 Jun, 15 & 16 Aug, 1 Nov, 25, 26 & 31 Dec

Adm: €16 (€8 ISIC under 26s, under 18s)

St Peter's Basilica: Piazza San Pietro ■ 06 6988 3731

Open 7am–7pm daily (until 6:30pm Oct–Mar)

Adm: free (basilica); €6 (treasury), €6 (dome via steps), €8 (dome via lift)

■ Within the museums complex, take a break at the cafeteria (with a terrace in the Cortile della Pigna) or the pizzeria in the gardens near the Pavilion of Carriages.

■ When in town, the Pope gives a mass audience on Wednesday mornings.

Book free tickets in advance (Prefecture of the Papal Household, fax 06 6988 5863).

Museum Guide

The Vatican Museums (a 15-minute walk from St Peter's) consist of 10 collections, the Sistine Chapel and the Papal Apartments. To see highlights only, first visit the Pinacoteca, to the right of the entrance turnstile. The Sistine and other collections are to the left.

Sistine Chapel Works of Art

Detail from Michelangelo's fresco *The Creation of Adam*

1 Adam and Eve
God imparts the spark of life to Adam in one of western art's best known scenes, *The Creation of Adam*, then pulls Eve from Adam's rib.

2 Creation
God separates darkness from light, water from land and creates the Sun and Moon. Michelangelo veers towards blasphemy by depicting God's dirty feet.

3 The Sacrifice, Flood and Drunkenness of Noah
After disassembling his scaffolding and gazing up from floor level, Michelangelo noticed that these three tumultuous scenes were too minutely drawn.

4 Life of Moses Scenes
Left wall highlights include Botticelli's *The Trials of Moses* and Signorelli and della Gatta's *Moses Giving his Rod to Joshua*.

5 Sibyls and Prophets
Hebrew prophets, including Jonah, mingle with the Sibyls who foretold Christ's coming.

6 Old Testament Salvation Scenes and Ancestors of Christ
Portraits from Jesus's family tree are above the windows, and bloody Salvation scenes, including David and Goliath, are on corner spandrels.

7 Life of Christ Scenes
The chapel's right wall stars Botticelli's *Cleansing of the Leper*, Ghirlandaio's *Calling of Peter and Andrew*, and Perugino's *Christ Giving the Keys to St Peter*.

8 Christ Giving the Keys to St Peter
Classical buildings form the backdrop to this pivotal scene of transferring power from Christ to the popes. Each scene is divided into three parts.

9 Botticelli's Punishment of the Rebels
Schismatics question Aaron's priestly prerogative to burn incense. A vengeful Moses opens the earth to swallow them.

10 Last Judgement
This vast work depicts figures nude, equalized and stripped of their earthly rank. This was considered indecorous and the figures were covered by fig leaves. Saints are identified by their medieval icons.

Plan of the Sistine Chapel

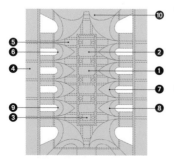

UNDERSTANDING THE SISTINE CHAPEL ART

The Sistine Chapel's frescoes are not merely decorations by some of the greatest artists of the Renaissance – the images tell a story and make a complex theological argument. Pope Sixtus IV commissioned wall frescoes for the Pope's Chapel in 1481–83. They were intended to underscore papal authority, in question at the time, by drawing a line of power from God to the pope. In the Life of Moses cycle, Moses' and Aaron's undisputed roles as God's chosen representatives are affirmed by the fate of those who oppose Aaron – significantly and anachronistically wearing a papal hat – in the *Punishment of the Rebels*. Directly across from this work, Perugino's *Christ Giving the Keys to St Peter* bridges the Old Testament with the New as Christ hands control of the church to St Peter – and therefore to his successors, the popes (who are pictured between the Sistine windows). Michelangelo's breathtaking frescoes on the ceiling (1508–12) later added Genesis, Redemption and Salvation to the story.

**TOP 10
PAINTERS OF THE
SISTINE CHAPEL**

1 **Michelangelo**
(1475–1564)

2 **Perugino** *(1450–1523)*

3 **Sandro Botticelli**
(1445–1510)

4 **Domenico
Ghirlandaio** *(c.1449–94)*

5 **Luca Signorelli**
(c.1450–1523)

6 **Rosselli** *(1439–1507)*

7 **Fra Diamante**
(1430–98)

8 **Pinturicchio**
(1454–1513)

9 **Piero di Cosimo**
(1462–1521)

10 **Bartolomeo della
Gatta** *(1448–1502)*

The Fall and Expulsion from the Garden of Eden, from Michelangelo's Genesis cycle, shows Adam and Eve being expelled from Eden for eating fruit from the forbidden Tree of Knowledge.

The Trials of Moses by Botticelli depicts scenes from the life of the prophet.

Features of St Peter's Basilica

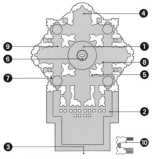

Plan of St Peter's Basilica

1 Dome

When Michelangelo designed a dome to span St Peter's massive transept, he made it 42 m (138 ft) in diameter, in deference to the Pantheon's 43.3 m (142 ft) dome. You can ride an elevator much of the way, but must still navigate by foot the final 330 stairs between the dome's inner and outer shell to the 132 m high (435 ft) lantern and sweeping vistas across the city.

2 Pietà

Michelangelo carved this statue (see p56) in 1499 at the age of only 25. It is at once graceful and

Michelangelo's
Pietà

mournful, stately and ethereal. It has been protected by glass since 1972, when a man screaming "I am Jesus Christ!" attacked it with a hammer, damaging the Virgin's nose and arm.

The magnificent Piazza San Pietro

3 Piazza San Pietro

Bernini's remarkable semi-elliptical colonnades transformed the basilica's approach into a pair of welcoming arms embracing the faithful (see p61). Sadly, the full effect of entering the square from a warren of narrow medieval streets was spoiled when Mussolini razed the neighbourhood to lay down pompous Via della Conciliazione. The obelisk came from Alexandria.

4 Apse

Bernini's exuberantly Baroque stained-glass window (1666) centres on a dove representing the Holy Ghost, surrounded by rays of the sun and a riot of sculptural details. Beneath the window sits the Chair of St Peter (1665), another Bernini concoction; inside is a wood and ivory chair said to be the actual throne of St Peter. Bernini also crafted the multicoloured marble *Monument to Urban VIII* (1644) to the right, based on Michelangelo's Medici tombs in Florence. It is of far better artistic quality than Guglielmo della Porta's similar one for Pope Paul III (1549) to the left.

5 Statue of St Peter

A holdover from the medieval St Peter's, this 13th-century bronze statue by the sculptor Arnolfo di Cambio has achieved holy status. The faithful can be seen lining up to rub (or kiss) Peter's well-worn foot for good luck.

6 Baldacchino

Whether you view it as ostentatious or glorious, Bernini's huge Baroque sculpted canopy above the high altar is at least impressive. Its spiralling bronze columns are said to have been made from the revetments (portico ceiling decorations) of the Pantheon (see pp18–19), taken by Pope Urban VIII. For his desecration of the ancient Roman temple the Barberini pope and his family (see pp58–9) were castigated

Crux Vaticana or the Cross of Justin II

with the waggish quip: "What even the barbarians wouldn't do, Barberini did."

7 Treasury

Among the ecclesiastical treasures here is a 6th-century, jewel-encrusted bronze cross – the Crux Vaticana – various fragments of the medieval basilica including a ciborium by Donatello (1432), and Antonio Pollaiuolo's masterful bronze slab tomb (1493) for Sixtus IV, the pope's effigy surrounded by representations of theological virtues and liberal arts.

8 Grottoes

Many of the medieval basilica's monuments are housed beneath the basilica's floor. During excavations in the 1940s, workers discovered in the Necropolis the legendary Red Wall behind which St Peter was supposedly buried. The wall was covered with early medieval graffiti invoking the saint, and a box of bones was found behind it. The late Pope John Paul II was buried in the crypt after his death in 2005.

9 Alexander VII's Monument

One of Bernini's last works (1678) shows figures of Justice, Truth, Chastity and Prudence gazing up at the pontiff seated in the deep shadows of the niche. A skeleton crawls from under the flowing marble drapery to hold aloft an hourglass as a reminder of mortality.

10 Vision of Constantine

The most dramatic statue in the basilica, this rearing equestrian figure shows Emperor Constantine at the moment in which he had a vision of the Cross at the Battle of the Milvian Bridge in 312 AD. Victorious, Constantine converted to Christianity and made it the official religion of the Empire.

Bernini's ornate *baldacchino*

TOP10 ⭐ The Pantheon

When Emperor Phocas donated this pagan temple to Pope Boniface IV in 608, he unwittingly ensured that one of the marvels of ancient Rome would be preserved unaltered in its new guise as the Christian church of Santa Maria ad Martyres. Designed by Emperor Hadrian in AD 118–25, it has been lightly sacked over the ages, yet the airy interior and perfect proportions remain, a wonder of the world even in its own time.

① Dome
The widest masonry dome in Europe is precisely as high as it is wide: 43.3 m (142 ft). Its airy, coffered space, cleverly shot through with a shaft of sunlight from the oculus, is what lends the Pantheon an ethereal air.

④ Oculus
The bold 8.3 m (27 ft) wide hole at the centre of the massive dome **(right)** provides light and structural support: the tension around its ring helps hold the weight of the dome.

⑥ Doors
The massive bronze doors are technically original, but were so extensively renovated under Pope Pius IV (1653) that they have been practically recast.

⑦ Marble Decorations
Red porphyry, giallo antico, and other ancient marbles grace the interior. More than half the polychrome panels cladding the walls are original, the rest careful reproductions, as is the floor **(below)**.

② Walls
The 6.2 m (20 ft) thick walls incorporate built-in brick arches to help distribute the weight downwards, relieving the stress of the heavy roof.

⑤ Portico
The triangular pediment **(above)** is supported by 16 pink and grey granite columns, all original save the three on the left (17th-century copies).

③ Royal Tombs
Two of Italy's kings are honoured by simple tombs. Vittorio Emanuele II (1861–78) unified Italy and became its first king. His son, Umberto I, was assassinated in 1900.

8 Fountain

Giacomo della Porta designed this stoop; Leonardo Sormani carved it in 1575. The marble basin was replaced by a stone one and the Egyptian obelisk of Rameses II was added in 1711 **(left)**.

9 Raphael's Tomb

Raphael, darling of the Renaissance art world but dead at 37, rests in a plain, ancient stone sarcophagus **(right)**. Poet Bembo's Latin epitaph says: "Here lies Raphael, whom Nature feared would outdo her while alive, but now that he is gone fears she, too, will die." Other artists buried here include Baldassare Peruzzi.

10 Basilica of Neptune Remains

Of the Pantheon's old neighbour, all that remains are an elaborate cornice and fluted columns against the Pantheon's rear wall.

THE FIRST PANTHEON

Emperor Augustus's son-in-law, Marcus Agrippa, built the first Pantheon in 27 BC, replaced in AD 118-125 by Hadrian's rotunda. The pediment's inscription "*M. Agrippa cos tertium fecit*" ("M. Agrippa made this") was Hadrian's modest way of honouring Agrippa. The pediment also provided the illusion of a smaller temple, making the massive space inside even more of a surprise (the Pantheon was originally raised and you couldn't see the dome behind). Bernini's "ass ears", tiny towers he added to the pediment, were removed in 1883.

NEED TO KNOW

MAP M3 ▪ Piazza della Rotonda ▪ 06 6830 0230

Open 9am–7:30pm Mon–Sat, 9am–6pm Sun (9am–1pm during hols); Mass: 10:30am Sun and 5pm Sat; closed 1 Jan, 1 May, 25 Dec

Free

▪ There's a good gelateria, Cremeria Monteforte *(see p102)*, on the Pantheon's right flank, and an excellent coffee shop, La Tazza d'Oro, just off the square *(see p79)*.

▪ Rather than bemoan a rainy day in Rome, head to the Pantheon to watch the water fall gracefully though the oculus and spatter on the marble floor and down a drain. Snowfall is even better.

🔟 ⭐ Roman Forum

Gazing on the picturesque ruins today, one would hardly guess that the Forum was the symbol of civic pride for 1,000 years. Its beginning, more than 3,000 years ago, was as a cemetery for the village on Palatine Hill. When the marshy land was drained in the 6th century BC, the Forum took on a more central role. It was at its most elegant starting with the reign of Augustus, who is said to have turned the city from brick to marble.

1 Temple of Vesta and House of the Vestal Virgins

A graceful round temple and its adjacent palace were the centre for one of the city's most revered cults. Noble priestesses tended the sacred flame and enjoyed the greatest privileges.

3 Arch of Septimius Severus

This well-preserved triumphal arch **(below)** celebrates the emperor's Middle Eastern victories. It was erected in AD 203 by his sons, Geta and Caracalla, then co-emperors.

2 Curia

The 3rd-century-AD Senate retains its original polychrome inlaid floor, its risers, where the 300 senators sat in deliberation, and the speaker's platform. For 2nd-century views of the Forum, examine the large marble reliefs, showing Emperor Trajan's good works.

4 Temple of Castor and Pollux

Three Corinthian columns remain of this temple **(left)** to the Dioscuri – twin brothers of Helen of Troy and sons of Jupiter and Leda. It marked the spot where they miraculously appeared in 499 BC to announce a crucial Roman victory.

6 Arch of Titus

The oldest extant arch in Rome was built in AD 81 by Emperor Domitian to honour his brother, Titus, and his father, Vespasian, for putting down the Jewish Revolt. Reliefs show the sacking of Jerusalem's Holy of Holies and sacred objects, such as a golden menorah, being taken.

5 Basilica of Maxentius and Constantine

Three vast, coffered barrel vaults proclaim the Forum's largest structure, built around AD 315 and used as the legal and financial centre of the Empire.

Original Plan of the Roman Forum

IMPERIAL FORA
see page 27

VIA DEI FORI IMPERIALI

(7) Temple of Vespasian
Until 18th-century excavations, these graceful columns (AD 79) from a temple to the former emperor stood mostly buried beneath centuries of detritus.

(8) Temple of Antoninus and Faustina
Dedicated by Antoninus Pius in AD 41 to his deified wife Faustina, this is one of the best preserved temples **(above)**. With its Baroque-style top-knot, it is also one of the oddest. Note the carvings of griffins along the side frieze.

(9) Via Sacra
Paved with broad, flat, black basalt stones, Rome's oldest road wound from the Arch of Titus through the Forum and up to the Capitoline. Triumphal processions were staged here, but it degenerated into a hang-out for gossips, pick-pockets and other idlers.

(10) Temple of Saturn
Eight grey-and-red Ionic columns **(left)** constitute what's left of this temple (also the state treasury) to the ruler of agriculture and of a mythic "Golden Age." Saturnalia, celebrated each December, was very similar to modern-day Christmas.

NEED TO KNOW

MAP Q5 ■ Via dei Fori Imperiali ■ 06 3996 7700

Open 1 Nov–15 Feb: 8:30am–4:30pm daily; 16 Feb–15 Mar: 8:30am–5pm daily; 16–31 Mar: 8:30am–5:30pm daily; 1 Apr–31 Aug: 8:30am–7:15pm daily; Sep: 8:30am–7pm daily; Oct: 8:30am–6:30pm daily; closed 1 Jan, 25 Dec

Adm: €12 (includes Palatine & Colosseum; valid for 48 hrs); free for under 18s; free for all first Sun of the month

■ The only option in the immediate area for drinks and snacks is one of the mobile refreshment vendors. For something more substantial, there are plenty of cafés and restaurants on Via Cavour.

■ In summer, it's best to visit the Forum either early or late in the day, to avoid the intense heat.

Forum Guide
You can access the Forum from Via Dei Fori Imperiali. However, for a great view of the whole site, enter from one of the high points at either end. From the northwest end, begin on the Capitoline (to the right and behind the huge, white Victor Emmanuel Monument) and take the stairs down from Largo Romolo e Remo. From the southeast end, start at the Colosseum (see pp26–7) and climb the small hill just to the northwest. Enter by the Arch of Titus, which is also near the main entry gate to the Palatine.

Palatine Hill Features

The ruins of Domus Augustana

1 Domus Flavia
Marked today mainly by the remains of two fountains, this imposing edifice was the official wing of a vast emperors' palace, built by Domitian in AD 81.

2 Livia's House
This 1st-century BC structure, now below ground level, formed part of the residence of Augustus and his second wife. Here you can examine a number of mosaic pavements and wall frescoes.

3 Palatine Museum and Antiquarium
This former convent houses a wealth of artifacts unearthed here, including pottery, statuary, ancient graffiti and very fine mosaics. You can also study a model of the Iron Age Palatine.

4 Romulus's Iron-Age Huts
Traces of the three 9th-century BC huts were uncovered in the 1940s. Legend says that this tiny village was founded by Romulus, who gave Rome its name *(see p46)*.

5 Stadium
Possibly a racetrack, or just a large garden, this sunken rectangle formed part of Domitian's palatial 1st-century abode.

6 Domus Augustana
All that remains of the private wing of Emperor Domitian's imperial extravaganza are the massive sub-structure vaults.

7 Temple of Cybele
The orgiastic cult of the Great Mother was the first of the Oriental religions to come to Rome, in 191 BC. Still here is a decapitated statue of the goddess. Priests worshipping Cybele ritually castrated themselves.

8 Farnese Gardens
Plants and elegant pavilions grace part of what was once an extensive pleasure-garden, designed by the noted architect Vignola and built in the 16th century over the ruins of Tiberius's palace.

Pavilions at the Farnese Gardens

9 Cryptoporticus
This series of underground corridors, their vaults decorated with delicate stucco reliefs, stretches 130 m (425 ft). It connected the Palatine to Nero's fabulous Domus Aurea or Golden House *(see p133)*.

10 Domus Septimius Severus
Huge arches and broken walls are all that remain of this emperor's 2nd-century AD extension to the Domus Augustana.

A DAY IN THE LIFE OF A ROMAN HOUSEHOLD

Most Romans lived in *insulae*, apartment buildings of perhaps six floors, with the poorest residents occupying the cheaper upper floors. An average Roman male citizen arose before dawn, arranged his toga, and breakfasted on a piece of bread. Then out into the alleys, reverberating with noise. First, a stop at a public latrine, where he chatted with neighbours. Next a visit to his honoured patron, who paid him his daily stipend. Lunch might be a piece of bread dipped in wine or olive oil, perhaps with a bit of cold meat. Bathing waited until late afternoon, when he met his friends at the public baths. There he lingered – conversing, exercising, reading, or admiring the artwork – until dinnertime. The main meal of the day was taken lying on couches, with his slaves in attendance. Then it was bedtime. Roman matrons, apart from their time at the baths (usually earlier than the men), spent the entire day at home, running the household.

Roman toga

TOP 10 ANCIENT ROMAN BELIEF SYSTEMS

1 State Religion of Graeco-Roman Gods (especially the Capitol Triad: Jupiter, Juno, Minerva)

2 Household Gods: Ancestors and Genii

3 Cult of Cybele, the Great Mother

4 Deification of Emperors, Empresses and Favourites

5 Orgiastic Fertility Cults

6 Mithraism

7 Cult of Attis

8 Cult of Isis

9 Cult of Serapis

10 Judeo-Christianity

Feasts held by wealthy Romans were usually extravagant affairs, served by slaves and eaten lying on couches, sometimes under garden pergolas.

TOP 10 ⭐ Galleria Borghese

The Borghese Gallery is one of the world's greatest small museums. Some of Bernini's best sculptures and Caravaggio's paintings sit alongside Classical, Renaissance and Neo-Classical works in a beautiful frescoed 17th-century villa set in the Villa Borghese park, all of which once belonged to the great art-lover of the early Baroque, Cardinal Scipione Borghese. He patronized the young Bernini and Caravaggio, in the process amassing one of Rome's richest private collections.

Sleeping Hermaphrodite ⑤
A Roman marble copy **(left)** of a notorious Greek bronze sculpture mentioned by Pliny. Walk around what appears to be a sleeping woman, to discover the reason for its notoriety.

① Bernini's Apollo and Daphne
A climactic moment frozen in marble (1622–5). As Apollo is inches from grabbing Daphne, the pitying gods transform her into a laurel.

③ Bernini's David
Young Bernini's *David* (1623–4) was the Baroque answer to Michelangelo's Renaissance version. The frowning face is a self-portrait.

⑥ Canova's Pauline Bonaparte
Napoleon's sister caused a scandal with this half-naked portrait (1805–8), lounging like a Classical goddess on a cushion carved of marble.

② Titian's Sacred and Profane Love
Titian's allegorical scene (1514), painted for a wedding, exhorts the young bride that worldly love is part of the divine, and that sex is an extension of holy matrimony **(above)**.

④ Bernini's Rape of Persephone
Bernini carved this masterpiece at the age of 23 (1621–2). Muscular Hades throws his head back with laughter, his strong fingers pressing into the maiden's soft flesh as she struggles to break free of his grasp **(right)**.

7 Caravaggio's Self-Portrait as a Sick Bacchus

This early self-portrait (1593) as the wine god was painted with painstaking detail, supposedly when the artist was ill. It shows finer brushwork than later works.

8 Raphael's Deposition

The Borghese's most famous painting (1507), although neither the gallery's nor Raphael's best **(below)**.

The Perugian matriarch Atalanta Baglioni commissioned it to honour her assassinated son (perhaps the red-shirted pall-bearer).

Key to Floorplan
- First floor
- Ground floor

Bernini's Aeneas and Anchises **9**

Titian's Sacred and Profane Love **2**

Raphael's Deposition **8**

Caravaggio's Self-Portrait as a Sick Bacchus **7**

10 Correggio's Danae

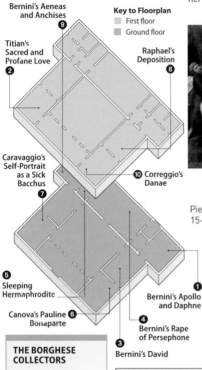

5 Sleeping Hermaphrodite

Canova's Pauline Bonaparte **6**

1 Bernini's Apollo and Daphne

4 Bernini's Rape of Persephone

3 Bernini's David

9 Bernini's Aeneas and Anchises

Pietro Bernini was still guiding his 15-year-old son in this 1613 work. The carving is more timid and static than in later works, but the genius is already evident.

10 Correggio's Danae

A sensual masterpiece (1531) based on Ovid's *Melamorphoses*. Cupid pulls back the sheets as Jupiter, the golden shower above her head, rains his love over Danae.

THE BORGHESE COLLECTORS

Scipione used this 17th-century villa as a showplace for a stupendous antiquities collection given to him by his uncle, Pope Paul V, to which he added sculptures by the young Bernini. When Camillo Borghese married Pauline Bonaparte, he donated the bulk of the Classical sculpture collection to his brother-in-law Napoleon in 1809. They now form the core of the Louvre's antiquities wing in Paris.

NEED TO KNOW

MAP E1 ■ Villa Borghese, off Via Pinciana ■ 06 328 10 ■ www.galleriaborghese. beniculturali.it, www. gebart.it (for reservations)

Open 9am–7pm Tue–Sun; closed 1 Jan, 25 Dec

Adm: €15; €8.50 students 18–25; €2 EU citizens under 18 and journalists (prices may change during exhibitions); free first Sun of the month; max. viewing time 2 hours (mandatory exit after that)

■ There's a decent café in the museum basement, although the Caffè delle Arti (06 3265 1236) at the nearby Galleria Nazionale d'Arte Moderna is better, with a park view.

■ Entrance to the gallery is strictly by reservation. Make sure you book well ahead of time – entries are strictly timed and tickets often sell out days, even weeks, in advance, especially if an exhibition is on.

The Colosseum and Imperial Fora

This rich archaeological zone, rudely intruded upon by Mussolini's Via dei Fori Imperiali, contains some of the most grandiose and noteworthy of Rome's ancient remains. Dominating the area is the mighty shell of the Colosseum, constructed in AD 72–80 under the Flavian emperors and originally known as the Flavian Amphitheatre. The Comune di Roma is constantly working on excavating the area and new discoveries are made every year.

Trajan's Column

1 Trajan's Forum and Column

Trajan's Forum left all who beheld it awed by its splendid nobility. Now cut off by modern roads, all that stands out is the magnificent column, commemorating in fine graphic detail the emperor's victories in what is now Romania. Access to part of it is through Trajan's Market.

3 Trajan's Markets

The emperor and his visionary architect, Apollodorus of Damascus, built this attractive, very modern looking shopping and office mall **(below)** in the early 2nd century AD. There were 150 spaces in all, the top floor utilized by welfare offices, the lower levels by shops of all kinds.

5 Colosseum

Built by Jewish slaves, this magnificent structure was where the imperial passion for bloody spectacle reached its peak of excess. When Emperor Titus inaugurated the amphitheatre **(above)** in AD 80, he declared 100 days of celebratory games, some involving the massacre of 5,000 wild beasts, such as lions. This slaughter-as-sport was finally banned in AD 523 *(see p48)*.

2 Domus Aurea

A result of the mad emperor Nero's self-indulgence, this "golden house" was the largest, most sumptuous palace Rome ever saw, yet it was for amusement only *(see p133)*. It covered several acres and had every luxury. Currently closed for restoration.

4 Mamertine Prison

Legend holds that Sts Peter and Paul were imprisoned here. Prisoners were dropped down through a hole in the floor and the only exit was death, often from starvation *(see p63)*.

6 House of the Knights of Rhodes

This 12th-century priory was owned by the crusading order of the Knights of Rhodes. Inside are the original portico, three shops and the Chapel of St John.

7 Arch of Constantine

This arch marks the victory of the first Christian emperor over his rival emperor Maxentius (see p46). Yet it is mostly a pastiche of pagan elements taken from several earlier monuments – the beautiful hunt-scene roundels come from a temple dedicated to Emperor Hadrian's male lover, Antinous.

Original Plan of the Imperial Fora

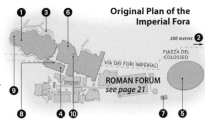

300 metres

PIAZZA DEL COLOSSEO

VIA DEI FORI IMPERIALI

ROMAN FORUM
see page 21

8 Forum of Julius Caesar

The first of Rome's great Imperial Fora. Caesar's line, the Julians, traced their ancestry back to Venus herself, so he erected the Temple of Venus Genetrix in 46 BC and placed there statues of himself and his great love Cleopatra, the queen of Egypt.

9 Palazzo Valentini

In 2005 two imperial Roman villas, retaining a spa bath, courtyards and traces of frescoed walls and mosaic floors, were found below Palazzo Valentini (see p49).

10 Forum of Augustus

Julius Caesar's successor (see p38) made the focus of his forum the Temple of Mars the Avenger (above), identified by the broad staircase and four Corinthian columns.

NEED TO KNOW

Colosseum: **MAP R6**
■ Piazza del Colosseo
■ www.coopculture.it

Open 8:30am–1 hr before sunset daily; closed 1 Jan, 1 May & 25 Dec

Adm: €12 (includes the Palatine & Roman Forum); concessions €7.50; free for under 18s; free for all first Sun of the month

Trajan's Markets: **MAP P4**
■ Via IV Novembre ■ www.mercatiditraiano.it

Open 9am–7:30pm daily; closed 1 Jan, 1 May & 25 Dec

Adm: €11.50; concessions €9.50; free for under 6s; free for all first Sun of the month

Mamertine Prison: **MAP P5** ■ Clivo Argentario 1 ■ 06 698 961 ■ www.tullianum.org

Open 8:30am–4:30pm daily (for more details, check website)

Adm: €10 (€5 for those aged 6–17 years) ; free first Sun of the month

■ A friendly place for a light meal is Caffè Valorani at Largo Corrado Ricci 30.
■ Student guides at the Colosseum work for tips and bring the place to life.
■ Via dei Fori Imperiali is pedestrianised to let visitors walk around the site.

Area Guide
Allow 3 hours to explore the site. Expect to queue for the Colosseum. The Forum of Augustus can be viewed from Via dei Fori Imperiali.

TOP 10 ⭐ Musei Capitolini

Ancient Rome's religious heart, Capitoline Hill now houses a magnificent museum. Take the Cordonata uphill, a theatrical experience planned by Michelangelo in the 16th century. At the top stands a statue of Marcus Aurelius in a star-shaped piazza, which is bordered by twin palaces containing some of Rome's greatest treasures. The collections in the Palazzo Nuovo (this page) and Palazzo dei Conservatori (overleaf) were established in 1471 with a donation of bronzes by Pope Sixtus IV.

3 Hall of the Emperors

The hall contains several portraits of the emperors and empresses of the Imperial Age. Among them is a bust of the brutal ruler Emperor Caracalla from the 3rd century AD.

4 Resting Satyr

Used to adorn an ancient grove or fountain, this young mythological creature is a copy of a 4th-century BC original by Greek sculptor Praxiteles. His pointed ears, panther-skin cape and flute are attributes of the nature god Pan. It inspired Nathaniel Hawthorne's novel *The Marble Faun (see p64)*.

1 Mosaic of the Masks

This floor mosaic of two Greek theatre masks is probably from the 2nd century AD. The use of perspective, light and shadow is highly skilled, employing small squares of marble to create dramatic effects (above).

2 Capitoline Venus

This fine 1st-century BC copy of a Praxiteles Aphrodite from the 4th century BC shows the goddess of love risen voluptuously from her bath, attempting to cover herself, as if reacting to someone's arrival.

NEED TO KNOW

MAP N5 ■ Piazza del Campidoglio ■ 06 0608 ■ www.museicapitolini.org

Open 9:30am–7:30pm daily; closed 1 Jan, 1 May, 25 Dec

Adm: €11.50 (free for under 6s); €15 during major exhibitions

The Capitolini Card costs €12.50 and is valid for 7 days. The card also gives admission to Centrale Montemartini (see p156).

■ The café behind the Palazzo dei Conservatori (Caffè Capitolino) has a terrace with a spectacular panorama of the city.

■ Part of the underground passage between the two museums is the ancient Tabularium, imperial Rome's Hall of Records, which offers an unusual view of the Roman Forum.

Museum Guide
The Palazzo Nuovo, on the left as you enter the piazza, contains mostly restored ancient sculpture. The finest pieces are on the upper floor. Take the stairs down to the underpass leading to the Palazzo dei Conservatori (see pp30–31) – the courtyard displays ancient marble fragments. The next floor up displays 16th-and 17th-century decorations and Classical statuary. On the top floor are paintings from the Renaissance and Baroque periods.

Marforio 5
This hirsute reclining giant **(right)** was originally a river god, and is believed to have come from the Forum of Augustus *(see p27)*. A Renaissance sculptor added the attributes of the god Ocean and placed him here, as overseer of this courtyard fountain.

Mosaic of the Doves 6
Once the centrepiece of a floor decoration in Hadrian's Villa *(see p158)*, this jewel-like composition **(above)** uses tiny marble and glass *tesserae* (chips) to achieve a sense of texture and volume.

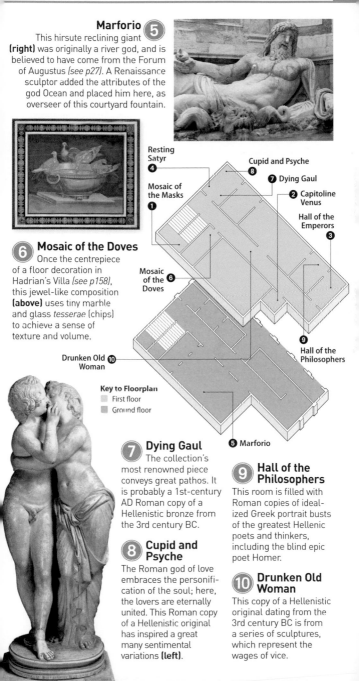

Resting Satyr 4

Mosaic of the Masks 1

Cupid and Psyche 8

Dying Gaul 7

Capitoline Venus 2

Hall of the Emperors 3

Mosaic of the Doves 6

Hall of the Philosophers 9

Drunken Old Woman 10

Key to Floorplan
First floor
Ground floor

Marforio 5

Dying Gaul 7
The collection's most renowned piece conveys great pathos. It is probably a 1st-century AD Roman copy of a Hellenistic bronze from the 3rd century BC.

Cupid and Psyche 8
The Roman god of love embraces the personification of the soul; here, the lovers are eternally united. This Roman copy of a Hellenistic original has inspired a great many sentimental variations **(left)**.

Hall of the Philosophers 9
This room is filled with Roman copies of idealized Greek portrait busts of the greatest Hellenic poets and thinkers, including the blind epic poet Homer.

Drunken Old Woman 10
This copy of a Hellenistic original dating from the 3rd century BC is from a series of sculptures, which represent the wages of vice.

Palazzo dei Conservatori Exhibits

Head, Colossal Statue of Constantine

1 Colossal Statue of Constantine Fragments

Found in the ruins of the Basilica of Maxentius and Constantine, these surreal outsized body parts (c.AD 313–24) formed the unclothed segments of an overwhelming seated effigy of the first Christian emperor, recognizable by his protuberant eyes. The rest of the sculpture was made of carved wood dressed in sheets of bronze.

2 Lo Spinario

One of the precious bronzes that comprised Sixtus IV's donation to the people of Rome, this charming sculpture dates from the 1st century BC. Hellenistic in its everyday subject matter, the head recalls more archaic models. The boy's unusual and graceful pose inspired many works during the Renaissance.

3 Caravaggio's St John the Baptist

Shocking in its sensuality, the boy's erotic pose, his arm around the ram, created an iconographic revolution when it was unveiled around 1600. Masterful *chiaroscuro* brought the holy image even more down to earth.

4 Bronze She-Wolf

The most ancient symbol of Rome, from the 5th century BC, of Etruscan or Greek workmanship. The she-wolf stands guard, at once a protectress and a nurturer, as the twins Romulus and Remus (see p46) feed on her milk. This was also part of the 1471 donation of Pope Sixtus IV.

Bronze statue of the Roman She-Wolf

5 Guercino's Burial of St Petronilla

The influence of Caravaggio is clearly evident in this huge altarpiece, executed for St Peter's Basilica between 1621 and 1623. Powerful effects of light and dark combined with pronounced musculature and individuality of the figures bring the work directly into the viewer's physical world.

6 Caravaggio's Gypsy Fortune-Teller

An earlier work by Caravaggio, but just as revolutionary as his St John

Palazzo dei Conservatori Floorplan

- 5
- 3
- 6
- 8
- 7
- 10
- 9
- 2
- 4
- 1

Key to Floorplan
- Second floor
- First floor
- Ground floor

Pietro da Cortona's Baroque artwork *Rape of the Sabines*

the Baptist. This subject is taken from everyday street life in late 16th-century Rome, which the painter knew intimately. Notice that the gypsy is slyly slipping the ring from the unsuspecting young dandy's finger.

7 Bust of Lucius Junius Brutus

Dating from between the 4th and 3rd centuries BC, this bronze bust is possibly the rarest object in the museum. Its identification as the first Roman consul is uncertain, because it also resembles Greek models of poets and philosophers. Its intense, inlaid glass eyes make it one of the most gripping portraits.

8 Pietro da Cortona's Rape of the Sabines

Baroque painting is said to have begun with this work (c.1630), where symmetry is abandoned and all is twisting, dynamic move-ment. It shows an early episode in

Roman history: the new city had been founded but the population lacked women, so they stole those of the neighbouring Sabine tribe (see p46).

9 Bust of Commodus as Hercules

The 2nd-century emperor, who loved to fight wild animals in the Colosseum, had himself represented as the demigod Hercules, to promote his own divinity. The club held in his right hand, the lion's mantle and the apples of the Hesperides in his left hand are all symbols of the labours of Hercules.

10 Equestrian Statue of Marcus Aurelius

A copy of this 2nd-century AD bronze masterpiece stands in the centre of the Capitoline star; the larger-than-life original is displayed in a glassed-in courtyard within the Palazzo dei Conservatori.

Equestrian statue of Marcus Aurelius

TOP 10 ⭐ Museo Nazionale Romano

The National Museum of Rome (MNR) is split across five sites. Much of the sculpture is at Palazzo Altemps (overleaf), while some of the best individual pieces, mosaics and frescoes are at Palazzo Massimo alle Terme (this page). Aula Ottagona has oversized bathhouse statues and the Baths of Diocletian house the epigraphic and *stele* collection. Crypta Balbi features remnants of ancient Roman city blocks and a 13 BC portico.

1 Statue of Augustus

The statue of Rome's first emperor once stood on Via Labicana. It shows him wearing his toga draped over his head – a sign that, in AD 12, he added the title *Pontifex Maximus* (high priest) to the list of honours he assigned himself.

2 Boats of Nemi

These elaborate bronzes (including lions, wolves and a head of Medusa) once decorated the two luxury boats that Emperor Caligula kept on the Lake of Nemi. The boats, used for parties, even had central heating.

3 House of Livia

These frescoes (20–10 BC) depicting a lush garden came from the villa of Augustus's wife, Livia **(above)**. They were in the *triclinium*, a dining room half-buried to keep it cool in summer.

4 Leucotea Nursing Dionysus

Discovered in 1879, a luxuriously frescoed villa included this bedroom scene of a nymph nursing the wine god **(above)** with additional scenes in the niches.

5 Wounded Niobid

Sculpted around 440 BC for a Greek temple and later acquired by Julius Caesar, this hauntingly beautiful figure of Niobid (daughter of Queen Niobe) is reaching for the fatal arrow that killed her siblings.

6 Discus Thrower

This 2nd-century AD marble copy **(right)** of the famous 450 BC Greek original by Myron is faithful to the point of imitating the original bronze's imperfect dimensions.

7 Four Charioteers Mosaic

The imperial Severi family must have been passionate about sports to have decorated a bedroom of their 3rd-century AD villa with these charioteers **(right)**. They are dressed in the traditional colours of the four factions of the Roman circus.

Previous pages the ruins of the Roman Forum

⑧ Bronze Dionysus

Few large Classical bronzes survive today, making this 2nd-century AD statue special beyond its obvious grace, skill and preserved decoration. You can still see the yellow eyes, red lips and a comb band in the grape-festooned hair.

⑨ Ivory Mask of Apollo

This exquisite mask was discovered by illegal excavators in 1995 near Lake Bracciano, northwest of Rome, and intercepted by the Carabinieri. It formed part of a larger chryselephantine statue – one whose face, hands and feet were made of ivory, placed on a wooden frame and "dressed" with textiles and gold.

⑩ Boxer at Rest

No idealised athlete, this is a muscled, tough, middle-aged man, resting between bouts, naked except for the leather strips binding his fists. Red copper highlights make his bruises look fresh **(below)**.

NEED TO KNOW

Palazzo Massimo alle Terme:
MAP F3 ■ Largo di Villa Peretti 1 ■ 06 3996 7700
Open 9am–7:45pm Tue–Sun; closed 1 Jan & 25 Dec

Palazzo Altemps: **MAP L2**
■ Piazza Sant'Apollinare 46 ■ 06 3996 7700
Open 9am–7:45pm Tue–Sun; closed 1 Jan & 25 Dec

Adm: the €7 ticket (valid 7 days) gives admission to all Museo Nazionale Romano sites; tickets cost an extra €3 for exhibitions; free first Sun of the month

■ From Palazzo Massimo alle Terme, walk down Via Nazionale for snack bars and restaurants. After exploring Palazzo Altemps, pop into Tre Scalini *(see p94)* on Piazza Navona for refreshments.

■ Call ahead for Palazzo Massimo alle Terme tickets, as the frescoes and mosaics on the top floor are timed-entry only.

Gallery Guide

Palazzo Massimo alle Terme exhibits its Republican and Early Imperial Rome (up to Augustus) statuary on the ground floor, along with a few precious older Greek pieces. The first floor exhibits art reflecting the political, cultural and economic spheres of Imperial Rome up to the 4th century. The second floor, which requires a timed-entry ticket, displays wonderful ancient mosaics and frescoes. In the basement, the numismatic collection illustrates the history of money from its origins. There is also ancient gold jewellery and a mummified eight-year-old girl.

Palazzo Altemps Collection

Dionysus with Satyr

1 Athena Parthenos

The 1st-century BC Greek sculptor Antioco carved this statue to match the most famed sculpture in antiquity, the long-lost Athena in Athens' Parthenon.

2 "Grande Ludovisi" Sarcophagus
This mid-3rd century AD sarcophagus, deeply carved and remarkably well-preserved, shows the Romans victorious over the barbarian Ostrogoth hordes.

3 Orestes and Electra

This 1st-century AD statue was carved by Menelaus, an imitator of the great Greek artist Praxiteles. The scraps of 15th-century fresco nearby depict some wedding gifts from the marriage of Girolamo Riario and Caterina Sforza.

4 Garden of Delights Loggia
The loggia frescoes (c.1595) are a catalogue of the exotic fruits, plants and animals then being imported from the New World.

5 Dionysus with Satyr

Imperial Rome was in love with Greek sculpture, producing copies such as this grouping of Dionysus, a satyr and a panther.

6 Ludovisi Throne
This set of 5th-century BC reliefs came to Rome from a Calabrian Greek colony and were discovered in the 19th century.

7 Apollo Playing the Lute
There are two 1st-century AD Apollos in the museum, both restored in the 17th century.

8 Suicidal Gaul
This suicidal figure supporting his dead wife's arm was part of a trio, including the Capitoline's Dying Gaul (see p28) commissioned by Julius Caesar to celebrate a Gaulish victory.

9 Egyptian Statuary
The Egyptian collections are divided into three sections related to that culture's influence on Rome: political theological, popular worship and places of worship. The showpiece is the impressive granite *Bull Api*, or *Brancaccio Bull* (2nd century BC).

10 Colossal Head of Ludovisi Hera
Goethe called this his "first love in Rome". It is believed to be a portrait of Claudius's mother, Antonia.

Garden of Delights Loggia

ANCIENT ROMAN ART

Ancient Rome's art was as conservative as its culture. From the middle Republican to the Imperial era, Romans shunned original sculpture for copies of famous Greek works. The Caesars imported Golden Age statuary from Greece, and Roman workshops churned out toga-wearing headless figures in stock poses to which any bust could be affixed. Romans excelled at bust portraiture, especially up to the early Imperial age when naturalism was still in vogue. Roman painting is divided into styles based on Pompeii examples. The First Style imitated marble; the Second Style imitated architecture, often set within the small painted scenes that became a hallmark of the Third Style. The Fourth Style was *trompe l'oeil* decoration. Mosaic, first developed as a floor-strengthening technique, could be simple black-on-white, or intricate work with shading and contour. *Opus sectile* (inlaid marble) was a style that was imported from the East.

The Ludovisi Throne is a sculpted marble block depicting the birth of Aphrodite. The goddess is seen rising from the sea wearing finely carved diaphanous drapery.

A 2nd-century BC Roman mosaic at the Museo Nazionale Romano

📻 ⭐ Santa Maria del Popolo

Few churches are such perfect primers on Roman art and architecture. Masters from the Early Renaissance (Bramante, Pinturicchio), High Renaissance (Raphael) and Baroque (Caravaggio, Bernini) exercised their genius in all disciplines here: painting, sculpture, architecture and decoration. It's also one of the few churches with major chapels still intact, preserving the artworks that together tell a complete story.

2 Crucifixion of St Peter

Caravaggio has avoided the goriness of his earlier works and filled this *chiaroscuro* work (1601) with drama **(left)**. The naturalistic figures quietly go about their business – the tired workers hauling the cross into place, Peter looking contemplative.

1 Pinturicchio's Adoration

Raphael's contemporary retained more of their teacher Perugino's limpid Umbrian style in this 1490 work in the della Rovere chapel. Also in the chapel is Cardinal Cristoforo's tomb by Francesco da Sangallo (1478), while Domenico's tomb (1477) features a *Madonna with Child* by Mino da Fiesole.

3 Conversion of St Paul

Again, Caravaggio leaves all drama to the effects of light, depicting an awe-struck Paul transfixed by blinding light (1601).

4 Sansovino Tombs

Tuscan Andrea Sansovino gave a Renaissance/Etruscan twist to the traditional lying-in-state look (1505–07). These effigies of Cardinal della Rovere and Cardinal Sforza recline on cushions as if merely asleep.

Santa Maria del Popolo

5 Daniel and Habakkuk

Sculpture as theatre by Bernini, as an angel seizes Habakkuk by the hair **(right)** to fly him to the imprisoned, starving Daniel, shown kneeling with a lion licking his foot.

6 Raphael's Chigi Chapel

Pagan and Christian imagery are fused in this exquisite chapel designed for Agostino Chigi. The skeleton inlaid in the floor **(left)** plays a role in Dan Brown's *Angels and Demons*.

MORS AD CAELOS

7 Marcillat's Stained-Glass Window

The only Roman work by Guillaume de Marcillat (1509), the undisputed French master of stained glass, this depicts the Infancy of Christ and Life of the Virgin (left).

Plan of Santa Maria del Popolo

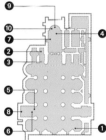

8 Sebastiano del Piombo's Nativity of the Virgin

This altarpiece in the Chigi Chapel (1530–34) is in contrast to the dome's Neo-pagan themes, the Eternal Father blessing Chigi's horoscope of planets symbolized by pagan gods.

NEED TO KNOW

MAP D2 ▪ Piazza del Popolo 12 ▪ 06 361 0836

Open 7:30am–12:30pm, 4–7pm Sun–Thu; 7:30am–7pm Fri–Sat

Free

▪ Canova and Rosati cafés (see p122) are both on Piazza del Popolo.

▪ Some of the church's treasures are behind the high altar in the choir and apse. When mass is not in session, go behind the curtain to the left of the altar and switch on the lights to see them.

9 Bramante's Apse

The Renaissance architect's first work in Rome, commissioned by Julius II around 1500, was this beautiful light-filled choir and scallop shell-shaped apse.

10 Delphic Sibyl

Pinturicchio, one of the most fashionable artists of the early 16th century, decorated the apse with antique grotesqueries including Sibyls and an intricate tracery of freakish and fantastic beasts.

TOP 10 ⭐ Villa Giulia

Villa Giulia was built in the mid-16th century by Vignola as a pleasure palace for Pope Julius III, who used to float up the Tiber on a flower-decked barge to the building site to keep an eye on progress. It is now a museum devoted to the Etruscans, whose upper classes at least shared Julius's love of luxury. Occupying the area bounded by the Arno and Tiber, they dominated Rome until ousted by an uprising in 509 BC.

5 Euphronios Krater

This exquisite red-figured Greek *krater* – used for mixing wine and water – holds 45 litres and depicts a scene from the Trojan War, in which the Olympian deity Hermes directs Hypnos, the god of sleep, and Thanatos, the god of death, to carry away the body of a slain warrior. It was sold to New York's Metropolitan Museum of Art after being looted from a tomb in the 1920s, and was returned to Italy in 2008 **(right)**.

1 Frescoed Tomb from Tarquinia

A reconstruction of a tomb at the Etruscan necropolis at Tarquinia, this is frescoed with scenes from a banquet, with dancers, acrobats and athletes providing entertainment **(above)**.

3 Lion Sarcophagus

This marvellous 6th-century BC terra-cotta sarcophagus **(below)**, with four roaring lions on its lid, was so huge that it had to be cut in two in order to fit in the kiln for firing.

2 Hydria

This vase, used for carrying water, was imported from Greece by the Etruscans and shows a lion and panther attacking a mule **(below)**.

4 Ficoroni Cista

A cylindrical bronze coffer in which women stored mirrors, cosmetics and beauty accessories, incised with intricately detailed scenes from the myth of Jason and the Argonauts.

6 Ex Votives

As with similar practices in contemporary Catholicism, models of body parts, including faces, feet, uteri and various other internal organs were offered to Etruscan Gods by sick people and their families, in the hope that they would be cured.

7 Sarcophagus of the Spouses
When it was discovered in 1881, this splendid 6th-century BC sarcophagus **(right)** was in 400 pieces. Painstakingly reconstructed, the intimate portrait of a married couple reclining on the lid, smiling as if sharing a joke, is perhaps the most evocative and human work of Etruscan art in existence.

8 Etruscan Temple
In the gardens is a 19th-century reconstruction of the Temple of Alatri.

9 Chigi Vase
Imported from Corinth, Greece, this vase is painted with hunting and battle scenes, including a fascinating frieze showing hoplites (foot soldiers) in formation with decorated shields.

10 Faliscan Krater of the Dawn
The Faliscans, who lived in southern Lazio, were an indigenous Italic tribe with their own language and culture. This elaborate 4th-century BC vase is decorated with scenes showing a personification of Dawn rising in a chariot.

NEED TO KNOW

MAP D1 ■ Piazzale di Villa Giulia 9 ■ 06 320 1706 ■ www.villagiulia.beniculturali.it

Open 8:30am–7:30pm Tue–Sun

Adm: €8; free for under 18s and over 65s; free for all first Sun of the month

Villa Giulia's vast collection continues in the Villa Poniatowski *(see p66)*, which also hosts temporary exhibitions. Check the website for information.

■ The Villa Giulia Café has tables on a terrace shaded by orange trees, and serves coffees, cold drinks pastries and sandwiches.

■ There are excellent audio guides available in English and Italian.

Museum Guide
This is a lovely museum with a lot to see and pleasant gardens to stroll around when you need to take a break. There are two main floors, plus a small basement section – an atmospheric home for the reconstructed tombs

from Etruscan necropolises at Tarquinia and Cerveteri. The ground floor is organised geographically, with sections devoted to the main Etruscan archaeological sites, including Cerveteri, Vulci and Veio. The first floor has a room devoted to important objects that have been returned after being illegally excavated and sold, as well as private collections that have been donated to the museum. There is also an interesting and well-explained epigraphic section.

TOP 10 ⭐ Ostia Antica

Some 2,000 years ago, this lively international port city was at the seashore (*ostium* means "river mouth"), but over the millennia the sea retreated and the river changed course. Ostia was founded in the 4th century BC as a simple fort, but as Rome grew, the town became important as an import hub. Its heyday ended in the 4th century AD, and it died completely as an inhabited area about 1,000 years ago.

3 Museum

Beautifully organized, the displays include precious sculptures, sarcophagi and mosaics found among the ruins. A highlight is a statue of the god Mithras about to sacrifice the Cosmic Bull **(left)**.

4 Forum

The rectangular heart of officialdom was originally encircled by columns. In the centre was a shrine to the Imperial Lares (household gods).

1 Decumanus Maximus

You enter this vast archaeological park by way of the ancient Via Ostiensis. The white marble goddess on the left marks the start of city's main street, lined with buildings, the Decumanus Maximus.

5 Mithraeum of the Serpents

One of 18 Ostian temples to Mithras. The cult was popular with Roman soldiers, and flourished especially well in port towns. The snake frescoes invoked the earth's fertility; the platforms were for lying on during mystic banquets.

6 Theatre

The original theatre was twice as tall as it now stands **(above)**. Behind the stage was a temple, of either Ceres (goddess of grain) or Dionysus (god of theatre).

7 Piazzale delle Corporazione

This large piazza is surrounded by the ruins of what were once the offices of various maritime businesses, each with a black and white mosaic advertising its trade – chandlers, ropemakers, importers of grain, ivory, wild animals. One has a charming elephant mosaic.

2 Casa di Diana and Thermopolium

You can climb up to the top of this *insula* (apartment block) for a great view across the site. Across the street is the Thermopolium, a tavern with a delightful wall painting of menu items **(above)**.

Terme di Nettuno
8 Built in the 2nd century, this bath complex **(left)** was enhanced with fine mosaics of sea gods and sea monsters, which you can view from a small terrace. You can also go down to the left to study close up the ingenious heating system of the baths.

Terme dei Sette Sapienti
9 This elaborate bath complex contains a painting of Venus; floor mosaics of hunters, animals, nude athletes and marine scenes; and humorous texts in Latin.

House of Cupid and Psyche **10**
The wealthy had villas like this refined example of a 3rd-century AD *domus* **(right)**. You can still admire the Doric columns, the fountain (*nymphaeum*) and the inlaid marble decorations.

NEED TO KNOW

MAP G2 ■ Viale dei Romagnoli 717 ■ 06 5635 8099

Metro B, trams 3 and 30, or buses 23, 75, 95, 280 to Piramide, then local train from Porta San Paolo Station (next to the metro station) to Ostia Antica

Open Nov–Feb: 8:30am–3:30pm Tue–Sun; Mar–Aug: 8:30am–4:30pm Tue–Sun; Sep–Oct: 8:30am–5:30pm Tue–Sun (last admission one hour before closing); closed 1 Jan, 1 May, 25 Dec

Adm: €8 (€4 EU citizens 18–25); free first Sun of the month

The port area (Trajan's Port) can be visited on request, 06 6501 0089

■ There's a snack bar behind the museum.

■ The ruined walls look confusingly similar –rent an audio guide where you buy your entrance ticket.

Park Guide
The trip by local train is easy, short and costs the same as one regular bus ticket. From the Ostia Antica train station, walk straight out to the footbridge that goes over the highway. Continue past the restaurant until you get to the ticket booth. The park is extensive and a decent visit will take at least 3 hours. Wear sturdy shoes, and bring sunscreen and water on hot days.

The Top 10 of Everything

**Museum staircase
at the Vatican**

Moments in Rome's History

1 Romulus and Remus

The foundation of Rome is said to have occurred in 753 BC. Twins Romulus and Remus, sons of Mars and a Vestal Virgin, were set adrift by their evil uncle and suckled by a she-wolf. They then founded rival Bronze Age villages on the Palatine, but Romulus killed Remus during an argument, and his "Rome" went on to greatness.

2 Rape of the Sabine Women

To boost the female population in the 750s BC, Romulus's men kidnapped women from the neighbouring Sabine kingdom. As Rome began to expand, however, the kingdoms were united. Rome was later conquered by the Etruscan Tarquin dynasty. In 510 BC, a patrician-ruled Republic was formed that lasted more than 450 years.

3 Assassination of Caesar

A series of military victories, adding Gaul (France) to Rome, increased General Julius Caesar's

Joseph Court's *The Death of Caesar*

popularity. He marched his army to Rome and declared himself Dictator for Life, but on 15 March 44 BC he was assassinated. Caesar's adopted son Octavian changed his name to Augustus and declared himself emperor in 27 BC.

4 Rome Burns

In AD 64 fire destroyed much of Rome. Emperor Nero rebuilt many public works, but also appropriated vast tracts of land to build his Domus Aurea or Golden House. Hounded from office, he committed suicide in AD 68 *(see p49).*

Julius Caesar

5 Battle at Milvian Bridge

In 312 Emperor Constantine, whose mother was a Christian, had a vision of victory under the sign of the Cross and defeated co-emperor Maxentius at Milvian Bridge. He declared Christianity the state religion.

Rape of the Sabine Women

6 Fall of the Empire

By the late 4th century Rome was in decline, as Barbarians from across the Rhine and Danube conquered outlying provinces. In 476, the last emperor was deposed and the Empire fell.

7 Papacy moves to Avignon

Following the departure of the papacy to France in 1309, the city became a backwater ruled by petty princes who built palaces out of marble from the great temples. In 1377 the papacy returned to Rome, and the city was reborn.

8 Sack of Rome

Rome was conquered for the first time in more than a millennium in 1527. Emperor Charles V's Germanic troops held the city for seven months until Pope Clement VII surrendered and promised to address the concerns of the new Protestant movement.

9 Unification of Italy

Piemontese King Vittorio Emanuele II and his general, Garibaldi, spent years conquering the peninsula's kingdoms and principalities to create a new country called Italy. In 1870, Garibaldi breached the Aurelian Walls and took the ancient capital, completing Italian Unification.

Mussolini with the Quadrumvirs

10 Mussolini Takes Power

Benito "Il Duce" Mussolini, leader of the nationalistic Fascist Party, marched on Rome in 1922 and was declared prime minister. Delusions of imperial grandeur led him to excavate many of the ruins we see today. He allied Italy with Hitler, but when the tides turned, Mussolini was deposed and Italy joined Allied troops. The current Republic was set up after a referendum in 1946.

TOP 10 INFLUENTIAL POPES

Pope John Paul II

1 St Peter
The Apostle (AD 42–67) called by Jesus to lead the church. After his martyrdom in Rome the city became the epicentre of Christianity.

2 St Leo the Great
Rome's bishop (440–61) made himself *pontifex maximus* of the Christian church.

3 St Gregory the Great
Affirmed the papacy as the western secular leader and converted England to Christianity (590–604).

4 Innocent III
This medieval pope (1198–1216) hand-picked emperors and approved monkish orders.

5 Boniface VIII
Imperious, pragmatic and power-hungry, Boniface (1294–1303) instituted the first Jubilee to make money.

6 Alexander VI
Ruthless Borgia pope (1492–1503), who used the pontificate to destroy rivals.

7 Julius II
A warrior pope and patron of the arts (1513–21), he hired Michelangelo for the Sistine Chapel and Raphael to decorate his apartment (see p12).

8 Paul III
Scholarly and secular, but fighting Protestant reforms, Paul III (1534–49) founded the Jesuits and the Inquisition.

9 Sixtus V
Cleansed Papal States of corruption (1585–90) and masterminded a Baroque overhaul of Rome.

10 John Paul II
The first non-Italian Pope for over 400 years, John Paul II (1920–2005), was famed for his extensive travelling.

🔟 Ancient Sites

The ruins of the Colosseum, the imposing 1st-century AD amphitheatre

1 The Colosseum
The intense labour to build the greatest of amphitheatres was carried out by Jewish slaves, brought here after the suppression of their revolt in Judaea. It has been the archetype for the world's sports stadiums ever since (see p26).

2 Trajan's Markets and Column
Trajan's Markets were the world's first shopping complex – 150 shops on five levels selling everything from fish (kept fresh in tanks), spices and fruit to wine, oil and fabrics. It opened onto Trajan's Forum, dominated by Trajan's Column. Bas reliefs spiral around the column, describing two Roman campaigns in Dacia, so detailed that they may have been based on Trajan's own war diaries (see pp26–7).

3 Roman Forum
In the centre of the Forum stands a humble ruined structure where fresh flowers are placed year-round. This is the foundation of the Temple to Julius Caesar, built by Augustus in the 1st century BC. The flowers indicate the exact spot of Caesar's cremation (see pp20–21).

4 The Pantheon
People originally approached this temple to all the gods by a steep staircase, but the street level has risen since the 2nd century. The present temple was built by Hadrian, after the 1st-century BC temple burned down (see pp18–19).

5 Palatine Hill
Most European languages derive their word for palace from the name of this hill. All-important in the history of early Rome, first as its birthplace, then as the site of its leaders' homes, it is now ideal for a romantic stroll (see pp22–3).

6 Pyramid of Caius Cestius
In the late 1st century BC, spurred by Cleopatra's fame, all things Egyptian were fashionable in Rome. Cestius built this pyramid as a tomb. It took 330 days to build and is his only claim to fame (see p126).

Trajan's Column

7 Column of Marcus Aurelius

A 2nd-century AD commemoration of conquests along the Danube, this colossus stands 30 m (100 ft) high and consists of 28 marble drums. The 20 spiral reliefs chronicle war scenes. A statue of the emperor and his wife once stood on top of the column, but it was replaced by one of St Paul in 1589 (see p98).

8 Baths of Caracalla

The most popular spa of ancient Rome, the baths included exercise areas, hot and cold pools, social lounges, art centres, brothels and libraries. Incredibly, access to the *terme* was free. Today, the complex hosts Rome's most important opera festival (see p125).

Baths of Caracalla

9 Crypta Balbi

In the 1980s, a private Roman theatre dating back to 13 BC was discovered here. By the 3rd century the area had gone downhill, with a lime kiln, glass factory and apartment blocks for workers. The museum brings to life all these stages, and there are regular tours around the excavations (see pp62–3).

10 Palazzo Valentini

The polychrome marble walls and mosaic floors are reconstructed using clever technology as visitors walk through the ruins of a private spa complex at these patrician villas, discovered in 2007. Another itinerary focuses on a newly excavated part of Trajan's Forum, and includes animations of scenes from Trajan's Column (see p62).

TOP 10 ROMAN EMPERORS

Emperor Constantine

1 Augustus
The first and most brilliant emperor (31 BC–AD 14) brought a reign of peace after 17 years of civil war.

2 Nero
The most notorious for his excesses, Nero (54–68) fancied himself a great singer and showman.

3 Vespasian
This emperor (69–79) ended civil war and the Jewish revolt, and started construction of the Colosseum.

4 Trajan
One of the most just rulers and successful generals, Trajan (98–117) pushed the Roman Empire to its furthest reaches.

5 Hadrian
A great builder and traveller, Hadrian (117–38) revived Greek ideals, including the fashion of growing a beard.

6 Marcus Aurelius
The closest Rome came to having a philosopher-king of the Platonic ideal (161–80).

7 Septimius Severus
Brought order after civil war, promoted cultural life and left an important architectural legacy (193–211).

8 Diocletian
Diocletian (284–305) set up a governing system of multiple emperors. A virulent persecutor of the Christians.

9 Constantine
Constantine (306–37) established Christianity as the state religion and moved the capital to Constantinople.

10 Romulus Augustulus
The last of the emperors (475–6), his deposition by German warrior Odoacer marked the fall of the Roman Empire.

TOP 10 Early Christian Churches

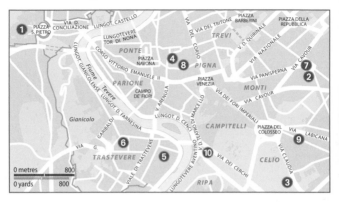

1 St Peter's Basilica

Should the opportunity arise, don't miss seeing the basilica's cavernous interior when all the lights are on – only then can you fully appreciate this giant jewel box of colour (see pp16–17).

2 Santa Prassede

Santa Prassede was founded in the 9th century by Pope Paschal II on the legendary site of a *titulus*, a private house where Christians worshipped in secret during the persecutions of the first and second centuries. The choir and the Chapel of St Zeno were decorated by Byzantine mosaic artists (see p132).

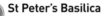

Santa Prassede

3 Santa Maria in Domnica

MAP E5 ■ Piazza della Navicella ■ 06 7720 2685 ■ Closed to visitors at time of publication; call for latest details ■ www.santamariaindomnica.it

Nicknamed Santa Maria della Navicella after the stone boat in the fountain outside – likely to be a votive offering by Roman sailors to the goddess Isis – the first church on this site was probably built over a disused Roman fire station, which Christians used for secret worship. Covering the apse are superb 9th-century mosaics, the figures lifelike and fluid – look at the different expressions of the angels, the wind stirring their drapery, or the sheep licking the gowns of the Apostles as they walk in a meadow.

4 The Pantheon

According to legend, in the 7th century, demons attacked Christians as they walked past the Pantheon, and permission was granted to convert this temple to all gods into a church. It is still a church, dedicated to the Madonna and all martyrs (see pp18–19).

5 Santa Cecilia in Trastevere

This church stands over the steam room or *caldarium* in which, according to legend, St Cecilia was locked for three days to suffocate to death for having tried to give her husband and his brother Christian burials. One story is that she sang throughout her imprisonment – the reason she is now the patron saint of music. In 1599, her tomb was opened and her perfectly preserved body briefly revealed before it disintegrated on contact with the air. Stefano Maderno made sketches, which he used for his haunting sculpture *The Martyrdom of Saint Cecilia (see p144)*.

6 Santa Maria in Trastevere

Probably Rome's oldest church, this is certainly one of the most intimate and charming. Dating from the time of Pope Calixtus I (AD 217–222), it was an early centre of Marian devotion and is Rome's only medieval church that has not been altered by either decay or enthusiastic Baroque renovators *(see p143)*.

7 Santa Maria Maggiore

One of Rome's greatest basilicas, this dates from the 5th century, as do its earliest mosaics, full of Byzantine splendour. The 16th-century Capella Sistina rare marbles were "quarried", in typical papal fashion, by destroying an ancient wonder – the Palatine's Septizonium, a tower built in AD 203 by Septimius Severus *(see p131)*.

Santa Maria Maggiore

8 Santa Maria sopra Minerva

Built in 1280 on the ruins of a temple dedicated to Minerva, Roman goddess of wisdom. In the 16th century it was the

Santa Maria sopra Minerva

headquarters of the Inquisition in Rome – Galileo was tried for heresy in the adjoining convent *(see p97)*.

9 San Clemente

A double decker-church above a Roman temple, San Clemente offers visitors a touch of Roman time travel. At street level is a 12th-century church with medieval mosaics, Cosmati-work pavements and choir enclosures and Renaissance frescoes by Massaccio and Masolino. Below is a 4th-century church with traces of frescoes, and below that a series of Roman foundations and a Mithras temple, where initiation rites and ritual feasts took place *(see p131)*.

10 Santa Maria in Cosmedin

This wonderfully atmospheric church has some of the city's finest Cosmati work (geometric mosaics made of coloured marble fragments reclaimed from ancient buildings) on its pavements, choir enclosure, and a twisting Paschal candlestick. A glass case holds the flower-crowned skull of St Valentine *(see p108)*.

🔟 Renaissance and Baroque Churches

Interior of Santa Maria del Popolo

1 Santa Maria del Popolo
Legend says that on this spot, where a great oak grew, Nero died and was buried. The site was thought cursed, but in 1099, in a vision, Pope Paschal II was told by the Virgin to fell the oak, dig up Nero's bones and build a chapel (see pp38–9).

2 Sant'Agostino
This church is home to the *Madonna del Parto*, a 15th-century marble statue inspired by Roman goddess Juno and surrounded by gifts from those whose wish for a child has been granted. Across the aisle, the realism of Caravaggio's *Madonna di Loreto* caused a scandal when it was unveiled in 1603 – the pilgrims' feet are filthy and even the Madonna has dirty toenails (see p90).

3 Santa Maria della Pace
One of the most fashionable churches in Renaissance Rome, Santa Maria was frequented by the beau monde. Fiammetta, courtesan lover of Cesare Borgia, donated property to the church, and banker Agostino Chigi commissioned a chapel which was decorated by Raphael with Sibyls, best seen from a window of the Bramante cloisters behind the church (see p90).

4 San Luigi dei Francesi
The great attraction here is Caravaggio's trio of huge paintings (see p57). The central oil on canvas, *St Matthew and the Angel*, is the second version. The first was rejected by the church because the saint was shown with dirty feet – and, some say, because of the overly familiar young angel (see p89).

5 Tempietto
MAP C5 ■ **Piazza San Pietro in Montorio** ■ **06 581 2806** ■ **10am–6pm Tue–Sun**
Rome's most quintessentially Renaissance building, the Tempietto is a perfectly circular Doric temple built by Bramante in 1501 on the site where St Peter was thought to have been crucified.

The 16th-century Tempietto

Frescoes at Sant'Ignazio di Loyola

6 Sant'Ignazio di Loyola

Construction of Sant'Ignazio di Loyola began in 1626, when the Catholic church was reeling from the blow dealt by Protestantism. The Jesuits who commissioned it were wary of appearing too wealthy – hence the austere façade. By the late 17th century, when the interior was decorated, they were more confident, and commissioned stunning illusionistic frescoes marking the triumphs of Jesuit missionaries (see p98).

7 Sant'Andrea al Quirinale

Created in a theatrical style by Bernini and completed in 1670, this church is an oval shape, with the main entrance located on its short axis – on entering, your eyes hit the high altar, where sculpted angels appear to be positioning a painting of St Andrew crucified on his diagonal cross. Above, a statue of the saint floats on a cloud towards heaven, as if he has just slipped through the broken pediment below (see p139).

8 Sant'Ivo

Borromini was a restlessly inventive architect, fascinated with intricate geometry. Sant'Ivo took over 20 years to build, spanning the reigns of three popes, and each has their family emblem included in the decor: bees for Barberini Pope Urban VIII, doves for Pamphilj Pope Innocent X, and star-topped blancmange – actually a mountain – for Chigi Pope Alexander VI (see p89).

9 San Carlo alle Quattro Fontane

Designed by Bernini's arch rival Borromini, San Carlo alle Quattro Fontane consists of an octagonal courtyard and oval building, and an ingenious geometrically coffered dome, constructed to create the illusion that it is higher than it really is (see p139).

10 Santa Maria della Vittoria

Caked with gold and stucco, this is one of Rome's most lavishly decorated churches. It holds Bernini's notorious statue, *Ecstasy of St Teresa*, showing the saint in the throes of what is possibly the art world's most famous orgasm (see p137).

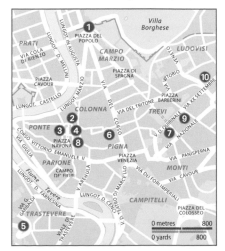

🔟 Museums and Galleries

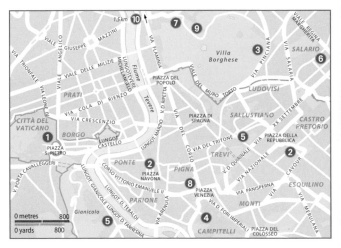

1.5 km 🔟

1 Vatican Museums

Occupying papal palaces dating from the 13th century onwards, these galleries include the Graeco-Roman antiquities, the Etruscan Museum, four Raphael Rooms, the Collection of Modern Religious Art, the Sistine Chapel and the Picture Gallery (see pp12–15).

2 Museo Nazionale Romano

Founded in 1889, this museum's holdings include archaeological finds and antiquities unearthed since 1870, plus pre-existing collections. The works are distributed between the Baths of Diocletian, nearby Palazzo Massimo, Palazzo Altemps, and the Crypta Balbi (see pp34–7).

Venus, Vatican Museums

3 Galleria Borghese

A tribute to the unbridled power of favoured papal nephews in the 1600s, this pleasure-palace, its restored gardens and priceless art collections comprise one of Rome's most gorgeous sights (see pp24–5).

4 Musei Capitolini

The glorious square, designed by no less than Michelangelo, is home to smaller papal art collections than the Vatican's, but equally invaluable (see pp28–31).

5 Galleria Nazionale d'Arte Antica

This state art collection is divided between two noble family residences, Palazzo Barberini (see p137) and Palazzo Corsini (see p146). The first boasts the Gran Salone, with its dazzling illusionistic ceiling by Pietro da Cortona, along with works by Filippo Lippi, El Greco, Holbein and Caravaggio. The second houses a Fra Angelico triptych, and paintings by Rubens, Van Dyck and Caravaggio.

6 MACRO

MAP F1 ▪ Via Nizza 138
▪ 06 0608 ▪ Open 10:30am–7:30pm Tue–Sun ▪ Adm

One of two branches of the Museo d'Arte Contemporanea Roma (the other is in Testaccio, see p127). The building, originally a Peroni

One of the spaces at MACRO

beer factory, is an imaginative triumph, with an aerial, glass-floored courtyard and reactive lighting systems. Although there is a permanent collection, the style is that of a contemporary gallery, with an ever-changing series of exhibitions and installations.

7 Villa Giulia

The building itself is a 16th century country retreat designed for Pope Julius III by Vignola. Since 1889, it has housed the state collection of pre-Roman art, including Etruscan artifacts and relics of the Latins and other tribes. The prize Etruscan work is the 6th-century BC Sarcophagus of the Spouses, a large terracotta showing a serenely smiling couple (see p117).

8 Galleria Doria Pamphilj

This aristocratic family's palace is filled with masterpieces by such painters as Raphael, Titian and Velázquez, whose portrait of the Pamphilj pope is famous for its psychological depth. This exhibit is accompanied by an audio-guide narrated by the present-day Prince Jonathan Doria Pamphilj (in English) that gives rare insight into the history of the collection (see p97).

9 Galleria Nazionale d'Arte Moderna

The *belle époque* home to this collection offers sculptures by Canova and an exhaustive view of 19th-century Italian and European painting. There is also an eclectic selection of modern works, including pieces by artists such as Rodin, Cézanne, Modigliani, Van Gogh, Monet, Klimt and Jackson Pollock (see p118).

10 MAXXI

Set in a futuristic concrete building, MAXXI hosts a rich season of frequently changing thematic exhibitions of contemporary art, photography and architecture. Short art films and videos are screened for free in a small cinema. The building alone makes a visit worthwhile, featuring a gravity-defying overhang, carbon-fibre lighting and freestanding stairways and walkways that look like something straight out of a sci-fi movie (see pp156–7).

The award-winning futuristic architecture of MAXXI

Artistic Masterpieces

1 Caravaggio's Deposition

Caravaggio strove to outdo Michelangelo's *Pietà* by making his Mary old and tired. Rather than a slender slip of a Christ, Caravaggio's muscular Jesus is so heavy (emphasized by a diagonal composition) that Nicodemus struggles with his legs and John's grasp opens Christ's wound *(see p13)*.

2 Raphael's Transfiguration

Raphael's towering masterpiece and his final work was found, almost finished, in his studio when he died. It is the pinnacle of his talent as a synthesist, mixing Perugino's clarity, Michelangelo's colour palette and twisting figures, and Leonardo's composition *(see p12)*.

3 Michelangelo's Pietà

The Renaissance is known for naturalism, but Michelangelo warped this for artistic effect. Here, Mary is too young, her dead son, achingly thin and small, laid

Michelangelo's Pietà

across her voluminous lap. Hearing the work being attributed to better known sculptors, the artist crept into the chapel of St Peter's one night and carved his name in the band across the Virgin's chest *(see p16)*.

4 Raphael's School of Athens

When Raphael first cast his contemporary artists as Classical thinkers in this imaginary setting, one was missing. After he saw the Sistine ceiling Michelangelo was painting down the hall, Raphael added the troubled genius, sulking on the steps, as Heraclitus *(see p12)*.

5 Michelangelo's Sistine Chapel

Although he considered himself a sculptor first, Michelangelo

Raphael's *Transfiguration*

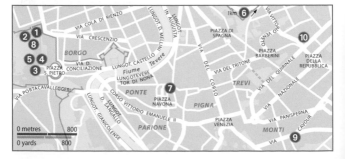

Detail from the frescoes of the Sistine Chapel

managed to turn this almost-flat ceiling into a soaring vault peopled with Old Testament prophets and *ignudi* (nude men). He did it virtually alone, firing all of his assistants save one to help him grind pigments *(see pp14–15)*.

6 Bernini's Apollo and Daphne

Rarely has marble captured flowing, almost liquid movement so gracefully. Bernini freezes time, windblown hair and cloak, in the instant the fleeing nymph is wrapped in bark and leaves, transformed into a laurel by her sympathetic river god father *(see p24)*.

Bernini's *Apollo and Daphne*

7 Caravaggio's Calling of St Matthew

Caravaggio uses strong *chiaroscuro* techniques here. As a naturalistic shaft of light spills from Christ to his chosen chronicler, St Matthew, who is sitting at a table with four other men, Caravaggio captures the precise moment of Matthew's conversion from tax collector to Evangelist *(see p89)*.

8 Leonardo da Vinci's St Jerome

Barely sketched out, yet compelling for its anatomical precision and compositional experimentation. Jerome forms a spiral that starts in the mountains, runs across the cave entrance and lion's curve, up the saint's outstretched right arm, then wraps along his left arm and hand into the centre *(see p13)*.

9 Michelangelo's Moses

This wall monument is a pale shadow of the elaborate tomb for Julius II that Michelangelo first envisaged and for which he carved this figure. Some claim there is a self-portrait in the beard and what are commonly thought to be horns may have been an attempt to create a radiating light effect *(see p131)*.

10 Bernini's Ecstasy of St Teresa

The saint here is being pierced by a smirking angel's lance, and is Bernini at his theatrical best. He sets this religious ecstasy on a stage flanked by opera boxes from which members of the commissioning Cornaro family look on *(see p137)*.

Villas and Palaces

Fresco at Villa Farnesina

1 Villa Farnesina

A little gem, Villa Farnesina is decorated by some of the greatest artists of the Renaissance, including Raphael. The loggias are now glassed in to protect the precious frescoes, but they were originally open, embodying the ideal of blending indoor and outdoor spaces – a concept borrowed from ancient Roman villa designers *(see p143)*.

2 Palazzi del Campidoglio

When Emperor Charles V visited Rome in 1536, Pope Paul III was so embarrassed at the Capitoline Hill's state that he enlisted Michelangelo's help. Work started 10 years later, but Michelangelo died long before its completion. True to his design, however, are the double flight of steps for the Palazzo Senatorio, the addition of Palazzo Nuovo, the fine façades and placement of ancient sculptures *(see p107)*.

3 Galleria Doria Pamphilj

Occupying an entire block of Via del Corso, this vast palazzo is still owned by the Doria Pamphilj family. In 1940, it was stormed by Nazi troops, but the labyrinthine layout allowed the family to escape. The palace, and its superb art collection – including the *Portrait of Innocent X* by Velázquez and *Rest on the Flight into Egypt* by Caravaggio – are open to the public *(see p97)*.

4 Villa Torlonia

Via Nomentana 70
■ Open 9:30am–7pm Tue–Sun
■ www.museivillatorlonia.it

Created in the 19th century for a wealthy banker, Prince Giovanni Torlonia, this aristocratic estate sprang to fame in the 1920s when it was rented out to Mussolini. He lived here until he was ousted in 1943. The park is open to the public, and there are several small museums, including the original Technotown *(see p70)*.

5 Palazzo Farnese

Considered the Renaissance palace *par excellence*, Palazzo Farnese reflects the genius of Antonio da Sangallo the Younger and Michelangelo. Home to one of Rome's most unscrupulous families, it was commissioned in 1517 by Alessandro Farnese, later Pope Paul III *(see p110)*.

6 Palazzo Barberini

When Maffeo Barberini became Pope Urban VIII in 1623, he decided to build a family palace on

Galleria Doria Pamphilj

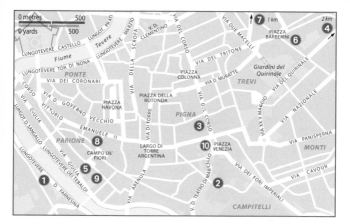

the (then) edge of town. Architect Carlo Maderno designed it as an outsize country villa with three floors of arcades. Bernini added the square staircase on the left; Borromini the spiral staircase on the right *(see p137)*.

7 Villa Giulia

Intended for hedonistic pleasure, this was a perfect papal retreat where Pope Julius III could indulge his tastes for young boys and Classical statuary. Designed by Vignola, Ammannati and Vasari, this 16th-century marvel is all loggias, fountains and gardens *(see pp40–41)*.

8 Palazzo della Cancelleria

One of the loveliest palaces from the Early Renaissance (late 1400s) – the purity of Palazzo della Cancelleria's façade and courtyard is unparalleled. Several ancient monuments were pillaged to provide the marble and the 44 portico columns inside *(see p110)*.

9 Palazzo Spada

Built around 1550 for a wealthy cardinal, the architect unknown, this palace houses an art gallery and has one of the most ornate Renaissance façades in Rome, featuring reliefs that evoke the city's glorious past. However, the courtyard is the masterpiece, with its figures of the 12 Olympian gods *(see p110)*.

Decorated passage, Villa Giulia

10 Palazzo Venezia

Built for the Venetian cardinal Pietro Barbo, Rome's first great Renaissance palace (1455–64) is usually attributed to two Florentine architects, Alberti and Maiano. You can admire the beautiful palm court with its 18th-century fountain from the museum café. Outside, Piazza Venezia is the de facto centre of Rome and converging point of traffic that is conducted with balletic brio by a white-gloved policeman during rush hour *(see p110)*.

🔟 Squares and Fountains

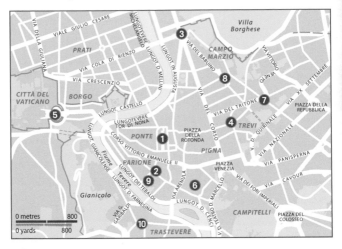

1 Piazza Navona

The elongated oval of Rome's loveliest square hints that it is built atop Domitian's ancient stadium (see p92). This pedestrian paradise is filled with cafés, street artists and splashing fountains. Bernini created the central Fountain of Four Rivers, and added the Moor figure to the most southerly of the piazza's fountains, constantly altered from the 16th to 19th centuries (see p89).

2 Campo de' Fiori

This "field of flowers" bursts with colour during the morning market, and again after dark when its pubs and bars make it a centre of Roman nightlife. The dour hooded statue overlooking all is in honour of Giordano Bruno, a theologian who was burned at the stake here for his progressive heresies in 1600 during the Counter-Reformation (see p107).

3 Piazza del Popolo

Architect Giuseppe Valadier expanded this site of festivals and public executions into an elegant Neo-Classical piazza in 1811–23, adding four Egyptian-style lion fountains to the base of one of Rome's oldest obelisks. The 1200 BC Rameses II monolith was originally brought to the Circus Maximus by Emperor Augustus, then placed here by Pope Sixtus V (see p116).

4 Trevi Fountain

Tradition holds that if you throw coins into this 1732 Nicola Salvi fountain, you ensure a return to Rome. Ingeniously grafted on to the back of a palazzo (even the window-sills mutate into rough rocks), the Trevi marks the end of the Acqua

Trevi Fountain

The lovely Piazza di Spagna

Vergine aqueduct, built by Agrippa in 19 BC from a spring miraculously discovered by a virgin (see p115).

5 Piazza San Pietro

Bernini's immense colonnade, 196 m (640 ft) across, encircles the piazza. Its perfect ellipse is confirmed by the optical illusion of disappearing columns viewed by standing at one of the focus points – marble discs set between the central 1st-century BC obelisk, carved in Egypt for a Roman Prefect, and the two fountains: Bernini's on the left, Fontana's on the right (see p16).

6 Fontana delle Tartarughe

Giacomo della Porta designed this delightful fountain between 1581 and 1584. The turtles (tartarughe) struggling up over the lip, however, were added in 1658, perhaps by Bernini (see p109).

7 Piazza Barberini

This busy piazza is centred on Bernini's Triton Fountain (1642–3), the merman spouting water from a conch shell. Commissioned by Pope Urban VIII, it features large bees – his family symbol – on its base. There are more chubby Barberini bees, poised as if to take a sip of water, on the other Bernini fountain across the piazza (see p138).

8 Piazza di Spagna

Overlooked by shuttered russet, cream and mustard palazzi, Piazza di Spagna attracts visitors from all over the world. The piazza has been at the heart of tourist and expatriate Rome since the 18th century, when artists, musicians and writers ranging from Keats, Shelley and Byron to Goethe, Liszt and Wagner flocked to the city. Come here early in the day to avoid the crowds (see p115).

9 Piazza Farnese
MAP K4

The elegant Piazza Farnese is dominated by two fountains incorporating giant granite bath tubs from the Baths of Caracalla. Overlooking the piazza is Palazzo Farnese, whose ceilings, frescoed by Annibale Caracci, are illuminated every night so that they can be seen through the unshuttered windows.

Fountains at the Piazza Farnese

10 Piazza Santa Maria in Trastevere
MAP K6

Lining this square are cafés, bars, shops and a 17th-century palazzo abutting a medieval church, its mosaics romantically floodlit at night (see p143). A fountain fitted with shells by Carlo Fontana (1682) atop a pedestal of stairs serves as benches for backpackers to strum guitars and tourists to eat ice cream.

🔟 Underground Sights

San Clemente church

1 San Clemente
The many layers of this fascinating church reveal the changing ideals of Rome in various eras. Over 2,000 years old, San Clemente is a three-tiered church whose foundations rest on an ancient Roman Mithraic temple, above which there is a 4th-century basilica with traces of frescoes. On ground level, the present-day church dates to the 12th century and has stunning mosaics (see p131).

2 Appian Way Catacombs
Underground cemeteries outside the city walls were created in accordance with the laws of the time, not as a response to suppression. San Sebastiano has some well-preserved stucco, while San Callisto's walls have early Christian art. Domitilla is Rome's largest and oldest catacomb network, and the only one to still contain bones. Frescoes of both Classical and Christian scenes can be seen in its passages, including one of the earliest images of Christ as the Good Shepherd. Many of its 1st- and 2nd-century chambers have no Christian connection; several religions practised burial of this sort (see p156).

3 Under the Colosseum
In the late 19th century, excavations revealed a network of tunnels, shafts and corridors. Wild animals were kept here in cages before being winched up to the arena, and released through a trapdoor. Archers stood by in case any of the beasts escaped (see p26).

4 Palazzo Valentini
MAP P3 ▪ Via IV Novembre 119/A ▪ Open 9am–1pm Mon, Wed, Fri; 9am–1pm, 2:30–4:30pm Tue & Thu ▪ Adm ▪ www.palazzovalentini.it
Below Palazzo Valentini were found not only Roman villas but also layers of detritus. Archaeologists concluded that the site was a Renaissance rubbish dump. A section has been replicated, using original finds – shells and bones – useful indicators about the Renaissance diet (see p49).

5 Vatican Grottoes
The famous Red Wall behind which St Peter was supposedly buried was discovered under the Vatican in the 1940s (see p17).

Fresco, Crypta Balbi

6 Crypta Balbi
MAP M4 ▪ Via delle Botteghe Oscure 31 ▪ Open 9am–7:45pm Tue–Sun ▪ Adm
A jumble of excavations from several eras, Crypta Balbi includes a piece of 13 BC *crypta* (porticoed courtyard)

attached to a destroyed theatre. The museum has didactic panels and several medieval frescoes (see p109).

Mamertine Prison

This was Rome's ancient central lockdown (built 7th–6th century BC). Among its celebrity inmates were Vercigetorix, a rebel Celtic chieftain, and St Peter, who left an impression of his face where guards reportedly slammed him against a wall (see p27).

8 Roman Houses under Santi Giovanni e Paolo

MAP E5 ■ Clivo di Scauro/Piazza SS Giovanni e Paolo ■ 06 7720 1975, 06 7045 4544 (call for reservations) ■ Open 10am–1pm, 3–6pm Thu–Mon ■ Adm

The houses under this church (see p133) belonged to two Constantinian officials, who were put to death under emperor Julian in AD 362 for refusing to worship pagan gods. The buildings include a frescoed nymphaeum dating from the 1st to 4th centuries.

9 Santa Maria della Concezione

MAP E2 ■ Via Veneto 27 ■ Open 7am–1pm, 3–6pm daily ■ Adm

Among the tenets of the Capuchin Order is the necessity of confronting the reality of death, the reason why the Capuchin catacombs below this church contain the skulls and bones of thousands of dead monks, wired together into crowns of thorns and sacred hearts. At the entrance a sign reads "What you are, we used to be; what we are, you will be".

10 Mithraeum under Santa Prisca

MAP D5 ■ Via di Santa Prisca 13 ■ 06 3996 7700 ■ Open 2nd and 4th Sat of the month, 11am and noon (by reservation only) ■ Adm

This 3rd-century AD shrine to Mithraism was popular among soldiers and the lower classes while Christianity was gaining status with the patricians.

TOP 10 VISTAS

Roman Forum

1 Roman Forum from Campidoglio
MAP P5
Walk around the right side of Palazzo Senatorio for a postcard panorama – floodlit at night.

2 Il Vittoriano
Climb the so-called "Wedding Cake" (or take the lift) for vistas over the Imperial Fora (see p110).

3 Gianicolo
The Eternal City is laid out at your feet from a lover's lane perch across the Tiber (see p145).

4 The Spanish Steps
Views spill down the steps to the tourist-filled piazza (see p115).

5 Musei Capitolini Café
A bird's-eye sweep over the archaeological park at Rome's heart can be seen from here (see p28).

6 St Peter's Dome
St Peter's Colonnade and Castel Sant'Angelo can be seen from Michelangelo's Dome (see p16).

7 Knights of Malta Keyhole
St Peter's Dome is perfectly framed through a gate keyhole in this garden (see p126).

8 Castel Sant'Angelo Ramparts
Lazy Tiber River vistas with the Ponte Sant'Angelo directly underneath (see p144).

9 Pincio
Valadier carefully designed this view from his gardens, across Piazza del Popolo to St Peter's (see p117).

10 Villa Mellini
MAP B1
A different panorama, near Rome's observatory above Piazzale Clodio, taking in the city and hills beyond from the northwest.

TOP10 Writers in Rome

Johann Wolfgang von Goethe, German writer and statesman

1 Goethe
The first Grand Tourist, German author Johann Wolfgang von Goethe (1749–1832) rented rooms on the Corso, now a museum dedicated to his life, between 1786 and 1788 (see p118). His book *Italian Journey* laid the blueprint for later tourists who came to Italy to complete their education.

2 John Keats
The English Romantic poet (1795–1821) came to Rome in 1820 for the antiquities and Italian lifestyle – and to bolster his ailing health, which nevertheless failed. Keats died at age 25 of tuberculosis in an apartment that overlooked the Spanish Steps (see p115).

3 Henry James
The New York author (1843–1916) spent half his life in Europe. Rome features in his novels *Daisy Miller* and *Portrait of a Lady*, and in the essay "A Roman Holiday" in

Mark Twain

his travelogue *Italian Hours*. In an 1869 letter he proclaimed "At last – for the first time – I live! It beats everything: it leaves the Rome of your fancy – your education – nowhere."

4 Nathaniel Hawthorne
During his Italian sojourn from 1857 to 1859, the American man of letters (1804–64) was so moved by an ancient sculpture in the Capitoline museums he crafted his final novel *The Marble Faun* around it.

5 Alberto Moravia
One of Italy's top modern authors (1907–90), Moravia wrote about Rome in *Racconti Romani*, *La Romana*, *La Ciociara*, *Gli Indifferenti* and *La Noia*, most of which have been translated many times.

6 Mark Twain
The American writer (1835–1910) spent little time in the Eternal City during his Grand Tour in 1867, but his satirical

impressions in *The Innocents Abroad* have become among the most quoted and memorable of any visitor.

7 Edward Gibbon

When English parliamentarian Gibbon (1737–94) stood in the Forum for the first time in 1764, he was struck by how "...each memorable spot where Romulus stood, or Tully spoke, or Caesar fell, was at once present to my eye." He resolved to write the history of Rome, and in 1788 finished his seminal work, *The Decline and Fall of the Roman Empire*.

8 Gore Vidal

The prolific American writer (1925–2012) was a resident of Rome and Ravello, south of Naples, for decades. His Roman experiences informed such books as *The Judgment of Paris*, *Julian* and his memoir *Palimpsest*.

Romantic poet Lord Byron

9 Lord Byron

The ultimate Romantic poet (1788–1824) lived, to varying degrees, the cavalier life so beloved by his genre. He spent years in Italy in the company of the Shelleys and other friends, and based a large part of *Childe Harold's Pilgrimage* and *Don Juan* on his experiences here.

10 Percy Bysshe Shelley

The English Romantic poet (1792–1822) lived in Italy with his wife Mary from 1818 until he drowned near Pisa. He visited Rome often, and penned the masterpiece *The Cenci* about the scandal of Roman patrician Beatrice Cenci.

TOP 10 CLASSICAL WRITERS IN ROME

1 Plautus
Formulaic comedies of errors by Plautus (250–184 BC) influenced Shakespeare.

2 Caesar
General, dictator and writer (100–44 BC). *De Bello Gallico* describes his campaigns in Gaul (France), *The Civil War* his fight against Pompey.

3 Cicero
Great orator and staunch republican (106–43 BC). His speeches grant insight into Roman political life.

4 Virgil
Poet and propagandist (70–19 BC). His epic *The Aeneid* tied Rome's foundation to the Trojan War.

5 Ovid
Greatest Roman Classical poet (43 BC–AD 17). His *Metamorphoses* codified many Roman myths, but *Ars Amatoria* detailed how to entice women and got him exiled.

6 Tacitus
Tacitus (55–117) wrote *Annals and Histories* covering Rome's early Imperial history; *Life of Agricola* his father-in-law's governorship of Britain.

7 Juvenal
Romans invented satire; Juvenal (60–130) perfected the form in his poems.

8 Pliny the Younger
The letters (*Epistulae*) of Pliny (61–113) give us a glimpse of imperial society.

9 Suetonius
The historian Suetonius (70–125) wrote *The Lives of the Caesars*.

10 Petronius
Petronius (70–130) parodied Roman life in *Satiricon*.

Virgil

TOP 10 Off the Beaten Track

Fontana delle Rane, Piazza Mincio

1 Quartiere Coppedè
Between Via Salaria and Via Tagliamento

A bijou neighbourhood of elaborate Art Nouveau palazzi and villas designed by Gino Coppedè. This is architecture at its most fanciful and eclectic, inspired by Assyria, ancient Greece and Gothic fairytale. The Fontana delle Rane in Piazza Mincio leapt to fame when the Beatles jumped in after playing a gig nearby.

2 Museo delle Anime del Purgatorio
MAP L1 ▪ Lungotevere Prati 12 ▪ 06 6880 6517 ▪ Open 7:30–11am, 4:30–7:30pm daily

The neo-Gothic church of Sacro Cuore del Suffragio hosts Rome's most arcane museum. After a church fire in 1897, priest Victor Jouet became convinced that certain scorch marks showed the face of a soul in purgatory, and started collecting objects he believed were proof of the dead trying to contact the living. The spookiest examples on display are the handprints burned onto surfaces.

3 Villa Poniatowski
Piazzale di Villa Giulia 34 ▪ 06 322 6571 ▪ Open Apr–Feb: 10am–1pm Thu, 2–6pm Sat ▪ Adm ▪ www.villagiulia.beniculturali.it

The restored frescoed rooms of this villa house Etruscan archaeological finds. Highlights are a tomb carved from a tree trunk, fine gold jewellery and decorated make-up containers.

4 San Teodoro
MAP P6 ▪ Via di San Teodoro 7 ▪ Open 9:30am–12:30pm Sun–Fri

This circular 6th-century Greek Orthodox church is one of Rome's hidden treasures. St Theodore was martyred on this spot, and the church was built into the ruins of a grain warehouse that stood here. The apse mosaic showing Christ seated on an orb is original.

5 Auditorium of Maecenas
MAP F4 ▪ Largo Leopardi 2 ▪ 06 0608 ▪ Guided tours by appt only (call the day before)

A bon viveur and patron of the arts, Maecenas was famous at the time of

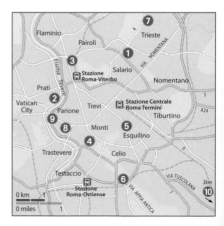

Emperor Augustus for his lavish parties. This space is thought to have been a summer dining room. The walls retain traces of exquisite *trompe l'oeil* windows with views of gardens, flowers and birds.

6 Museo delle Mura

MAP F6 ■ Via di Porta San Sebastiano 18 ■ Open 9am–2pm Tue–Sun ■ www.museodelle muraroma.it

Porta San Sebastiano is the most impressive surviving gate in the Aurelian Walls. It now houses a small museum containing prints and models that illustrate the history of the walls *(see p157)*.

Catacombs of Priscilla

7 Catacombs of Priscilla

Via Salaria 430 ■ 06 8620 6272 ■ Open 9–noon, 2–5pm Tue–Sun ■ Adm ■ www.catacombepriscilla.com

Few people visit the Catacombs of Priscilla, which date back to the 1st century AD. Benedictine nuns take visitors on fascinating tours that include the tombs of over 40,000 Christians and the earliest known image of the Madonna and Child.

8 Theatre of Pompey

MAP L4 ■ Da Pancrazio: Piazza del Biscione 92 ■ Open 12:30–2:30pm, 7:30–11pm Thu–Tue

A hint of Pompey's 61–55 BC theatre is evident in the medieval curve of Largo del

Ancient corridors, Da Pancrazio

Pollaro. Its fabric is now visible only in the ancient travertine corridors of the downstairs rooms of the Da Pancrazio restaurant.

9 Museo Criminologico

MAP J3 ■ Via del Gonfalone 29 ■ 06 6889 9442 ■ Open 9am–1pm Tue–Sat, 2:30–6:30pm Tue & Thu ■ Adm ■ www.museocriminologico.it

Part of a former prison, the museum is devoted to crime and punishment. It includes replicas of medieval instruments of torture and items confiscated from prisoners, including a letter written on a pair of underpants and a knife inside a hairbrush.

10 Cinecittà si Mostra

Via Tuscolana 1055 ■ 06 722 931 ■ Open 9:30am–7pm Wed–Mon, guided tours only (at 11:30am and 3:15pm in English) ■ Adm ■ cinecittasimostra.it

Step behind the scenes at Italy's legendary film studio. Tours of film sets take in a Broadway created for director Martin Scorsese's 2002 *Gangs of New York* and an ancient Rome made of polystyrene built for the television series *Rome*, but also used for other shows including *Doctor Who*.

Cinecittà si Mostra

🔟 Green Spaces

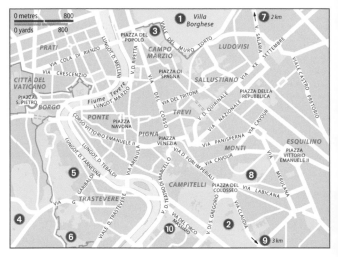

1 Villa Borghese

Extensive, elegant and full of shady glades and beautiful fountains, this is a great park for a stroll, a picnic or a jog. You can also go boating on the artificial lake, and rent a bicycle or in-line skates (see p117).

Villa Celimontana

2 Villa Celimontana
MAP E5 ■ Piazza della Navicella 12 ■ Open dawn–dusk

Picnics have been a tradition here since 1552, when the Mattei family gave pilgrims a simple meal during the Visit of the Seven Churches begun by Filippo Neri. Lovely dinner-concerts are held here in summer.

3 Pincio

The traditional time to enjoy the most famous panorama of Rome is at sunset. Other charms at these terraced gardens – a walkers' favourite – include the water clock, the busts of various notables and an Egyptian-style obelisk Emperor Hadrian erected on the tomb of his beloved Antinous (see p117).

4 Villa Doria Pamphilj

This is Rome's largest green area, extending from the Gianicolo along the ancient Via Aurelia. It's a terrific place for a run and offers a course of exercise posts. Its hills are adorned with villas, fountains, lakes and orangeries and are perfect for strolls, or you can enjoy a picnic under the umbrella pines (see p146).

5 Orto Botanico

The graceful botanical gardens and grounds of Palazzo Corsini provide one of the most enjoyable places to while away an hour or two and breathe in air richly perfumed by more than 7,000 plant species that thrive here. The gardens, which now belong to the University of Rome, include indigenous and exotic varieties, grouped according to ecosystems (see p146).

6 Villa Sciarra
MAP C5 ■ Via Calandrelli
■ Open dawn–dusk

This small park is replete with fountains, gazebos, ponds, loggias and statuary. There are leafy lanes for walking and lawns for relaxing and enjoying a picnic. It's a good place for children, too.

7 Villa Ada
MAP E1 ■ Via Salaria 265
■ Open dawn–dusk

This huge public park, originally the hunting reserve of King Vittorio Emanuele III, has rolling lawns, serene waters and copses. It's worth the trip out if you need an antidote to the fumes and noise of the city. On summer nights the lake at the northern end of the park hosts food stalls and concerts.

8 Parco del Colle Oppio
MAP E4 ■ Via Labicana

After hours of walking around the Forum and the Colosseum in the high summer heat, these green slopes can be a welcome sight. Most of the Colle Oppio park is actually the roof of Nero's Golden House (see p133), and you can see skylight structures for its rooms. If you haven't had enough of sightseeing,

you can also examine the massive remains of the Baths of Trajan scattered about the area.

9 Parco della Caffarella
Via della Caffarella
■ www.caffarella.it

Combining farmland and wilderness with abundant wildlife, these fields and meadows are dotted with the remains of Roman temples. There is also a large children's playground.

Fountain, Parco Savello, Aventine

10 Aventine
MAP D5 ■ Via del Circo Massimo

One of the seven hills of Rome, the Aventine is lush, leafy and little-trafficked. With romantic *fin de siècle* villas set among public gardens, it is a haven from city chaos. The roses of the Roseto Comunale are in flower in May and June; up the hill is Parco Savello, also known as the Giardino degli Aranci, planted with orange trees and offering magnificent views.

The charming Parco del Colle Oppio

🔟 Rome for Children

Exhibit with bubbles at the interactive children's museum Explora

1 Explora
MAP C1 ▪ Via Flaminia 80-86 ▪ 06 361 3776 ▪ Children must be accompanied ▪ 1-hour 45-minute visits 10am (except in Aug), noon, 3pm, 5pm Tue–Sun ▪ Booking recommended ▪ Adm ▪ www.mdbr.it

Youngsters can interact with life-size dioramas and models, which give a child's eye view of the world. There's a popular create-your-own TV show.

2 Villa Borghese
Scipione Borghese's private Renaissance park and the adjacent 19th-century Pincio gardens, with statues and fountains, are a joy to explore, especially on two wheels. There are bike rental stands scattered throughout the park. You can also rent paddle boats for the little lake or take the kids to the park's small funfair *(see pp117)*.

3 MAXXI
Futuristic MAXXI, designed by Iraqi architect Zaha Hadid, is a fabulous building for children to explore, with its illuminated stairways, suspended walkways, and floors that curve up to meet the walls without a joint. Exhibitions are presented in a way that children will find stimulating and exploration is made fun with one of the museum's interactive guides *(see p156)*.

4 Bioparco
MAP E1 ▪ Piazzale del Giardino Zoologico 1 ▪ Open Apr–Oct: 9:30am–6pm Mon-Fri, until 7pm Sat & Sun; Nov–Mar: 9:30am–5pm daily ▪ Adm ▪ www.bioparco.it

Rome's once run-down zoo has been overhauled to become a pretty "biological garden" in a corner of Villa Borghese park.

Children's train at the Bioparco

5 Technotown
MAP F2 ▪ Via Lazzaro Spallanzani 1a ▪ 06 0608 ▪ Open 9:30am–7pm Tue–Sun ▪ Adm ▪ www.technotown.it

Occupying a 20th-century house in the lush Villa Torlonia gardens, Technotown is a multimedia playhouse for kids, with educational and fun interactive exhibits including robotics, special effects and 3D photography *(see p58)*.

6 Time Elevator

MAP D3–4 ■ Via dei Santi Apostoli 20 ■ 06 6992 1823 ■ Open 10:30am–8:15pm (last show 7:30pm) daily ■ www.time-elevator.it ■ Adm

The panoramic movies shown here come complete with surround-sound, flight simulator and 5D technology. Not advisable for those suffering from motion sickness.

7 Casina di Raffaello

MAP D2 ■ Via della Casina di Raffaello (Villa Borghese) ■ 06 0608 ■ Open 10am–6pm Tue–Fri, 10am–7pm Sat & Sun ■ www.casina diraffaello.it ■ Adm

This city-run playhouse for kids aged 3–10 years offers educational toys and games, a toy library, a theatre and a bookshop, plus weekly events and workshops. Park entrance free.

8 Castel Sant'Angelo

Little visitors will enjoy spending a few hours at Castel Sant'Angelo with its winding passageways, hidden lookouts, dungeons and moat. The castle has had many uses over the years, and the museum's extensive collection of weapons and artworks that illustrate the millennia-long

history make this an interesting trip for adults too *(see p144)*.

9 Pony Rides

Ride a pony in one of Rome's parks – short rides are available in most of the city's parks, including the Villa Borghese, Villa Celimontana and Villa Lazzaroni.

Traditional puppets, Gianicolo

10 Puppet Shows on the Gianicolo

MAP B4 ■ Teatro di Pulcinella, Gianicolo ■ Shows at 10:30, check days

You can appreciate Punch and Judy without understanding Italian (the pugilistic characters are native to Italy). This is the last of the old puppet kiosks that once peppered Rome's public parks, offering appealing shows for free.

🔟 Restaurants

1 La Pergola

Top chef Heinz Beck has been awarded three Michelin stars for his extraordinary, innovative Mediterranean dishes in this refined restaurant at the Cavalieri hotel. The wine cellar is among Europe's most prestigious *(see p153)*.

2 Imàgo

MAP D2 ■ Piazza Trinità dei Monti 6, Hotel Hassler ■ 06 6993 4726 ■ Closed L ■ €€€

Housed on the sixth floor of the Hassler hotel *(see p170)*, this elegant restaurant has panoramic views of Rome. Chef Francesco Apreda won his first Michelin star here for his creative Italian fusion cuisine.

3 Il Pagliaccio

MAP J3 ■ Via dei Banchi Vecchi 129a ■ 06 6880 9595 ■ Closed Sun, Mon ■ €€€

A tiny, exclusive and understated restaurant in the centro storico,

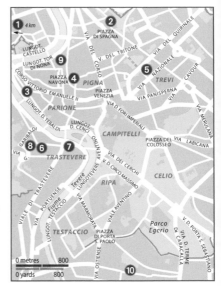

Intimate Il Pagliaccio

Il Pagliaccio has two Michelin stars for its inventive and refined contemporary Italian fusion food. Book well in advance as there are only 28 places.

4 La Rosetta

This sophisticated restaurant is run by renowned chef Massimo Riccioli who personally handpicks the ingredients. The seafood arrives daily from nearby harbours, and the bread and desserts are prepared in-house by the maître pâtissier. The gourmet offerings include fish tapas, rock lobster with artichokes and spaghetti with calamari, and a four-course tasting menu *(see p103)*.

5 Open Colonna

Housed in the rooftop conservatory of Palazzo della Esposizioni, Antonio Colonna's restaurant has the advantage of being particularly affordable at lunchtime with a stellar all-you-can-eat buffet at only €30. It offers great service and amazing views *(see p141)*.

The chic modern decor of Glass Hostaria

6 Glass Hostaria

Exquisite, intelligent fusion food, partnered with cutting-edge, contemporary chic decor, have won chef Cristina Bowerman a Michelin star in the heart of Trastevere. Combining Italian dishes with flavours from other parts of the world, the fine-dining, inventive menu changes seasonally. Despite the minimalist interior, the ambience is warm and friendly (see p153).

7 Osteria La Gensola

MAP M6 ■ Piazza della Gensola 15 ■ 06 5833 2758 ■ €€

This wonderful family-run Sicilian restaurant has a well-balanced menu with a focus on fish and seafood, which is freshly caught and cooked to perfection. There is a good selection of meat dishes too. The atmosphere is intimate, with attentive and friendly service.

8 Antica Pesa

MAP C4 ■ Via Garibaldi 18 ■ 06 580 9236 ■ Closed Sun ■ €€€

Many Hollywood names have dined here, as attested to by the pictures at the entrance. A classy ambience, contemporary frescoes and a lovely garden act as the perfect backdrop for the high-quality Roman cuisine at this well-established restaurant dating to 1922. There is an extensive but pricey wine list.

9 Il Convivio Troiani

The elegant feel of this restaurant is reflected in its classic dishes, all prepared only with certified local and organic ingredients that meet the highest standards. The three brothers who run this establishment have made it their mission to celebrate Italian cuisine by offering a creative menu based on traditional recipes, earning the restaurant a well-deserved Michelin star. It also has an impressive wine cellar (see p95).

People eating at Eataly

10 Eataly

Piazzale 12 Ottobre 1492 ■ 06 9027 9201 ■ €€

Sponsored by Slow Food, Rome's Eataly is the flagship for this chain of gastronomic emporia (also at Piazza della Repubblica 41). Everything from sustainable fish and Gragnano pasta to Alpine ice cream is on offer. Every month a different Roman osteria is hosted on the second floor.

For a key to restaurant price ranges see p95

Roman Dishes

1 **Saltimbocca**
This savoury veal dish is so good they call it "jumps-in-the-mouth". A veal escalope is layered with sage leaves and prosciutto then sautéed in white wine.

2 **Bucatini all'Amatriciana**
Named after Amatrice, the northern Lazio town high in the Abruzzi mountains where it originated. The sauce consists of tomatoes mixed with Italian bacon – *guanciale* (pork cheek) or *pancetta* (pork belly) – laced with chilli pepper and liberally dusted with grated Pecorino romano cheese. The classic pasta accompaniment are *bucatini* (thick, hollow spaghetti). The original *amatriciana bianca* version (before tomatoes, a New World food, entered Italian cuisine) adds parsley and butter.

Carciofi alla romana

3 **Carciofi alla Romana**
Tender Italian artichokes, often laced with garlic and mint, are braised in a mixture of olive oil and water.

Coda alla vaccinara

4 **Coda alla Vaccinara**
Oxtail braised in celery and tomato broth. Like *pajata*, this is a product of trying to make something out of the *quinto quarto* (the unusable "fifth fourth" of the day's butchering), which was part of the take-home pay of 19th-century slaughterhouse workers. Checchino dal 1887, the restaurant that created this delicacy, is one of Rome's finest *(see p129)*.

5 **Carciofi alla Giudia**
Artichokes, flattened then fried. This typical Roman Jewish dish is often accompanied by fried courgette (zucchini) flowers stuffed with mozzarella cheese and anchovies.

6 **Spaghetti alla Carbonara**
Piping hot pasta is mixed with a raw egg, grated Parmesan and black pepper so that the eggy mixture cooks with the heat of the pasta. It is then tossed with pieces of *pancetta* (bacon). One of several

Spaghetti alla carbonara

stories has it that the recipe was born out of US army rations after World War II, but no one seems to have proven or discarded the theory.

7 Pajata

It may sound revolting but it's actually delicious: suckling calf intestines boiled with its mother's milk still clotted inside. Usually the intestines are chopped, coated with a tomato sauce and served over pasta.

8 Abbacchio Scottadito

Roasted Roman spring lamb, so succulent the name claims you'll "burn your fingers" in your haste to eat it. When *abbacchio* (lamb) is unavailable, once the spring slaughter is over, they switch to less tender *agnello* (young mutton).

A bowl of gnocchi in sauce

9 Gnocchi

Dense and bite-sized potato and flour dumplings, gnocchi originated in Northern Italy but have infiltrated nearly every regional cuisine. Rome's version of the dish is made with semolina and/or corn flour, doused in butter and parmesan and oven-baked. The original gnocchi are served much more frequently, however. Try them with tomato sauce, gorgonzola cheese or simply *burro e salvia* (with butter and sage).

10 Cacio e Pepe

Sometimes the simplest dishes are the best. Perfectly *al dente* ("with a bite") spaghetti is tossed hot with cracked black pepper and grated Pecorino romano (a local sharp, aged sheep's milk cheese rather similar to Parmesan).

TOP 10 WINES AND LIQUEURS

1 Frascati
Lazio's only high profile wine, a dry, fruity, not always perfect white from the hills south of Rome.

2 Castelli Romani
Cousin to Frascati from the neighbouring hill towns and also made with Trebbiano grapes.

3 Colli Albani
Another Trebbiano-based white from the slopes of Lazio's dormant volcano.

4 Orvieto Classico
Dry white from southern Umbria – so good that the Renaissance artist Signorelli once accepted it as payment.

Glass of grappa

5 Est! Est! Est!
A bishop's taste-tester, sampling this sweet white in a northern Lazio lakeside village, excitedly ran to the door and scribbled *"Est! Est! Est!"* (Latin for "This is it!").

6 Torre Ercolana
One of Lazio's unsung reds, made from Cabernet and Cesanese grapes.

7 Chianti
This old favourite from over the border in Tuscany is one of the most common reds you'll find in Rome's bars and restaurants.

8 Lacrima Christi
"Tears of Christ", a white wine from the slopes of the infamous Mount Vesuvius near Pompeii *(see p158)*.

9 Campari
A bitter red apéritif, best diluted in soda water, or lemonade for a sweet drink.

10 Grappa
The most powerful of Italy's *digestivi* (drunk after a meal), this is quite a harsh-tasting liqueur.

Campari

🔟 Osterias, Trattorias and Pizzerias

① Casa e Bottega
At this contemporary and chic new-wave *osteria*, a short distance from Piazza Navona, carefully sourced, top-quality ingredients, including gourmet eggs by legendary egg chef Paolo Parisi, bring traditional Roman dishes such as spaghetti carbonara to new heights (see p95).

② Roscioli
MAP L4 ▪ Via dei Giubbonari 21–5 ▪ 06 687 5287 ▪ Closed Sun ▪ €€

This casual and very popular *osteria*-deli-wine bar is run by the family who make some of the best bread and pizza in Rome (see also p112). Come for a snack or a full meal – the spaghetti carbonara is particularly recommended.

Menus outside Casa e Bottega

Deli products on sale at Roscioli

③ Casa Bleve
Run by Anacleto Bleve, one of Rome's most respected foodies and a pioneer in the rigorous sourcing of ingredients from local, artisanal producers, this gourmet *osteria* in a 16th-century palazzo has won multiple national awards. Try the *sfizi di Casa Bleve*, a visual and olfactory feast of innovative antipasti, such as pumpkin flower stuffed with pistacio and

ricotta. Ask if they have *burrata*, a creamier variant of mozzarella that is flown in several times a week from Puglia and served with a rich fig jam. The wine list offers a great selection (see p95).

④ Felice
This Testaccio trattoria is famous for two things – grumpy owners and excellent, utterly traditional Roman food centering on meat and offal – given its proximity to the one-time slaughterhouse. Classics are *tonnarelli cacio e pepe*, lamb baked with potatoes, *carciofi alla romana* and offal cooked in a variety of ways. Advance booking is recommended (see p129).

⑤ Sora Margherita
This tiny, traditional, no-frills *osteria* has a cult following. Insta-gram it in black and white and your friends will be convinced you walked onto a neo-Realist film set. Food is

Margherita pizza

hearty Roman-Jewish – homemade pasta (an excellent *cacao e pepe*); stuffed, deep-fried courgette flowers; and anchovies baked with endive. They don't accept credit cards *(see p113)*.

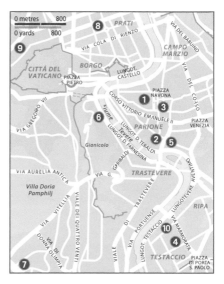

6 Da Giovanni

This tiny, good-value trattoria has a lovely atmosphere and serves up simple pasta dishes and legume soups. An ideal spot for lunch after visiting the Vatican and St Peter's, it encapsulates utter period authenticity – decor, food and staff could all belong to the 1950s *(see p152)*.

7 La Gatta Mangiona

Via F Ozanam 30/32 ▪ 06 534 6702 ▪ Open 7:45–11:30pm Tue–Sun ▪ €

Head to Monteverde Nuovo for one of the best pizzas in Rome. High-crust Neapolitan-style pizzas are made from specially selected flours and slow-rise pizza dough. They offer all the classics, but innovative combinations as well.

8 La Pratolina

MAP C2 ▪ Via degli Scipioni 248 ▪ 06 3600 4409 ▪ Open 7:30pm–1am Mon–Sat ▪ €

Busy and buzzy, this is the perfect place for dinner after a day of exploring the Vatican Museums. Oval-shaped, slow-risen pizzas are baked in a lava-stone wood-burning oven. Particularly recommended is the Genovese, with mozzarella di bufala, pesto, Pachino tomatoes and ham.

9 Pizzarium Bonci

MAP A2 ▪ Via della Meloria 43 ▪ 06 3974 5416 ▪ Open 11am–10:30pm Mon–Sat ▪ €

Esteemed pizza-maker Gabriele Bonci is known as "the Michelangelo of pizza" and his restaurant serves the best *pizza a taglio* (pizza by the slice) in Rome. Toppings range from the classic margherita to ricotta, black pepper and courgette. The *suppli* (croquette-type antipasti) are also delicious, and there is a range of regional beers and drinks.

10 Da Remo

Scrocchiarella (crispy thin crust) Roman-style pizzas with all the classic toppings are served at this ebullient Testaccio pizzeria. It is also a great choice for families with children as there is a play-ground in the piazza *(see p129)*.

Chefs at work at Da Remo

For a key to restaurant price ranges see p95

Cafés and Gelaterie

The cosy interiors of the 18th-century Antico Caffè Greco

1 Antico Caffè Greco

Rome's 1760 answer to all the famed literary cafés of Paris. Just off the Spanish Steps on the busiest shopping street in town, it is an elegant holdover from yesteryear, its tiny tables tucked into a series of genteel, cosy rooms plastered with photos, prints and other memorabilia from the 19th-century Grand Tour era. The A-list of past customers runs from Goethe and Wagner to Byron and Casanova (see p122).

2 Caffè Sant'Eustachio

Rome's most coveted *cappuccini* come from behind a chrome-plated shield that hides the coffee machine from view so no

Rome's iconic Caffè Sant'Eustachio

one can discover the owner's secret formula. All that is known is that the water comes from an ancient aqueduct and the brew is pre-sweetened. Always crowded (see p102).

3 San Crispino
MAP P2 ■ Via della Panetteria 42

Navigate the glut of inferior ice cream parlours infesting the Trevi neighbourhood to reach this elegantly simple little *gelateria*. The signature ice cream contains honey but there are other velvety varieties made with fresh fruit or nuts and sinful delights laced with liqueurs.

4 Tre Scalini

This café's claim to fame is Rome's most decadent *tartufo* (truffle) ice cream ball, which is almost always packaged in other outlets. Dark chocolate shavings cover the outer layer of chocolate ice cream, with a heart of fudge and cherries (see p94).

5 Giolitti

This 19th-century café is the best known of Rome's *gelaterie*. Touristy but excellent (see p102).

6 Café Doney

Still the top café on the famous Via Veneto, but long past its prime as the heartbeat of Rome's 1950s heyday (along with the

Gelato

now-defunct rival Café de Paris across the road) – when celebrities in sunglasses hobnobbed with starlets at outdoor tables under the magnolias. The lifestyle was documented in – and in part created by – Fellini's seminal film *La Dolce Vita*, whose shutterbug character Paparazzo lent a name to his profession of bloodhound photographers (see p140).

7 Caffè Rosati

The older, more left-wing of Piazza del Popolo's rival cafés (the other is Caffè Canova), this was founded by two of the Rosati brothers (a third continued to

Local favourite, La Tazza d'Oro

manage the family's original Via Veneto café). It sports 1922 Art Nouveau decor and its patrons park their newest Ferrari or Lotus convertibles out front (see p122).

8 Gelarmony

MAP C2 ■ Via Marcantonio Colonna 34

The ingredients at this hugely popular ice cream parlour come directly from Sicily. More than 60 flavours are available, and the presentation is second to none. Their pistachio flavour is especially good.

9 Grom

Artisanal, organic *gelato* made with top-quality local ingredients is on offer here. The company has its own organic farm where they grow the fruit they use. Expect long queues (see p102).

10 La Tazza d'Oro

Here only top quality Brazilian beans go into the coffee. There's nothing fancy in this unassuming place and no touristy gimmicks (despite being just off the Pantheon's piazza). Just a long, undulating bar counter where regulars enjoy a heavenly *espresso* that, amazingly, manages to be both among the best and the cheapest in Rome (see p102).

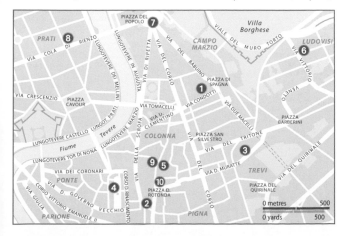

🔟 Shopping Streets

1 Piazza di Spagna

This is Rome's prime designer shopping area, with Fendi, Versace and Ferrè on Via Borgognona; Gucci, Bulgari, Prada, Hermès, Ferragamo, Trussardi and Valentino on Via Condotti; Chanel and Tiffany & Co on elegant Via del Babuino; and Fendi, Missoni and Krizia on the piazza itself. Babuino and Via Margutta also have some superb art, antique and furniture shops – don't miss nos. 45, 86 and 109 on Margutta (see p120).

2 Monti
MAP R4

Lying behind the Imperial Fora, Monti is Rome at its most hip, with vintage clothes shops and an eclectic selection of jewellery and home accessories by upcoming designers. Head to Via dei Serpenti and Via Leonina.

3 Via del Corso
MAP N1–3

Up and down Rome's central axis street that bisects the north from the south, more commonly known as the Corso, you'll find the entire range of shopping options, including stylish clothes, handbags, shoes, music and stationery. The prime shopping arena here is the Art Nouveau Galleria Alberto Sordi.

Galleria Alberto Sordi shopping arcade

Vintage store, Via dei Coronari

4 Via dei Coronari

Named for the rosary makers and sellers that used to line the way when it was on the main pilgrimage route to St Peter's, this street now has a reputation for antiques. Prices, however, are usually inflated and most pieces are imported (see pp92–3).

5 Via del Governo Vecchio

Running behind Piazza Navona, this street has long been known for its vintage clothes shops, now joined by one-off shops devoted to new designers.

6 Trastevere

Reflecting the area's changing demographics, jewellery, book, food and boho clothes shops now rub shoulders with niche designers. Piazza San Cosimato has a small, bustling daily produce market and Porta Portese a vibrant Sunday morning flea market (see p142).

7 Via Appia Nuova

A popular shopping street in the San Giovanni district, Via Appia Nuova has high-end boutiques such as Leam (see p134).

8 Via Cola di Rienzo

Less crowded than Via del Corso, this is Rome's best street for mid-range clothing. Castroni is the city's best shop for hard-to-find international and traditional food items, while nearby Franchi is famous for its cheese (see p147).

Delicatessen on Via Cola di Rienzo

9 Via Nazionale
MAP R2

The shops lining this busy major thoroughfare that runs from Termini Station to Piazza Venezia include such brand names as Desigual, G Star and Furla.

10 Campo de' Fiori

Central Rome's bustling fruit and veg market sets the tone for this area, which is known for its fantastic food shops, both traditional and innovative. Via Giubbonari is lined with affordable clothes shops, while Via dei Pellegrini and Via dei Ballauri have several chic stores (see p107).

TOP 10 MARKETS

Flea market, Porta Portese

1 Porta Portese
MAP C5 ▪ Via Ippolito Nievo
Mammoth flea market with genuine and fake antiques, memorabilia, plants, clothing and more. Sunday morning.

2 Campo de' Fiori
MAP L4
Fruit, vegetable and fish market in an authentic medieval square.

3 Via Mamiani
Rome's largest market for the freshest meat and fish. Monday to Saturday mornings (see p134).

4 Via Sannio
Vintage clothing and designer fakes. Weekday mornings and Saturday (see p134).

5 Antique Print Market
MAP M1 ▪ Largo della Fontanella di Borghese
Antique and reproduction prints. Monday to Saturday mornings.

6 Testaccio Market
MAP D6
Lavish displays of nature's bounty. Monday to Saturday mornings.

7 Via Trionfale Flower Market
MAP B2
Fresh cut flowers and all sorts of plants at bargain prices. Tuesday morning.

8 Borghetto Flaminio
MAP D1 ▪ Adm ▪ Piazza della Marina 32
A flea market in a former bus depot. Every Sunday, September to July.

9 Piazza San Cosimato
MAP C5
Trastevere's lively fruit and vegetable market. Monday to Saturday mornings.

10 Quattro Coronati
MAP E4
Off-beat produce market. Monday to Saturday mornings.

ᵀᵒᵖ**10** Rome for Free

Sphere Within a Sphere by Arnaldo Pomodoro, Vatican Museum

① Museums for Free

State and city museums are free for under 18s. All state museums, including archaeological sites such as the Roman Forum and the Colosseum, are free for all visitors on the first Sunday of every month. The Vatican Museums are free on the last Sunday of the month.

② Free Medieval-Style Lie Detection Service

The *Bocca della Verità* – made famous by Gregory Peck and Audrey Hepburn in *Roman Holiday* – is in the narthex of Santa Maria in Cosmedin. It was believed that if someone told a lie while their hand was in the mouth, it would be bitten off *(see p108)*.

③ Aerial View of the Forum

MAP P4 ■ **Via San Pietro in Carcere** ■ 06 678 0664 ■ **Open 9am–6:30pm daily in summer, 9:30am–5:30pm daily in winter**

Entry to the Vittoriano monument – with some of the best views in Rome – is free, as long as you are prepared to walk up the steps to the top instead of taking the lift.

Bocca della Verità

④ World's Best Preserved Roman Temple

The Pantheon is the only one of Rome's ancient monuments to which entry is free. The ancient temple was converted to a church in the Byzantine era *(see pp18–19)*.

⑤ Mussolini's Muscle Men

Stadio dei Marmi, encircled by 60 travertine muscle-bound athletes, was built by Mussolini in the hope of bringing the Olympics to Rome. Now an icon of Fascist kitsch, it is free and open to the public *(see p157)*.

⑥ The Caravaggio Trail

There are six magnificent Caravaggio canvasses that can be seen for free in the churches of San Luigi dei Francesi *(see p89)*, Sant'Agostino *(see p90)* and Santa Maria del Popolo *(see pp38–9)*.

⑦ Michelangelo for Free

Admire Michelangelo masterpieces for free at San Pietro in Vincoli and Santa Maria sopra Minerva. The latter has Michelangelo's *Risen Christ (see p97)*, while his muscle-bound *Moses* was created for San

Pietro and is still there. It does cost 50c to switch the lights on, but there are usually plenty of other people around to take care of that *(see p131)*.

⑧ Byzantine Splendour

Admire magnificent, jewel-like Byzantine mosaics at Santa Maria in Domnica *(see p50)* and Santa Prassede *(see p132)*, although you'll need to wait for others to put money in the slot to turn the lights on.

⑨ St Peter's

Access to the Basilica, Necropolis and Grottoes of St Peter is free, but to make the experience special – and avoid the queues that begin to build up from around 9am – go early, before breakfast, when usually the only other people there will be nuns, monks, priests and pilgrims *(see pp16–17)*.

⑩ Contemporary Architecture

Although an entrance fee is charged for the exhibitions at MAXXI *(see pp156–7)*, MACRO *(see pp54–5)* and MACRO Testaccio *(see p127)*, there are usually free video presentations at all three, and large parts of these stunning buildings – including MACRO's roof terrace – can be enjoyed free of charge.

Intertwining walkways at MAXXI

TOP 10 BUDGET TIPS

Good-value bakery food

1 Rome is full of marvellous bakeries and delicatessens offering fabulous food for a fraction of the prices charged in cafés and restaurants.

2 At restaurants and trattorias, order the house wine – it is served by the quarter, half or litre and is vastly cheaper than bottled wine.

3 To save money when self catering, avoid the *centro storico* delis and mini-supermarkets. Instead shop at neighbourhood markets such as Piazza Vittorio or Testaccio.

4 Look out for *aperitivo* "happy hours", where customers pay a set price for a drink and can serve themselves from an ample buffet.

5 The Roma Pass is valid for 2 or 3 days and includes free public transport, free entry to two museums, and discounted entry at many others.

6 Once you have a Roma Pass, plan ahead to select the most expensive museums as your free choices.

7 The Roma Archeologia Card, a 7-day ticket, is valid for the Colosseum, the Palatine, monuments along the Via Appia and the museums of the Museo Nazionale Romano.

8 Organise your days to make the most of public transport passes, which are available for 1, 2, 3 and 7 days.

9 Several museums (including the Museo Nazionale Romano) have multiple sites for which the same ticket is valid.

10 You can visit state museums for free on the last Sunday of every month.

Cultural Festivals

1 RomaEuropa Festival
End Sep–early Dec
■ www.romaeuropa.net

A fast-growing performing arts festival with a pronounced emphasis on the provocative, held every autumn in various superlative venues, including the French Academy, Palazzo Farnese and the Spanish Academy. All kinds of music, dance and theatre, including several international artists.

2 Rome Film Fest
October ■ www.romacinemafest.it

The Rome Film Fest is Rome's answer to the Venice film festival. Hosted by the Auditorium Parco della Musica complex, the fest organizes film premieres and gala events starring Italian and international movie celebrities. Many of the screenings are open to the public, but it is advisable to book ahead.

3 Luglio Suona Bene
Viale Pietro de Coubertin 30 ■ **06 802 41281** ■ **www.auditorium.com**

The "July Sounds Good" concert series brings big international names in pop, jazz and folk music to Auditorium Parco della Musica's outdoor arena.

Rome's Birthday celebrations

4 Rome's Birthday
Every 21 April there's a gala civic observance in the Piazza del Campidoglio, in celebration of Rome's traditional founding in 753 BC (see p46). Music, fireworks, costumed processions and a speech by the mayor mark the event, and the Musei Capitolini (see pp28–9) are free of charge.

5 Summer Opera Festivals
The Rome Opera Company offers its usual summer programme in the Baths of Caracalla (see p125), with other opera programmes all over the city, and workshops to make opera accessible to all. Singers come from around the globe.

6 ¡Fiesta! and Rock in Roma
Parco Rosati, Via delle Tre Fontane; Ippodromo delle Capannelle, Via Appia Nuova 1245 ■ **Metro Colli Albani then bus** ■ **mid-Jun–mid-Aug** ■ **www.fiesta.it, www.rockinroma.com**

The converted racetrack of Capannelle hosts Rock in Roma, bringing world-renowned rock stars to the outdoor stage, while ¡Fiesta! at Parco Rosati celebrates Latin American culture in all its forms.

Performance, Luglio Suona Bene

7 Festa dell'Unità

Put on by the PD, the former Communist Party, this lively evening event features music, films, dancing, games and more. The venue changes every year, as do the dates, but it's usually held in a central park from mid-June to late July.

8 Isola Tiberina
Isola Tiberina, Lungotevere de' Cenci

Seasonal pop-up bars and cafés on Tiber Island and along the river banks every summer. There's also live music, a market and an outdoor film festival (including English-language screenings).

9 International Horse Show
MAP E1 ▪ Piazza di Siena, Villa Borghese ▪ last week May

Villa Borghese's annual splash-out for the equestrian classes, with international showjumping in a garden setting. Much of the park is closed off for the event and parties.

International Horse Show

10 May Day Concert
MAP F5 ▪ Piazza S Giovanni ▪ 1 May

Held in front of the Basilica of San Giovanni in Laterano *(see p131)*, this is a vast, free event, boasting a line-up of top Italian popstars and the occasional international luminary. It's in celebration of socialist Italy's "Day of the Worker", when just about everything shuts down.

TOP 10 RELIGIOUS FESTIVALS

Pentecost at the Pantheon

1 Pentecost
MAP M3 ▪ Whitsunday
Rose petals shower down through the Pantheon's oculus *(see p18)*, followed by pageantry.

2 Christmas Market
MAP L3 ▪ 1 Dec–6 Jan ▪ Piazza Navona
Sugar candy, nativity figurines and all the Christmas trimmings.

3 Epiphany
6 Jan
Friendly witches land in Piazza Navona to give free candy to children.

4 Easter Week
Good Friday Procession of the Cross at the Colosseum and Easter Sunday blessing from the balcony of St Peter's.

5 Madonna della Neve
5 Aug
Commemorating a papal vision of an August snowfall in the 4th century, white petals float down from the ceiling of S Maria Maggiore.

6 Christmas Eve Midnight Mass
Most churches celebrate the Saviour's birth, but tickets are required for St Peter's.

7 "Urbi et Orbi"
The noontime Christmas Day blessing by the pope from St Peter's balcony.

8 Carnival
Late Jan–Feb ▪ www.carnevale.roma.it
Dressing up, parties and pranks.

9 All Souls' Day
1 Nov
Romans visit the graves of loved ones.

10 Feast of Sts Peter and Paul
MAP D6 ▪ 28–29 Jun ▪ Piazza S Paolo and Via Ostiense
Fireworks and partying to celebrate the founders of the Catholic Church.

Rome
Area by Area

The Spanish Steps at dusk

TOP 10 Around Piazza Navona

This is Baroque Rome in all its glory, with curvaceous architecture and elaborate fountains by the era's two greatest architects, Bernini and Borromini, and churches filled with works by Caravaggio and Rubens. The street plan was overhauled by 16th- to 18th-century popes, although ancient Rome peeks through in the curve of Palazzo Massimo alle Colonne and the shape of Piazza Navona. This is also a district of craftsmen and antiques restorers, and more recently, a centre of Roman nightlife.

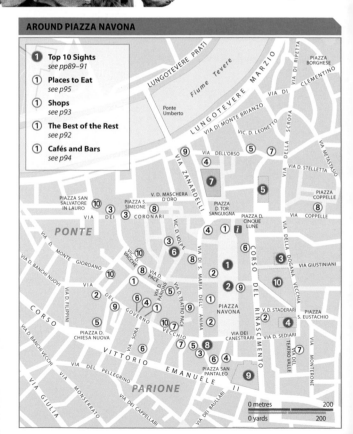

The Ganges, Four Rivers Fountain

AROUND PIAZZA NAVONA

❶	**Top 10 Sights** see pp89–91
①	**Places to Eat** see p95
①	**Shops** see p93
①	**The Best of the Rest** see p92
①	**Cafés and Bars** see p94

0 metres 200
0 yards 200

Fountain, Piazza Navona

1 Piazza Navona
MAP L3

One of Rome's loveliest pedestrian squares (see p60) is studded with fountains and lined with palaces, the church of Sant'Agnese, and classy cafés such as Tre Scalini (see p94).

2 Four Rivers Fountain
MAP L3 ■ Piazza Navona

The statues ringing Bernini's theatrical 1651 centrepiece symbolize four rivers representing the continents: the Ganges (Asia, relaxing), Danube (Europe, turning to steady the obelisk), Rio de la Plata (the Americas, bald and reeling), and the Nile (Africa, whose head is hidden since the river's source was then unknown). The obelisk, balancing over a sculptural void, is a Roman-era fake, its Egyptian granite carved with the hieroglyphic names of Vespasian, Titus and Domitian.

3 San Luigi dei Francesi
MAP L2 ■ Piazza S Luigi dei Francesi 5 ■ 06 688 271 ■ Open 9:30am–12:45pm & 2:30–6:30pm Mon–Fri, 9:30am–12:15pm & 2:30–6:30pm Sat, from 11:30am Sun

France's national church in Rome has some damaged Domenichino frescoes (1616–17) in the second chapel on the right, but everyone makes a beeline for the last chapel on the left, housing three large Caravaggio works. His plebeian, naturalistic approach often ran foul of Counter-Reformation tastes. In a "first draft" version of the *Inspiration of St Matthew*, called *St Matthew and the Angel*, the angel guided the hand of a rough labourer-type saint; the commissioners made the artist replace it with this more courtly one (see p52). Underlying sketches in the *Martyrdom of St Matthew* and the *Calling of St Matthew* (see p57) show how Caravaggio was moving from symbolism to realism.

4 Sant'Ivo
MAP L3 ■ Corso del Rinascimento 40 ■ Closed for restoration, call 06 0608 for latest details

Giacomo della Porta's Renaissance façade for the 1303 Palazzo della Sapienza, the original seat of the university of Rome, hides the city's most gorgeous courtyard. The double arcade is closed at the far end by Sant'Ivo's façade, an intricate Borromini interplay of concave and convex curves. The crowning glory is the spiralling ellipse of the dome. The interior, however, is somewhat disappointing despite its Pietro da Cortona altarpiece. When the courtyard is closed, you can see the dome from Piazza Sant'Eustachio.

San Luigi dei Francesi

Palazzo Altemps

⑤ Sant'Agostino
MAP L2 ■ Piazza di Sant'Agostino 80 ■ Open 7:30am– noon, 4–7:30pm daily

Raphael frescoed the prophet Isaiah (1512) on the third pillar on the right, and Jacopo Sansovino provided the pregnant and venerated *Madonna del Parto*, but Sant'Agostino's pride and joy is Caravaggio's *Madonna di Loreto* (1603–6). The master's strict realism balked at the tradition of depicting Mary riding atop her miraculous flying house (which landed in Loreto). The house is merely suggested by a travertine doorway and flaking stucco wall where Mary, supporting her overly large Christ child, is venerated by a pair of scandalously scruffy pilgrims.

⑥ Santa Maria della Pace
MAP L2 ■ Arco della Pace 5 ■ Open 9–11:45am Mon, Wed, Sat

Baccio Pontelli rebuilt this church for Pope Sixtus IV in 1480–84, but the lovely and surprising façade (1656–7), its curved portico squeezed into a tiny piazza, is a Baroque masterpiece by Pietro da Cortona. Raphael's first chapel on the right is frescoed with *Sibyls* (1514), which was influenced by the then recent unveiling of the Sistine Chapel ceiling (*see pp14–15*). Peruzzi decorated the chapel across the aisle and Bramante's first job

in Rome was designing a cloister based on ancient examples. It now hosts frequent concerts.

⑦ Palazzo Altemps
This beautiful 15th-century palace was overhauled in 1585 by Martino Longhi, who is probably also responsible for the stucco and travertine courtyard (previously attributed to Antonio da Sangallo the Younger or Peruzzi). Its series of elegant rooms now provide an excellent home to one wing of the Museo Nazionale Romano, its frescoed galleries filled with ancient sculptures (*see pp34–7*).

⑧ Pasquino
MAP L3 ■ Piazza Pasquino

That this faceless and armless statue was part of "Menelaus with the body of Patroclus" (a Roman copy of a Hellenistic group) is almost irrelevant. Since this worn fragment took up its post here in 1501, it has been Rome's most vocal "Talking Statue" (*see box*).

***Pasquino*, Piazza Pasquino**

⑨ Palazzo Massimo alle Colonne

MAP L3 ■ Corso Vittorio Emanuele II 141 ■ Open 7am–1pm 16 Mar only

This masterpiece of Baldassare Peruzzi, built in 1532, marks the transition of Roman architecture from the High Renaissance of Bramante and Sangallo into the theatrical experiments of Mannerism that would lead up to the Baroque. The façade is curved for a reason; Peruzzi honoured Neo-Classical precepts so much he wanted to preserve the arc of the Odeon of Domitian, a small theatre incorporated into the south end of the emperor's stadium *(see p58)*.

⑩ Palazzo Madama

MAP L3 ■ Piazza Madama 11 ■ Open for guided tours 10am–6pm 1st Sat of month (closed Aug)

Based around the 16th-century Medici Pope Leo X's Renaissance palace, the Baroque façade of unpointed brick and bold marble window frames was added in the 17th century. Since 1870 it's been the seat of Italy's Senate, so public admission is obviously limited.

Grand interiors of Palazzo Madama

A MORNING AROUND PIAZZA NAVONA

▶ **MORNING**

Start in the courtyard of the Sapienza, marvelling at the remarkable façade of **Sant'Ivo** *(see p89)*. Head around the church's right side and out the back exit on to Via della Dogana Vecchia. If you need a morning pick-me-up, turn left and then right into **Piazza Sant'Eustachio** (if the namesake church is open, pop in for a look around the early 18th-century interior). In the elongated piazza to the left are fine views of Sant'Ivo's dome and two great cafés to choose from, **Camillo** and **Sant'Eustachio**.

Return to Via della Dogana Vecchia and turn right to visit the Caravaggio works inside **San Luigi dei Francesi** *(see p89)*. Continue up the street to Via delle Coppelle and turn left for more works of art by Caravaggio at **Sant'Agostino**. Continue into Piazza delle Cinque Lune and walk a few yards to the left down Corso del Rinascimento, stopping for a pastry or cake at **Pasticceria Cinque Lune** *(see p94)*.

Around the corner is **Palazzo Altemps**, now home to a wing of the Museo Nazionale Romano and full of Classical statuary. Spend a good hour admiring the works of art. Then relax from the sight-seeing with a stroll amid the street performers and splashing fountains of **Piazza Navona** *(see p89)*. Enjoy a *tartufo* ice cream or a full lunch at the wonderful **Tre Scalini** *(see p94)*, before ending the morning window-shopping along the antiques of **Via dei Coronari** *(see p92)*.

See map on p88 ←

The Best of the Rest

1 Sant'Agnese in Agone
MAP L3 ▪ Piazza Navona
▪ Open 9:30am–12:30pm, 3:30–7pm Mon–Sat, 9am–1pm, 4–8pm Sun & hols

This church was built in honour of a young girl whose hair miraculously grew to cover her nakedness after she was stripped in a brothel. Borromini's façade combines concave and convex shapes.

2 Palazzo Pamphilj
MAP L3 ▪ Piazza Navona 14
▪ Open for guided tours only (to book call 06 683 981)

This 17th-century palace was commissioned by Pope Innocent X and has a wonderful Pietro da Cortona fresco upstairs.

3 Via dei Coronari
MAP K2

Lined with antiques shops, this street is at its torch-flickering best during the May and October antiques fairs (see p80).

4 Santa Maria dell'Anima
MAP L2 ▪ Via di Santa Maria dell' Anima 66 ▪ Open 9am–12:45pm, 3–7pm daily

Highlights in this breathtaking church include a Giulio Romano altarpiece and Peruzzi's Hadrian VI tomb (1523).

5 Chiesa Nuova
MAP K3 ▪ Piazza della Chiesa Nuova/Via del Governo Vecchio 134
▪ Open 7:30am–7pm

Pietro da Cortona painted the dome and apse, and Rubens painted three sanctuary canvases for this imposing 1575 church with a lavish interior.

6 Palazzo Braschi
MAP L3 ▪ Piazza San Pantaleo 10 ▪ Open 10am–7pm Tue–Sun ▪ Adm

The last papal family palace was built 1791–1811. Cosimo Morelli used a Renaissance design to match the piazza. Inside is a small museum dedicated to Roman history.

7 Sant'Antonio dei Portoghesi
MAP L2 ▪ Via dei Portoghesi 2
▪ 8:30am–1pm, 3–6pm Mon–Fri, 8:30am–noon, 3–6pm Sat, 9am–noon Sun

A Baroque gem of a church. Out front is the Torre della Scimmia, a rare remnant of medieval Rome.

8 Domitian's Stadium
MAP L3 ▪ Via di Tor Sanguigna 13 ▪ Open daily 10am–7pm (to book call 06 6880 5311) ▪ Adm

The outline of this AD 86 stadium is echoed in Piazza Navona, built on top of its remains.

9 Museo Napoleonico
MAP L2 ▪ Piazza di Ponte Umberto I ▪ Open 10am–6pm Tue–Sun ▪ Adm

This collection of paintings, furnishings and objets d'art once belonged to the Bonaparte clan.

10 San Salvatore in Lauro
MAP K2 ▪ Piazza S Salvatore in Lauro 15 ▪ Open 9am–noon, 3–7pm daily

This church houses da Cortona's Adoration of the Shepherds (1630).

Santa Maria dell'Anima

Shops

 Al Sogno
MAP L2 ■ Piazza Navona 53

Enjoy a nostalgic trip browsing dolls, doll's houses, life-size teddy bears and wooden toys. Although hard for children to resist, staff disapprove of them touching anything.

Dolls on display at Al Sogno

 Murano Piú
MAP L3 ■ Corso Rinasci-mento 42

A large selection of blown-glass vases, tableware and jewelry from Murano are available in a variety of colours at this shop.

3 SBU Store
MAP L3 ■ Via di San Pantaleo 68–9

A former draper's shop on the ground floor of a historic building is now one of Rome's most fashionable menswear stores selling everything from casual jeans to formal suits.

 Antica Cappelleria Troncarelli
MAP L2 ■ Via della Cuccagna 15

This tiny hat shop is older than the Italian nation – it opened in 1857, and has changed little over the years. It offers a range of stylish models for men and women.

5 Massimo Maria Melis
MAP L2 ■ Via dell'Orso 57

A film costume designer turned goldsmith, Massimo Melis creates breathtaking jewellery inspired by Roman and Etruscan pieces and techniques, and often incorporating ancient stones, seals and coins.

6 Cinzia Vintage
MAP K3 ■ Via del Governo Vecchio 45

A historic second-hand shop on Via del Governo, Cinzia Vintage sells every-thing from old Levis to the occasional brand name.

7 Altro-quando
MAP L3 ■ Via del Governo Vecchio 80

This art and photography bookshop also doubles as event venue and movie theatre. In addition to books, they also sell magnets, posters and fun gadgets.

8 Kouki
MAP K2 ■ Via dei Coronari 26

Buy bags of beads at this Aladdin's cave, or make your own selection and have it strung while you wait.

9 Nicotra di San Giacomo
MAP C3 ■ Via del Governo Vecchio 128

The elegant and unique jewellery at this shop is handcrafted by artisans and combines Italian tradition with contemporary fashion.

10 Josephine De Huertas & Co
MAP L3 ■ Via del Governo Vecchio 68

Owned by a French-Italian fashion designer duo, this sophisticated boutique carries international and Italian brands for women.

See map on p88

Cafés and Bars

Abbey Theatre Irish Pub

① Abbey Theatre Irish Pub
MAP K3 ▪ Via del Governo Vecchio 51–53

Removed from the hubbub of the nightlife core nearby, this cosy Irish-themed pub serves Guinness and an Irish and Italian all-day food menu

② Tre Scalini
MAP L3 ▪ Piazza Navona 28

This historic café, right on Piazza Navona, is renowned for its delectable chocolate homemade *tartufo* ice cream ball *(see p78).*

③ Bistrot Chiostro del Bramante
MAP K3 ▪ Arco della Pace 5

A modern museum café with out-door tables overlooking the Baroque cloister. Stop by for a cup of coffee or to enjoy one of the tasty salads.

④ Fluid
MAP K3 ▪ Via del Governo Vecchio 46

Space-inspired interiors and cosmic forests define this high-level cocktail bar, which is frequented by young professionals and a trendy crowd that spill out into the piazza.

⑤ Emporio alla Pace
MAP K3 ▪ Via della Pace 28

A small, friendly café, Emporio alla Pace serves very good-value coffees, pastries and light meals in a relaxed atmosphere. In the evening it transforms into a cocktail bar.

⑥ Pasticceria Cinque Lune
MAP L3 ▪ Corso del Rinascimento 89

This old-school Italian bakery is packed to the brim with pastries, biscuits and cakes. The speciality is the "imperatore": pastries filled with ricotta cheese and aromatic herbs, to be had plain or with chocolate.

⑦ Enoteca Il Piccolo
MAP K3 ▪ Via del Governo Vecchio 74

A small wine bar with a personal touch, the friendly Enoteca il Piccolo is a great choice for wine with tasty homemade snacks and salads, and *vin brulè* (mulled wine) in winter.

⑧ Bar del Fico
MAP K3 ▪ Piazza del Fico 26

Large *aperitivo* (happy-hour) buffets, delicious cocktails and a marvellous Sunday brunch are served at this popular bar-cum-restaurant.

⑨ Caffè Domiziano
MAP L2 ▪ Piazza Navona 88

Service is slightly slow but this café features one of the most beautiful views in Rome, with a wide terrace directly on Piazza Navona.

⑩ Etabli
MAP K2 ▪ Vicolo delle Vacche 9/A

The perfect spot for a drink or an *aperitivo* with friends. The decor is inspired by the French countryside.

Places to Eat

PRICE CATEGORIES
For a three-course meal for one with half a bottle of wine (or equivalent meal), taxes and extra charges.

€ under €40   €€ €40–60   €€€ over €60

Da Francesco
MAP K2–3 ■ Piazza del Fico 29 ■ 06 686 4009 ■ €

Popular with tourists, this has an excellent appetiser buffet offering hand-cut prosciutto, fresh seafood salads and many vegetarian options. It also has great pizza and pasta.

2 Da Tonino
MAP K3 ■ Via del Governo Vecchio 18–19 ■ 06 908 6508 ■ Closed Sun ■ €

Massive portions of pasta, and mains ranging from traditional veal stew to lamb with crisp roast potatoes, are served at this cheerful trattoria.

3 Casa e Bottega
MAP K2 ■ Via dei Coronari 183 ■ 06 686 4358 ■ Open daily ■ €

Quality ingredients and bistro-type decor make this stylish lunch place a top choice in the area (see p76).

4 Il Convivio Troiani
MAP L2 ■ Vicolo dei Soldati 31 ■ 06 686 9432 ■ Closed Sun ■ €€€

A top restaurant in the historic centre, Il Convivio Trioiani offers seasonal cuisine based on Italian traditions. It has an excellent wine list (see p73).

5 Cul de Sac
MAP L3 ■ Piazza Paquino 73 ■ 06 6880 1094 ■ €

One of Rome's oldest wine bars has a wide range of labels. It's a bit of a squeeze, but it's a better option than most bars in nearby Piazza Navona.

6 Pizzeria La Montecarlo
MAP K3 ■ Vicolo Savelli 13 ■ 06 686 1877 ■ Closed Mon ■ €

The offspring of Baffetto's owners run this joint. It has less ambience than its famous parent, Pizzeria da Baffetto in Via del Governo Vecchio, but benefits from shorter queues.

7 Casa Bleve
MAP L3 ■ Via de Teatro Valle 48 ■ 06 686 5970 ■ Closed Sun ■ €€€

Anacleto Bleve sources the freshest ingredients from small producers to create exquisite dishes at this traditional osteria (see p76).

8 Casa Coppelle
MAP M2 ■ Piazza delle Coppelle 49 ■ 06 6889 1707 ■ €€

This relaxed, contemporary restaurant serves French and Roman food, such as caramelised artichoke tarte tatin, and fabulous gorgonzola and pear risotto.

Cosy interior of Lo Zozzone

9 Lo Zozzone
MAP L3 ■ Via Teatro della Pace 32 ■ 06 6880 8575 ■ €

The wonderful Lo Zozzone serves slices of crisp pizza bianca (with a base of olive oil and salt), filled with any combination from the deli counter. Eat on the terrace or take away.

10 Antica Taverna
MAP K3 ■ Via Monte Giordano 12 ■ 06 6880 1053 ■ €

The owners get their ricotta, goat's milk and rabbit from their hometown in the Sabine Hills. Suckling pig and roast duck are house specialities.

See map on p88

🔟 Around the Pantheon

During the Roman Empire the Tiber Bend area was a military training ground called the Campo Marzio. After the fall of Rome, this riverside district was all but forgotten until the Baroque boom gave the area's palaces their distinctive look. Mussolini cleaned up the quarter in the 1920s and 1930s to bring out its ancient character, adding Fascist buildings complete with self-aggrandizing bas-reliefs.

Detail, Piazza della Rotonda

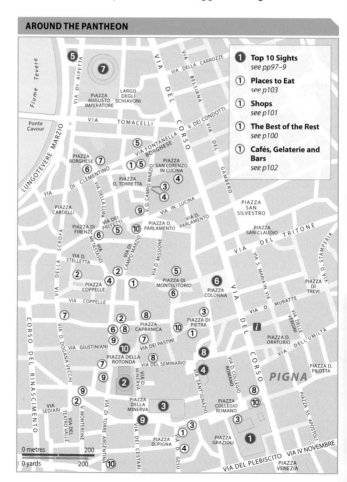

AROUND THE PANTHEON

- ① Top 10 Sights
  see pp97–9
- ① Places to Eat
  see p103
- ① Shops
  see p101
- ① The Best of the Rest
  see p100
- ① Cafés, Gelaterie and Bars
  see p102

The Pantheon, fronted by the Fontana del Pantheon and obelisk of Rameses II

1 Galleria Doria Pamphilj
MAP N3 ■ Via del Corso 305 ■ **Open 9am–7pm daily** ■ **Adm** ■ www.doriapamphilj.it

The best of the private collection galleries in Rome. In addition to paintings by Rubens, Correggio, Tintoretto, Carracci and Brueghel, star works include Caravaggio's *Mary Magdalene*, *Rest on the Flight into Egypt*, and *Young St John the Baptist* (a copy he made of his Capitoline version), Titian's *Salome with the Head of John the Baptist* and Bernini's bust of Pope Innocent X *(see p55)*.

Santa Maria sopra Minerva

2 The Pantheon
"Simple, erect, severe, austere, sublime" – even Lord Byron struggled to find adequate words to describe this marvel of Roman architecture, the only ancient Roman temple to survive virtually intact through the millennia *(see pp18–19)*.

3 Santa Maria sopra Minerva
MAP M3 ■ Piazza della Minerva 42 ■ **Open 7:30am–7pm Mon–Fri, 7:30am–12:30pm, 3:30–7pm Sat, 8am–12:30pm, 3:30–7pm Sun**

This is the only truly Gothic church in Rome, possibly built, as the name suggests, above a temple to Minerva. Michelangelo's *Risen Christ* (1514–21), to the left of the main altar, is a muscular rendition of the Saviour so shockingly nude that church officials added the bronze wisp of drapery. Filippino Lippi frescoed the last chapel on the right; the lower scene on the right wall includes portraits of young Giovanni and Giulio de' Medici (known as Popes Leo X and Clement VII), who are buried in tombs by Antonio Sangallo the Younger, in the apse, with Fra Angelico and (most of) St Catherine of Siena *(see p51)*.

Sant'Ignazio di Loyola

4 Sant'Ignazio di Loyola
MAP N3 ▪ Piazza di S Ignazio ▪ Open 7:30am–7pm Mon–Sat, 9am–7pm Sun

When the Jesuits' new Baroque church was finished, it still lacked a dome. Master of *trompe l'oeil* Andrea Pozzo used the technique in 1685 to create the illusion of an airy dome on the flat ceiling over the church's crossing; stand on the yellow marble disc for the full effect, then walk directly under the "dome" to see how skewed the painting actually is. Pozzo also painted the nave vault with the lovely *Glory of Sant'Ignazio*.

RECYCLED TEMPLES
Romans are ingenious recyclers. The Pantheon became a church, Hadrian's Temple a stock exchange. Santa Maria sopra Minerva was built atop a temple to Minerva; San Clemente on one to Mithras. In the 11th century, the walls of San Lorenzo in Miranda in the Forum and San Nicola in Carcere on Via Teatro di Marcello were both grafted onto temple columns.

5 Ara Pacis Museum
MAP D2 ▪ Lungotevere in Augusta ▪ 06 0608 ▪ Open 9:30am–7:30pm daily ▪ Adm ▪ www.arapacis.it

Augustus Caesar built this "Altar of Peace" between 13 BC and 9 BC to celebrate the famed *pax romana* (Roman peace) he instituted – largely by subjugating most of Western Europe, the Levant and North Africa. Fragments of the altar were excavated over several centuries, and in the 1920s Mussolini placed the reconstituted Ara Pacis by Augustus's Mausoleum. The altar is now housed in a Richard Meier-designed museum, the first modern structure to be built in the centre of Rome in more than 70 years.

6 Column of Marcus Aurelius
MAP N2 ▪ Piazza Colonna

Trajan's Column was such a success *(see p26)* that this one was erected to honour Marcus Aurelius in AD 180–93. The reliefs celebrate his battles against the Germans (169–73) on the bottom and the Sarmatians (174–6) on the top. In 1588, Pope Sixtus V replaced the statues of the emperor and his wife with that of St Paul.

Detail, Column of Marcus Aurelius

7 Augustus's Mausoleum
MAP D2 ▪ Piazza Augusto Imperatore ▪ Closed for restoration until 2019 (guided tours by prior arrangement – call 06 0608)

Augustus built this grand imperial tomb in 27 BC, his ashes later joined by those of emperors Tiberius and Nerva, and worthies such as Agrippa and Marcellus. Barbarian invaders later made off with the urns and locals mined its travertine facing for their palaces. The ancient rotunda has served time as a circus for bear-baiting fortress, hanging garden and concert hall. In the 1920s its crown was restored to the ancient style, covered with grass and cypress, and Mussolini laid out the Fascist piazza around it.

Augustus's Mausoleum

8 Piazza di Sant'Ignazio
MAP M2

Francesco Raguzzini laid out this masterpiece of Baroque urban design for the Jesuits in 1727–8, creating a piazza carefully planned right down to the ornate iron balconies and matching dusty pink plaster walls.

9 Bernini's Elephant Obelisk
MAP M3 ■ Piazza della Minerva

An example of Bernini's fun-loving side. This baby elephant, carved to the master's designs in 1667 by Ercole Ferrata, carries a miniature 6th-century BC Egyptian obelisk on its back. It is a playful reference to Hannibal's war elephants, which carried siege towers across the Alps to attack the Romans in 218 BC.

10 Piazza della Rotonda
MAP M3

This piazza hosted a busy daily market until 1847; some of the Pantheon's portico columns still bear holes from the stall posts once set into them. The square is now filled with cafés and visitors, ranged around Giacomo della Porta's 1575 fountain, which has a tiny Egyptian obelisk dedicated to Rameses II.

A WALK AROUND THE PANTHEON

▶ Start with a *cappuccino* at **Caffè Sant'Eustachio** (see p102). Follow Salita de' Crescenzi to **Piazza della Rotonda** and the stunning beauty of the **Pantheon** (see pp18–19). Head down to Piazza della Minerva to admire **Bernini's Elephant Obelisk** and **Santa Maria sopra Minerva** (see p97).

Via S Caterina da Siena becomes Via Pie' di Marmo (look right to see the famous ancient marble foot). The street meets the piazza in front of **Galleria Doria Pamphilj** (see p97). After paying homage to the works inside, take a coffee break at the elegant **Caffè Doria** (see p102). Then head out the east end of the piazza to Via Lata, then on to the Corso to **Santa Maria in Via Lata** (see p100). Turn left up the Corso to the Baroque Piazza di Sant'Ignazio for Rome's best *trompe l'oeil* frescoes in **Sant'Ignazio di Loyola**. Work your way past the square's mini palaces onto Piazza di Pietra. An alley leads to the **Column of Marcus Aurelius**. Lunch with politicians and lobbyists from the nearby Parliament at reliable and deeply traditional **Dal Cavalier Gino** (see p103) or head to **Giolitti** for ice cream (see p102).

Walk west on Via del Leone into Piazza Borghese, home to an antiques print market and the **Palazzo Borghese** (see p100). Two blocks north you'll come to Piazza Augusto Imperatore, where this walk ends after you've visited its churches, **Augustus's Mausoleum** and the **Ara Pacis Museum**.

See map on p96 ◀

The Best of the Rest

Hadrian's Temple

1 Hadrian's Temple
MAP M2 ▪ Piazza di Pietra 9A
▪ Access to outside only (inside for cultural events only)

Eleven huge columns still stand from a Temple to Hadrian built in AD 145 by his adoptive son, Antoninus Pius.

2 Santa Maria Maddalena
MAP M2 ▪ Piazza della Maddalena 53 ▪ Open 8:30–11:30am, 5–6:30pm Sun–Fri, 9am–11:30am Sat

The 1735 façade of this church by Giuseppe Sardi is Rome's best monument to the Rococo movement.

3 Piè di Marmo
MAP N3 ▪ Via S Stefano del Cacco, Via del Piè di Marmo

This large, marble foot belonged to an unidentified ancient statue, thought to be around 26 ft (8 m) high.

4 San Lorenzo in Lucina
MAP M2 ▪ Piazza S Lorenzo in Lucina 16A ▪ Open 8am–8pm daily

Founded in the 5th century, this church was overhauled in 1090–1118. Guido Reni painted the Crucifixion altarpiece, while Bernini designed the second chapel on the right.

5 Palazzo di Montecitorio
MAP M1 ▪ Piazza di Montecitorio 33 ▪ 06 676 01
▪ Open 1st Sun of month except in Jul, Aug & 1st week of Sep

Bernini's palace houses the Chamber of Deputies. The south façade is the 17th-century original; the north is Art Nouveau.

6 Piazza di Montecitorio
MAP M1

The square's obelisk was once part of the Augustus's giant sundial, which used to be flanked by the Ara Pacis (see p98).

7 Palazzo Borghese
MAP M1 ▪ Via Borghese & Via di Ripetta ▪ Access to outside only

The oddly shaped "harpsichord of Rome", begun by Vignola in 1560, was finished with a Tiber terrace by Flaminio Ponzio.

8 Fontanella del Facchino
MAP N3 ▪ Via Lata

This small wall fountain (probably from the 1570s) is fashioned as a water-seller whose barrel forever spouts fresh water.

9 Piazza Sant'Eustachio
MAP M3

The lovely Piazza Sant'Eustachio is home to two cafés competing for the title of Rome's best cappuccino, as well as an 1196 bell tower, and an excellent view of Sant'Ivo (see p89).

10 Santa Maria in Via Lata
MAP N3 ▪ Via del Corso 306
▪ Open 5–10:30pm daily

Pietro da Cortona designed this church's façade (1660) and Bernini designed the high altar (1639–43). Its frescoes can now be seen in the Crypta Balbi (see p62). The church is also famous for its fascinating underground crypt.

Santa Maria in Via Lata

Shops

Art supplies at Ditta G. Poggi

1 Ditta G. Poggi
MAP M3 ▪ Via del Gesù 74

One of Rome's most famous art supplies stores sells everything from oil paints and sketchbooks to pencils and charcoal.

2 Davide Cenci
MAP M2 ▪ Via di Campo Marzio 1–8

Founded in 1926, Davide Cenci is a men's and women's clothes boutique. Their own classic but highly fashionable line is sold alongside international labels such as Ralph Lauren, Church's, Brooks Brothers, Fay, Burberry and Giorgio Armani.

3 Campo Marzio
MAP M2 ▪ Via di Campo Marzio 41

Accessories and luxury writing instruments here include silver-plated fountain pens and calligraphy sets; exquisite, vividly coloured leather notebooks; leather iPad and phone covers; and leather computer cases, briefcases and hand luggage.

4 Vittorio Bagagli
MAP M2 ▪ Via di Campo Marzio 42

Purveyor of fine houseware since 1855, this store sells design-led Alessi kitchen gadgets, Pavoni coffee machines and Solimene pottery.

5 Michele di Loco
MAP M1 ▪ Via del Leone 7

Exquisite men's and women's shoes and boots by a carefully selected clique of niche designers are sold here. There is also a branch at Via de Baullari 22, near Campo de' Fiori.

6 Mercato dell'Antiquariato
MAP M1 ▪ Piazza Borghese

This lovely antiquarian market consists of about 17 stalls specializing in antique prints and books.

7 Città del Sole
MAP L1 ▪ Via della Scrofa 65

Part of an Italian chain of high-class toy stores with the very best in educational playthings, this shop places an emphasis on innovative design and natural materials.

8 Il Papiro
MAP M3 ▪ Via del Pantheon 50

The Rome branch of the renowned Florentine chain sells marbled paper products, souvenir pens and calligraphy tools.

9 Campomarzio70
MAP M2 ▪ Via di Campo Marzio 70

A luxurious perfume shop carrying the finest Italian brands and sophisticated cosmetic treatments. It also stocks hand-made fragrances.

10 Bartolucci
MAP M2 ▪ Via dei Pastini 98

The toys, clocks and furniture are all made of wood by Italian artisans in this delightful shop. Its fairytale creations include rocking horses and wooden Pinocchio dolls.

See map on p96

Cafés, Gelaterie and Bars

 Giolitti
MAP M2 ■ Via degli Uffici del Vicario 40

This 19th-century landmark café is widely regarded as serving Rome's best ice cream *(see p79)*.

Tables outside Giolitti

2 Caffè Sant'Eustachio
MAP M3 ■ Piazza Sant'Eustachio 82

Another best – this café is renowned for serving the best cappuccino in Rome. Their technique is a closely guarded secret *(see p78)*.

3 Caffè Doria
MAP N3 ■ Galleria Doria Pamphilj, enter on Via della Gatta 1A

With the atmosphere of an English tea room, this elegant café has coffees and pastries, light lunches, afternoon tea, and evening drinks with nibbles.

4 Grom
MAP M2 ■ Via della Maddalena 30A

This 100% organic ice cream chain has classic recipes *(see p79)*.

5 Enoteca al Parlamento
MAP M1 ■ Via dei Prefetti 15

Popular with politicos from the nearby parliament buildings, this wine bar is atmospheric and stylish.

6 San Crispino
MAP M2 ■ Piazza della Maddalena 3

San Crispino has been making artisan gelato from pure organic ingredients since the early 1990s. It has several branches around town, and the ice creams, sorbets and meringues are as good as ever.

 La Tazza d'Oro
MAP M2 ■ Via degli Orfani 84

A die-hard locals' joint, La Tazza d'Oro has been serving what devotees swear is Rome's best coffee since 1946 *(see p79)*.

8 Enoteca Capranica
MAP M2 ■ Piazza Capranica 99

This wine bar-cum-restaurant is just the place for a quick *aperitivo* (happy hour buffet) or a more leisurely alfresco lunch. The bottle-lined interior shows that this is a serious wine bar with a well-stocked cellar and a great choice.

9 Cremeria Monteforte
MAP M3 ■ Via della Rotonda 22 ■ Closed Dec & Jan

Despite its touristy location, this gelateria guarded by a wooden Pinocchio doorman serves the best *fragola* (strawberry) ice cream in town, as well as innovative flavours such as orange chocolate *(see p19)*.

10 Pascucci Frullati Bar
MAP M4 ■ Via di Torre Argentina 20

This bar has the frothiest milk shakes and smoothies in Rome. They come in all flavours and in any combination.

Italian gelato on sale

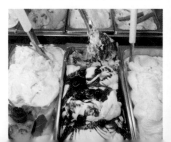

Places to Eat

 Matricianella
MAP M1 ■ Via del Leone 3–4 ■ 06 683 2100 ■ Closed Sun ■ €€

Try the *carciofi alla giudia* (Jewish-style crispy fried artichokes), *fritto vegetale* (lightly-battered fried vegetables) and *saltimbocca* (veal rolled up with prosciutto and sage), at this quintessential Roman trattoria in the *centro storico*.

2 Il Bacaro
MAP M2 ■ Via degli Spagnoli 27 ■ 06 687 2554 ■ €€

Il Bacaro's decor is contemporary inside, but the vine-clad terrace outside has the feel of old Rome. The menu has traditional dishes from across Italy. Booking is essential.

3 Osteria dell'Ingegno
MAP N2 ■ Piazza di Pietra 45 ■ 06 678 0662 ■ €€

This popular wine bar serves up huge meat and cheese platters.

4 Trattoria Enoteca Corsi
MAP N3 ■ Via del Gesù 88 ■ 06 679 0821 ■ Closed Sat night & Sun ■ €

As well as a huge wine selection, this popular restaurant offers traditional dishes at affordable prices. Check the blackboard for the daily specials.

5 Settimio all'Arancio
MAP M1 ■ Via dell'Arancio 50–52 ■ 06 687 6119 ■ Closed Sun ■ €€

Excellent classic Roman cuisine is served at this family-run trattoria.

6 Obicà
MAP M1 ■ Via dei Prefetti 26A ■ 06 683 2630 ■ €

This café-restaurant specializes in dishes containing very high-quality buffalo mozzarella.

7 Armando al Pantheon
MAP M3 ■ Salita dei Crescenzi 31 ■ 06 6880 3034 ■ Closed Sat night & Sun ■ €€€

Roman classics as well as lighter dishes are served at this long-standing, friendly family run trattoria.

Diners at Armando al Pantheon

8 Taverna del Seminario
MAP M3 ■ Via del Seminario 105 ■ 06 8110 9909 ■ €

Authentic Italian food and great house Chianti are offered at this place, all for a reasonable price.

9 La Rosetta
MAP M2 ■ Via della Rosetta 8/9 ■ 06 686 1002 ■ €€€

Tuna tartare and lobster pasta are a real treat, as is the variety of other shellfish and seafood dishes featured on the menu at this fish restaurant and oyster bar founded in 1966.

10 Dal Cavalier Gino
MAP M1 ■ Vicolo Rosini 4 ■ 06 687 3434 ■ Closed Sun ■ €€€

Largely unchanged since opening in 1963 and popular with politicians, this restaurant with *trompe l'oeil* frescoes has Roman classics such as *tonnarelli cacio e pepe* (pasta with cheese and black pepper). Book ahead.

See map on p96 ←

TOP 10 Campo de' Fiori to the Capitoline

This area is where Caesar was assassinated, but it is also home to the glory of Capitoline Hill. In ancient times, this district was full of important public monuments, but when the papacy moved to France and Rome was close to extinction, it was here that the remaining citizens lived in squalor. With the return of the popes, commerce flourished and the area revived. Today, Rome's most authentic neighbourhood bears clear signs of its long history.

Musei Capitolini

CAMPO DE' FIORI TO THE CAPITOLINE

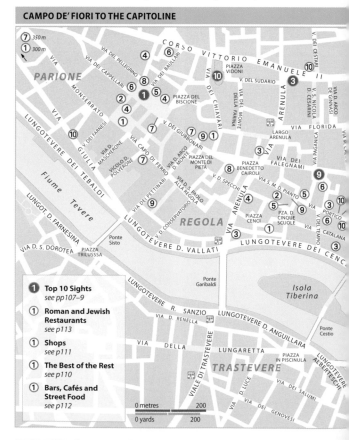

1 Top 10 Sights
see pp107–9

1 Roman and Jewish Restaurants
see p113

1 Shops
see p111

1 The Best of the Rest
see p110

1 Bars, Cafés and Street Food
see p112

0 metres   200
0 yards   200

Previous pages the vast dome of the Pantheon

1 Campo de' Fiori
MAP L4

The "Field of Flowers" occupies what was, in ancient times, the open space in front of the Theatre of Pompey. Since the Middle Ages, it has been one of Rome's liveliest areas, a backdrop for princes and pilgrims alike. It was also the locus of the Inquisition's executions, as attested to by the statue of Giordano Bruno, burned here in the Jubilee celebrations of 1600 (see p60).

2 Capitoline Hill
MAP N5

Everything in Rome is built on top of something else. The Capitoline (see pp28–9) was originally two peaks: the Arx, with the Temple of Juno, and the Cavo, with the Temple of Jupiter, now mostly occupied by the Palazzo dei Conservatori (see pp30–31). The huge Tabularium (Record Office) was built between them in 78 BC, thus forming one hill, called the Capitol; and over that the Palazzo Senatorio was built in the 12th century.

Capitoline Hill

3 Largo di Torre Argentina
MAP M4

The ruins of four Republican temples (one dating back to the 4th century BC) were uncovered here in 1925. To the west is the 18th-century Teatro Argentina, with its inscription to the Muses. Many 19th-century operas debuted here, including Rossini's *Barber of Seville*. It was a flop on its first night, but only because his enemy, Pauline Bonaparte, had hired a gaggle of hecklers to disrupt it.

4 Theatre of Marcellus
MAP N5 ■ Via del Portico d'Ottavia 29 ■ Archeological area open 9am–sunset daily

One of three ancient theatres in this district, the Theatre of Marcellus dates back to 23 BC, and was probably the most frequented of all Imperial theatres in Ancient Rome until the Colosseum captured the public's favour. The lower archways once housed picturesque medieval shops. To the right stand three columns and a frieze fragment that belonged to a Temple of Apollo, also from the 1st century BC.

The simple interior of Santa Maria in Cosmedin

5 Santa Maria in Cosmedin
MAP N6 ■ Piazza della Bocca della Verità 18 ■ Open 9.30am–6pm daily (to 5pm winter)

Originally a bread distribution centre, the site became a church in the 6th century and, 200 years later, the focus of Rome's Greek exile community. The Greek title "in Cosmedin" means "decorated". Little remains of the earliest ornamentation; most of it is from the 12th and 13th centuries, although there is a graceful altar screen characteristic of Eastern Orthodox churches. The most popular element is the *Bocca della Verità* (Mouth of Truth), an ancient cistern cover. Legend has it that the mouth snaps shut on the hands of liars.

6 Foro Boario
MAP N6

The name refers to the ancient cattle market that once existed here. Now the area is a little park with two small 2nd-century BC temples and an Arch of Janus. Dating from the reign of Constantine or later, the arch is unprepossessing, but the temples are amazingly well preserved. The rectangular Temple of Portunus, god of rivers and ports, was converted in the 9th century into a church dedicated to St Mary the Egyptian, a prostitute who became a desert hermit. The pretty, circular shrine is a Temple of Hercules Victor.

7 Chiesa del Gesù
MAP N4 ■ Piazza del Gesù ■ Open 7am–12:30pm, 4–7:45pm daily

This prototype Counter-Reformation church, enormous and ornate, was meant to proclaim the pre-eminence of the Jesuit faith. The façade is elegant, but the interior is dazzling – first impressions are of vibrant gold, bathed in sunlight, and the vision of angels and saints being pulled into heaven through a miraculous hole in the roof. The tomb of Ignatius, the order's founder, is adorned with the world's largest chunk of lapis lazuli.

8 Santa Maria in Aracoeli
MAP N4 ■ Scala dell'Arce Capitolina 14 ■ Open 9:30am–5:30pm daily (9am–6:30pm in summer)

This 6th-century church stands on the site of the ancient Temple of

THE JEWS IN ROME

Since the 2nd century BC, Jews have been a significant presence in Rome. They thrived throughout the Middle Ages, until, in 1556, Pope Paul IV, founder of the Inquisition, confined them to the squalid Ghetto, where they remained until 1870. Sixty years later they again suffered deadly persecution under the Fascists, but today Roman Jews number about 14,000 and are an integral part of civic life.

Juno Moneta (Juno the Sentinel), which was also the Roman mint – and the origin of the word "money". Legend says you can win the lottery by climbing on your knees up the 14th-century front steps – but what you will definitely gain is a fine view. The nave's columns come from older structures; the third one on the left is inscribed "a cubiculo Augustorum" ("from the emperor's bedroom").

⑨ Fontana delle Tartarughe

MAP M5 ▪ Piazza Mattei

The "Fountain of the Tortoises" is the work of three artists. It was designed by Giacomo della Porta for the Mattei family. Taddeo Landini added the bronze boys. Later, an unknown artist added the tortoises that gave the fountain its name (see p61).

Fontana delle Tartarughe

⑩ Sant'Andrea della Valle

MAP L4 ▪ Piazza Sant'Andrea della Valle ▪ Open 7:30am–12:30pm, 4:30–7:30pm daily

Why has one of the most impressive 17th-century Baroque churches been left with an asymmetrical façade? Only one angel supports the upper tier. Upon its completion, when Pope Alexander VII dared to criticize the work, sculptor Cosimo Fancelli refused to produce a second angel, saying "If he wants another he can make it himself!". Many come to see the setting of Act I of Puccini's *Tosca*, but the church also has Rome's second-largest dome and some wonderful Domenichino frescoes.

ROMAN CULTURE, LAYER UPON LAYER

▶ Because of church opening times, you should take this walk (which lasts about 2 to 4 hours) beginning either at about 10am or 4pm. Starting with the **Theatre of Marcellus** (see p107), notice the soaring buttresses that support the palace, added in the 16th century. Heading round the next corner, in the 17th-century **Santa Maria in Campitelli** (see p110) use binoculars to espy the oak leaves depicted in the altar's tiny icon. Continuing west, as you approach the **Fontana delle Tartarughe**, listen for the sound of splashing water echoing off the medieval walls. To the north, the **Crypta Balbi Museum** (see pp62–3) has fascinating displays about the neighbourhood's history. One block north is the awe-inspiring **Chiesa del Gesù**.

🍴 For one of the best cappuccino-cornetto combinations in town, stop off at **Bernasconi** (Piazza Cairoli 16).

At **Sant'Andrea della Valle** look up at the unusual barrel-vaulted ceiling. Then head south to Via di Grotta Pinta for the remains of the **Theatre of Pompey** (see p67). A block northwest, in the piazza of the **Palazzo Farnese** (see p110), admire the twin fountains, composed of stone tubs from the Baths of Caracalla. Walk across **Campo de' Fiori** (see p107) to **Palazzo della Cancelleria** (see p110) to contemplate its Renaissance perfection.

🍷 End with a drink or a meal at **La Curia di Bacco** (Via del Biscione 79), set in 1st-century BC vaults of the ancient Theatre of Pompey.

See map on pp106–7 ⟵

The Best of the Rest

① Palazzo Farnese
MAP K4 ▪ Piazza Farnese 67 ▪ 06 686 011 ▪ 45-minute tours at 5pm Wed & Fri; book ahead on www.inventerrome.com

One of Rome's largest palaces is graced with art by Michelangelo, such as the wonderful cornice *(see p58)*.

② Il Vittoriano
MAP N4 ▪ Piazza Venezia ▪ Open 9:30am–5:30pm daily (to 4:30pm in winter)

The pastiche of motifs on this monument to Victor Emmanuel II inspired the Romans to nickname it "The Wedding Cake".

③ Synagogue and Jewish Museum
MAP M5 ▪ Lungotevere dei Cenci ▪ 06 6840 0661 ▪ Museum: Open 10am–5pm Sun–Thu, 10am–2pm Fri (winter); 10am–6pm Sun–Thu, 10am–4pm Fri (summer)

Dating from 1904, this large synagogue is also home to the city's Jewish museum.

④ Palazzo della Cancelleria
MAP L4 ▪ Piazza della Cancelleria 1 ▪ Open 7:30am–8pm Mon–Sat, 9:30am–7pm Sun ▪ Adm

Once the Papal Chancellery, this lovely Renaissance structure has an unparalleled courtyard *(see p59)*.

⑤ Portico d'Ottavia
MAP M5

Built in honour of Octavia, Augustus's sister, this was an entrance to the Circus Flaminius. You can view the ruins and archaeological digs from scaffolding.

⑥ Museo Barracco
MAP L4 ▪ Corso Vittorio Emanuele II 168 ▪ 06 0608 ▪ Open 10am–4pm Tue–Sun (to 7pm summer)

This palazzo has a small but important collection of ancient sculpture and some ceramics.

⑦ Galleria Spada
MAP L5 ▪ Piazza Capo di Ferro 13 ▪ 06 683 2409 ▪ Open 8:30am–7:30pm Wed–Mon ▪ Adm (free first Sun of the month)

The Palazzo Spada houses a fine collection of Baroque paintings amassed in the 17th century by Bernardino and Virginio Spada. Don't miss Borromini's incredible perspective gallery. The palace also houses the Council of State *(see p59)*.

⑧ Palazzo Venezia
MAP N4 ▪ Via del Plebiscito 118 ▪ 06 678 0131 ▪ Open 8:30am–7:30pm Tue–Sun ▪ Adm (free first Sun of the month)

Pope Paul II used to watch carnival horse races from the balcony in the 15th century; it's also where Mussolini shouted his Fascist harangues *(see p59)*.

⑨ Santa Maria in Campitelli
MAP N5 ▪ Piazza Campitelli 9 ▪ Open 7am–7pm daily

One of the most lavish tabernacles in Rome can be found in this church.

⑩ Via Giulia
MAP K4

This fashionable street was laid out by Bramante in the early 16th century and is lined with elegant palazzi.

Palazzo della Cancelleria

Shops

1 Calzoleria Petrocchi
MAP J3 ■ Vicolo Sugarelli 2
■ Open on weekends by appt only

Bruno Ridolfi keeps alive the high fashion, made-to-measure cobbler traditions of his uncle Tito Petrocchi, who shod glamorous stars in the 1950s and 1960s *dolce vita* heyday.

2 Beppe e I Suoi Formaggi
MAP M5 ■ Via di Santa Maria del Pianto 9A/11

This shop has cheeses created by Beppe in Piemonte, along with salami, hams, preserves, olive oil, bread and wine sourced from Italian artisans. Buy to take home, or stay for a lunch of choice produce with a glass of wine.

3 Cartolerie Internazionali
MAP D4 ■ Via Arenula 85

An array of art supplies, pens, gift ideas, photo albums and greetings cards are sold at this stationery shop.

Fahrenheit 451

4 Fahrenheit 451
MAP L4 ■ Campo de' Fiori 44

Cinema, art and photography books fill this shop from floor to ceiling.

5 Boccione Limentani
MAP M5 ■ Via del Portico d'Ottavia

Known simply as the kosher bakery or the Ghetto bakery, this neighbourhood institution offers *biscotti*, *pizze* and three kinds of *crostate* (tarts) – ricotta and cherry, ricotta and chocolate and almond paste and cherry. There's always a queue.

Acqua Madre Hammam

6 Acqua Madre Hammam
MAP M5 ■ Via di S Ambrogio 17
■ Closed Mon

Recharge your batteries with a visit to this luxury *hammam*. There's a sauna and Turkish bath, plus a wide choice of body treatments.

7 Alimentari Ruggeri
MAP L4 ■ Campo de' Fiori 1

This fabulous deli has a dizzying selection of cheeses, cured meats and many food souvenirs.

8 Momento
MAP L5 ■ Piazza Benedetto Cairoli 9

Chiffon ball gowns, wool coats, printed tops and a collection of funky accessories can be found at this eclectic boutique.

9 Orologeria Timezone
MAP L4 ■ Via dei Pettinari 41

Name brands (including Swatch) are available at about 30–50 per cent below retail prices at this shop.

10 Leone Limentani
MAP M5 ■ Via del Portico d'Ottavia 47

The best-known Italian brands in kitchen design and utensils are sold in this vast warehouse-like space.

See map on pp106–7

Bars, Cafés and Street Food

1 Antico Forno Roscioli
MAP L4 ▪ Via dei Chiavari 34
▪ 06 686 4045 ▪ 7am–7:30pm Mon–
Sat, closed Sat in Jul–Aug

Pizza, *rustici* (small puff pastries with a filling), focaccia and hot dishes are served fresh from the oven. The classic is *pizza bianca* (pizza with olive oil and salt).

2 Antica Latteria
MAP K4 ▪ Vicolo del Gallo 4
▪ 06 686 5091 ▪ Closed Wed

Serving bowls of hot chocolate and milky coffee, this bar has remained largely unchanged for 50 years or so.

3 Bar del Cappuccino
MAP L5 ▪ Via Arenula 50
▪ 06 6880 6042 ▪ Closed Sun

This unassuming, friendly bar serves some of the best cappuccinos in town, with decorated foam on request.

4 O'Cartoccio
MAP L5 ▪ Via Arenula 25
▪ Closed Mon

Great Roman fried street food to take away here includes cod, courgette flowers and other vegetables.

5 Antica Norcineria Viola
MAP L4 ▪ Campo de' Fiori 43
▪ 06 6880 6114 ▪ Closed in August

Viola specializes in Umbrian ham and salami, which are considered to be the best in Italy.

Antica Norcineria Viola

Forno Campo de' Fiori

6 Forno Campo de' Fiori
MAP K4 ▪ Campo de' Fiori 22
▪ 06 6880 6662

Run by a branch of the Roscioli family, this bakery specializes in *pizza bianca*, *pizza rosso* (with a tomato sauce) and *crostate* (tarts).

7 Bar Giulia
MAP J3 ▪ Via Giulia 84
▪ 06 686 1310 ▪ Closed Sun

This simple snack bar serves good sandwiches. The barman prepares great cappuccinos with fancy foam designs.

8 Obicà
MAP L4 ▪ Campo de' Fiori 16
▪ 06 6880 2366 ▪ Open daily

A range of mozzarellas is used in salads and sandwiches at this chic mozzarella bar, part of a chain.

9 Dar Filettaro a Santa Barbara
MAP L4 ▪ Largo dei Librari 88
▪ 06 686 4018 ▪ Closed Sun

This tiny place is a Roman food institution selling crisp, deep-fried salt cod. Perfect for a quick lunch.

10 Mercerie High Street Food
MAP D4 ▪ Via S Nicola de 'Cesarini 4/5
▪ 340 997 2996

Chef Igles Corelli creates stunning finger-food-style portions of his recipes at this modern eatery.

Roman and Jewish Restaurants

PRICE CATEGORIES

For a three-course meal for one with half a bottle of wine (or equivalent meal), taxes and extra charges.

€ under €40 ■ €€ €40–60 ■ €€€ over €60

1 Piperno

MAP M5 ■ Monte de'Cenci 9 ■ 06 6880 6629 ■ Closed Sun D, Mon ■ €€

Roman-Jewish cuisine is at its finest at Piperno, located in a beautiful quiet piazza. Traditional dishes include *carciofi alla giudia* (Jewish-style fried artichokes). Booking is a must.

Crispy fried artichokes

2 Vecchia Roma

MAP N5 ■ Piazza Campitelli 18 ■ 06 686 4604 ■ Closed Wed, 2 weeks Aug ■ €€

One of Rome's top institutions, Vecchia Roma is noted for its historic interior, superb service and wine list.

3 La Taverna del Ghetto

MAP N5 ■ Via Portico d'Ottavia 8 ■ 06 6880 9771 ■ Closed Fri D, Sat L ■ €€

Enjoy kosher cooking in the medieval dining rooms, or outside on the piazza. Grilled fish is the speciality.

4 Ar Galletto

MAP K4 ■ Piazza Farnese 104 ■ 06 686 1714 ■ Closed Aug ■ €€€

This hearty trattoria with a pleasant terrace serves traditional Roman food.

5 Sora Margherita

MAP M4 ■ Piazza delle Cinque Scole 30 ■ 06 687 4216 ■ Open Mon–Thu L, Mon–Sat D ■ €€

Enjoy wonderful, hearty Roman-Jewish delicacies at this small *osteria*. There is no sign – look for the red streamers in the doorway.

6 Ba'Ghetto

MAP M5 ■ Via del Portico d'Ottavia 57 ■ 06 6889 2868 ■ Closed Fri D, Sat L ■ €€

Jewish certified kosher dishes from Rome and Northern Africa are served at this modern trattoria.

7 Filetti di Baccalà

MAP M4 ■ Largo dei Librari 88 ■ 06 686 4018 ■ Closed Sun ■ No credit cards ■ €

A Roman institution, this tiny traditional restaurant specializes in delicious battered and deep-fried salt-cod fillets.

8 Da Giggetto

MAP M5 ■ Via del Portico d'Ottavia 21A–22 ■ 06 686 1105 ■ Closed Mon ■ €€

This busy eatery is next to the Portico d'Ottavia (*see p110*). It serves an exquisite version of *carciofi alla giudia* along with hearty pasta and sustaining meat and offal stews.

9 Sheva

MAP M5 ■ Via Santa Maria del Pianto 1B ■ 06 9259 7940 ■ €

Jewish specialities here include kosher dried meat and saffron, risotto with pumpkin and chestnut and pasta with courgette.

10 Nonna Betta

MAP M5 ■ Via del Portico d'Ottavia 16 ■ 06 6880 6263 ■ Closed Tue ■ €

This kosher-style restaurant's long menu features Rome's favourite Jewish specialities, from famous fried artichokes to anchovies with endive and a variety of pastas.

See map on pp106–7

TOP 10 The Spanish Steps and Villa Borghese

Detail, Trevi Fountain

Here is Rome at its most elegant, laid out under 16th-century papal urban planning schemes. Baroque popes redeveloped the area around the Corso, now called the Tridente after the three streets exiting Piazza del Popolo. The district exudes theatricality and stylishness, with Rome's most fashionable *passeggiata* unfolding down the length of Via del Corso.

THE SPANISH STEPS AND VILLA BORGHESE

Galleria Borghese
Worth seeing for its setting alone, this gallery is home to Rome's best collection of early Bernini sculptures *(see pp24–5)*.

2 The Spanish Steps and Piazza di Spagna
MAP D2

This elegant, off-centre sweep of a staircase is Rome's most beloved Rococo monument. Although it is at its most memorable in May, when it is covered in azaleas, it is littered with people drinking in *la dolce vita* all year round. Francesco De Sanctis designed the steps in 1723–6 for

Spanish Steps and Piazza di Spagna

King Louis XV, and their true name in Italian is Scalinata della Trinità dei Monti, after the church at the top *(see p116)*. Hourglass-shaped Piazza di Spagna, named after the Spanish Embassy nearby, is centred on Bernini's Barcaccia fountain. Bernini's father, Pietro, possibly helped train his son in making this tongue-in-cheek 1629 fountain of a sinking boat The design ingeniously solved the problem of low water pressure by having a boat sprouting leaks rather than the more usual jets and sprays.

3 Santa Maria del Popolo
This spectacular church offers a priceless lesson in Renaissance and Baroque art, architecture and sculpture *(see pp38–9)*.

4 Trevi Fountain
MAP P2 ■ Piazza di Trevi

Anita Ekberg bathed in it in *La Dolce Vita; Three Coins in a Fountain* taught us to throw coins in it over our shoulder to ensure a return visit (healthier than the original tradition of drinking the water for luck) – thanks to the movies, Trevi is one of Rome's most familiar sights. The right relief shows a virgin discovering the spring from which Agrippa built the aqueduct that still feeds the fountain. Salvi's Baroque confection is grafted onto a Classical triumphal arch.

ROME'S EXPATS

Since Goethe wrote his *Italian Journey* (see p64), other Europeans have come here to study and enjoy the sunny climes. Although the Spanish Steps are known as the "English Ghetto" for the Keats residence and Babington's Tea Rooms, Goethe lived here too. It's also home to McDonald's and American Express, and top students from the French Academy are awarded the Prix de Rome to study at the Villa Medici.

twin-towered façade (1584) is by Giacomo della Porta; the double staircase outside (1587) is by Domenico Fontana. The Baroque interior has three chapels. Daniele da Volterra frescoed the third chapel on the right and painted the *Assumption* altarpiece (which depicts his teacher Michelangelo on the far right); he also painted the *Deposition* in the second chapel on the left.

⑤ Keats-Shelley Memorial
MAP D2 ■ Piazza di Spagna 26 ■ 06 678 4235 ■ Open 10am–1pm, 2–6pm Mon–Sat ■ Adm ■ www.keats-shelley-house.org

The apartment overlooking the Spanish Steps, in which John Keats took his last, consumptive breath in 1821, has been turned into a modest museum about the Romantic-era British poets who lived part of their lives in Rome (see pp64–5). Documents, letters, copies of publications and Keats' death mask are on display. Joseph Severn cradled Keats' head as he died; his resultant sketch *Keats on his Deathbed* is also exhibited.

⑥ Trinità dei Monti
MAP D2 ■ Piazza Trinità dei Monti ■ Open 10am–7pm Tue–Sat, 10am–5pm Sun

Crowning the French-commissioned Spanish Steps, this church was originally part of a convent founded by Louis XII in 1503. The eye-catching

The grounds of Villa Medici

⑦ Villa Medici
MAP D2 ■ Viale Trinità dei Monti 1 ■ Open 9:30am-5:30pm Tue–Sun (English tour at noon) ■ Adm ■ www.villamedici.it

Built in 1540, this villa was used as a prison for those who fell foul of the Inquisition – its most famous inmate was Galileo. Now home to the French Academy, it is used for concerts and exhibitions. The gardens and apartments can be visited on guided tours. Highlights are the Stanza degli Uccelli, frescoed with flowers and birds, and the Niobidi, ancient Greek art showing the massacre of Niobe and her 14 children.

⑧ Piazza del Popolo
MAP D2

Rome's elegant public living room started as a trapezoidal piazza in 1538. In 1589, Sixtus V had Domenico Fontana build a fountain crowned with a 3,200-year-old obelisk – the 25-m (82-ft) megalith, honouring Ramses II, was originally brought to Rome from Heliopolis by Augustus. Napoleon's man in Rome hired

Twin towers of Trinità dei Monti

Giuseppe Valadier to overhaul the piazza to its current Neo-Classical look in 1811–23, a giant oval that heads up the steep slope of the Pincio via a winding road (see p60).

9 Villa Borghese
MAP D2 ■ Entrances on Piazza Flaminio, Piazza del Popolo, Via Trinità dei Monti and Corso Italia

One of Rome's largest green spaces, this is made up of public park, landscaped gardens, statuary, fountains, groves, pavilions and a water clock. There are also four museums: ancient Etruscan artifacts at Villa Giulia (see pp40–41), Renaissance and Baroque art at Galleria Borghese (see pp24–5), modern art at Galleria Nazionale d'Arte Moderna (see p55), and the Museo Carlo Bilotti (see p118) has contemporary works by Giorgio de Chirico (1888–1978). In 1608 Cardinal Scipione Borghese turned these vast family lands just outside the Aurelian Walls into a private pleasure park, opened to the public in 1901. In 1809–14, Giuseppe Valadier turned the adjacent space within the city walls into the Pincio gardens, a favourite *passeggiata* destination containing an elaborate tea house and an obelisk (see p68).

Lake and pavilion, Villa Borghese

10 Villa Giulia
MAP D1 ■ Piazzale di Villa Giulia 9 ■ Open 8:30am–7:30pm Tue–Sun ■ Adm (free first Sun of the month)

Italy's top Etruscan collection, celebrating the peninsula's first great civilization, which flourished from the 8th to the 3rd centuries BC, is contained here (see pp40–41).

AN AFTERNOON ROMAN PASSEGGIATA

Piazza del Popolo
Santa Maria del Popolo
Caffè Canova
S. Maria in Montesanto
Il Brillo Parlante
Spanish Steps
Piazza di Spagna
Galleria d'Arte Moderna
Trevi Fountain
San Crispino
Piazza SS Apostoli

▶ Begin in **Piazza SS Apostoli** to see its namesake church (see p118) and the 2nd-century AD relief of an Imperial eagle against the portico's right wall. Continue straight across Via dell'Umiltà and through the elaborate iron, glass, and frescoed 1880s pedestrian passage. Turn right on Via di Muratte to get to the beautiful **Trevi Fountain** (see p115). Three coins tossed backwards over your shoulder should ensure a return trip to Rome. Leave the square on Via del Lavatore and turn left on Via della Panetteria for some of Rome's best *gelato* at San Crispino (see p78).

Turn right up Via del Tritone and left on Via Francesco Crispi for the **Galleria d'Arte Moderna** at No.24 to admire some contemporary art. Walk down Via Capo le Case and right on Via dei Due Macelli into **Piazza di Spagna** and the **Spanish Steps** (see p115). Spend as long as you like window-shopping along the grid of streets west of the piazza, but try to finish up by 5pm so you can work your way north – weaving between Via del Babuino and Via Margutta to see the art and antiques shops (see p119) – to **Piazza del Popolo**.

Pause for a cappuccino at **Caffè Canova** (see p122). Visit **Santa Maria del Popolo** (see pp38–9) to admire its Caravaggios, Raphaels and Berninis. Stop at **Santa Maria in Montesanto** (see p118) around 7pm for the Gregorian chant, then get a pizza at **Il Brillo Parlante** (Via della Fontanella 12), always popular with locals and visitors.

See map on pp114–15 ←

The Best of the Rest

1 Via dei Condotti
MAP D2

The "Fifth Avenue" of Rome is lined with chic shops and top designer fashion and haute couture boutiques.

2 Galleria Nazionale d'Arte Moderna
MAP D1 ▪ Viale delle Belle Arti 131 ▪ 06 322 981 ▪ Open 8:30am–7:30pm Tue–Sun ▪ Adm (free first Sun of the month)

The national modern art museum covers 19th- and 20th-century works of mostly Italian art but there are also some pieces by international artists.

3 Museo Carlo Bilotti
MAP D2 ▪ Viale Fiorello la Guardia (Villa Borghese) ▪ Open 10am–4pm (winter), 1–7pm (summer) Tue–Sun, 10am–7pm Sat & Sun ▪ Adm

This small art museum includes works by Giorgio de Chirico, Gino Severini and Andy Warhol.

4 SS Ambrogio e Carlo al Corso
MAP N1 ▪ Via del Corso 437 ▪ Open 7am–7pm daily

Pietro da Cortona designed the tribune, cupola and stuccoes of this Roman Baroque church in 1669.

5 Canova's Studio
MAP D2 ▪ Via del Babuino 150a ▪ Open 8am–8pm Mon–Sat

The artist's studio walls are embedded with fragments of statuary.

6 Galleria Colonna
MAP N2 ▪ Via della Pilotta 17 ▪ Open 9am–1:15pm Sat or by appt (06 678 4350) ▪ Closed Aug ▪ Adm

This gallery features work by Tintoretto, Lotto and Veronese in a lavish Baroque palace.

7 Porta del Popolo
MAP D2 ▪ Piazza del Popolo

Architect Nanni di Baccio Bigio used the Arch of Titus as the model for this gateway in the 16th century.

8 Casa di Goethe
MAP D2 ▪ Via del Corso 18 ▪ Open 10am–6pm Tue–Sun (guided tours on request) ▪ Adm

German author Goethe lived here from 1786 to 1788 (see p64); his letters are on display.

9 Santi Apostoli
MAP N2 ▪ Piazza dei S Apostoli 51 ▪ Open 7am–noon, 4–7pm

Built in the 6th century, this basilica was restructured in 1702–8. It has a trompe-l'oeil vault above the altar.

10 Santa Maria dei Miracoli and Santa Maria in Montesanto
MAP D2 ▪ Miracoli: Via del Corso 528 ▪ Open 7am–12:30pm, 4–7:30pm daily ▪ Montesanto: Via del Babuino 198 ▪ Open 5:30–8pm Mon–Fri, 11am–1:30pm Sun

Carlo Fontana built these late 17th-century "twin" churches, although Bernini is said to have guided him in the decoration of the more elaborate Montesanto.

Santa Maria dei Miracoli

Art and Antiques Shops

Libreria Il Mare, a bookshop focusing on all things nautical

1 Dott. Cesare Lampronti
MAP D2
■ Via di San Giacomo 22

Artists ranging from the school of Caravaggio to Canaletto are represented by this internationally recognised dealer in Italian Old Master paintings, specializing in 17th- and 18th-century landscapes and still life paintings.

2 Benucci
MAP D2 ■ Via del Babuino 150C

The presitigious Benucci gallery specialises in museum-quality 17th- and 18th-century art and antique furniture, as well as some modern and contemporary pieces.

3 Erica Ravenna Fiorentini
MAP D2 ■ Via Margutta 17

This large art gallery showcases leading Italian contemporary artists. It hosts exhibitions and events throughout the year.

4 Maurizio Grossi
MAP D2 ■ Via Margutta 109

Marble reproductions are sold here, such as Classical and Renaissance sculptures, statues, busts and inlaid coloured marble tables.

5 Alberto di Castro
MAP D2 ■ Piazza di Spagna 5

Etchings, lithographs and other prints from the 1660s to the 1920s are on sale in this lovely shop.

6 Libreria Il Mare
MAP D2 ■ Via del Vantaggio 19

All the books and posters in this shop are about the ocean. They also have charts and a small selection of navigation instruments.

7 Galleria Valentina Moncada
MAP D2 ■ Via Margutta 54

This is one of Italy's most important contemporary art galleries. Trained in New York, Moncada is an internationally recognized curator and talent scout who discovered Chen Zhen and was the first to exhibit Tony Cragg in Italy. She has worked with artists ranging from Anish Kapoor and Damien Hirst to Gillian Wearing and Rachel Whiteread.

8 Monogramma Arte Contemporanea
MAP D2 ■ Via Margutta 102

Exhibitions at this contemporary art gallery aim to present Italian artists to an international audience.

9 Danon
MAP D2 ■ Via Margutta 36–7

Danon is a leading, long-established dealer of antique Oriental rugs.

10 Il Marmoraro
MAP D2 ■ Via Margutta 53B

Pieces of marble are engraved with various inscriptions by the owner of this small shop.

See map on pp114–15

High Fashion Boutiques

1 **Giorgio Armani**
MAP D2 ▪ Via dei Condotti 77

One of Italy's top designers offers luxury womenswear, menswear and accessories. The Emporio Armani branch at Via del Babuino 140 sells the designer's couture line at lower prices. The lowest-end line, Armani Jeans, is at Via del Babuino 70A.

2 **Ferragamo**
MAP D2 ▪ Via dei Condotti 73–4

The shoemaker to the stars during Hollywood's Golden Age of the 1950s hasn't lost its touch, but it now mass-produces styles rather than creating unique works.

3 **Gucci**
MAP D2 ▪ Via dei Condotti 8

The Florentine saddle-maker turned his leather-working skills into one of Italy's early fashion successes. This flagship store has top-notch bags, shoes and other accessories .

4 **Valentino**
MAP D2 ▪ Piazza di Spagna 38

The *prêt-à-porter* collection of this native Roman designer in the top echelon of fashion since Jackie Kennedy and Audrey Hepburn donned his clothes in the 1960s.

5 **Prada**
MAP D2 ▪ Via dei Condotti 88

This Milan fashion house with minimalist, slightly retro clothing is the most highly priced of the top Italian designers.

Mannequin at Giorgio Armani

6 **Gianni Versace**
MAP D2 ▪ Piazza di Spagna 12

The house of the late fashion designer never compromises the clothing's flamboyant cuts and use of colour.

7 **Fausto Santini**
MAP D2 ▪ Via Frattina 120

Beautiful and elegant men's and women's shoes and bags of supreme quality are available here.

8 **Fendi**
MAP D2 ▪ Largo Goldoni 420

Founded by Adele and Edoardo Fendi and nurtured by their five daughters, this Roman fashion empire reigns over Italy's rage for furs.

9 **Boutique Alberta Ferretti**
MAP D2 ▪ Via Condotti 34

The well-cut women's clothing here is feminine yet powerful and modern.

10 **Laura Biagiotti**
MAP D2 ▪ Via Mario de' Fiori 26

This is one of the largest fashion houses in Italy, making couture for women since 1972 and for men since 1987. The late Biagiotti earned the moniker "Queen of Cashmere" for her use of soft wool.

Shop windows at Prada

Specialist Shops

 Saddlers Union
MAP D2 ■ Via Margutta 11

The prime-quality leather products sold at this shop are very popular with celebrities and style icons. Browse through their range of travel bags, briefcases and belts, as well as computer and iPad cases.

2 **Profumum**
MAP D2 ■ Via di Ripetta 248

The fragrances created by this Roman luxury perfumery include Alba, Acqua Viva and Confetto. Be prepared to empty your wallet.

3 **Buccone**
MAP D2 ■ Via di Ripetta 19–20

A vast selection of wines at excellent prices are available at this historic wine shop. Homemade pasta, honey and jam are sold here as well.

Wines and speciality foods, Buccone

 Lelli
MAP D2 ■ Via Margutta 5

This shop has the best of European interior design, from fabrics and wallpaper to cutlery and kitchen utensils.

5 **Il Pesciolino Rosso**
MAP D2 ■ Via Bocca di Leone 49

A beautiful selection of aesthetically pleasing toys and craft activities, including the innovative Djeco range,

Toys and crafts at Il Pesciolino Rosso

is available at this niche toyshop. Toys are handcrafted from natural, non-toxic materials and colours.

 c.u.c.i.n.a.
MAP D2 ■ Via Mario de' Fiori 65

The motto of this shop, which carries superb minimalist kitchenware, translates as "How a kitchen inspires new appetites".

 Fabriano Boutique
MAP D2 ■ Via del Babuino 173

This luxury stationery shop carries Italian-made product lines for the office and school, all manufactured to the highest quality.

8 **'Gusto**
MAP D2 ■ Piazza Augusto Imperatore 9

Heaven for fashionable foodies, Gusto abounds with cookbooks (there are plenty in English), kitchen gadgets, wine, glasses and table accessories.

9 **Vertecchi**
MAP D2 ■ Via della Croce 70

The queen of Rome's stationery stores, Vertecchi has hundreds of types of pens (the fancier ones are sold next door at No. 72), a large selection of notebooks, as well as the very best in art supplies.

10 **Quetzalcoatl**
MAP D2 ■ Via delle Carrozze 26

Taking the name of Aztec deity Quetzalcoatl – who the Aztecs believed gifted cacao seeds to mankind – this chocolatier offers elaborately presented, exquisitely crafted chocolates.

See map on pp114–15 ←

Pubs, Cafés and Bars

 Enoteca Antica
MAP D2 ■ Via della Croce 76b

Delicious antipasti and wine by the glass are served in this old-fashioned lively establishment.

 Gregory's Jazz Club
MAP D2 ■ Via Gregoriana 54a

Enjoy great live jazz and blues here every night of the week, accompanied by good food and wine, and a wide variety of fine whiskeys.

3 **Antico Caffè Greco**
MAP D2 ■ Via Condotti 86

Rome's premier literary café since 1760, Antico Caffè Greco is best known for being frequented by 19th-century English Romantic poets *(see p78)*.

4 **Stravinskij Bar**
MAP D2 ■ Via del Babuino 9

Impeccably prepared dry martinis, a classy atmosphere and the enchanting garden of the Hotel de Russie *(see p170)* make this one of the most exclusive bars in town. Light Mediterranean dishes are served for lunch.

5 **VyTa Santa Margherita**
MAP E2 ■ Largo Marcello Mastroianni 1

Located in the grounds of Villa Borghese, this café serves drinks and light lunches, including salads, sandwiches and some seafood.

 Ciampini al Café du Jardin
MAP D2 ■ Piazza Trinità dei Monti ■ Closed Nov–Feb

Enjoy a drink while watching the sunset at this enchanting café.

7 **Caffè Rosati**
MAP D2 ■ Piazza del Popolo 4–5

Art Nouveau rival to the formerly right-wing Canova across the piazza, this café has long been the haunt of left-wing intellectuals *(see p79)*.

8 **Caffè Canova**
MAP D2 ■ Piazza del Popolo 16–17

The previously right-wing bastion in the long-standing Piazza del Popolo café war, this place has cheaper espresso and better ice cream (but the Rosati is more stylish).

9 **Babington's Tea Rooms**
MAP D2 ■ Piazza di Spagna 23

Opened in 1893 by a Derbyshire lady, this was the expat hub of the later Grand Tour era. It serves pricey tea and dainty British edibles.

10 **Ginger**
MAP N1 ■ Via Borgognona 43/44

Aimed at the health-conscious, Ginger serves salads, vegan dishes, smoothies and inventive mains.

Stylish, light-filled interior of Ginger

Places to Eat

Fiaschetteria Beltramme

1 Fiaschetteria Beltramme
MAP D2 ▪ Via della Croce 39 ▪ 06 6979 7200 ▪ No credit cards ▪ €€
Regulars and tourists sit around communal tables at this ultra-traditional trattoria just down the block from the Spanish Steps.

2 Edy
MAP D2 ▪ Vicolo del Babuino 4 ▪ 06 3600 1738 ▪ Closed Sun L ▪ €
Some of the best food and lowest prices in the neighbourhood can be found at Edy. It serves a mix of sea-food and Roman dishes. The candle-lit tables out front are a nice touch.

3 'Gusto
MAP D2 ▪ Piazza Augusto Imperatore 9 ▪ 06 322 6273 ▪ €€
Modern, hip 'Gusto is a combination of wine bar, restaurant and pizzeria.

4 Antica Birreria Peroni
MAP N3 ▪ Via San Marcello 19/Piazza SS Apostoli ▪ 06 679 5310 ▪ Closed Sun ▪ €
This 1906 beer hall sponsored by Italy's premier brewery has excellent, inexpensive local Roman food.

5 Massimo Riccioli
MAP E2 ▪ Via Veneto 50 ▪ 06 4214 4715 ▪ Closed Sun ▪ €€€
Sicilian-Roman chef Massimo Riccioli made his name with seafood, but his talents stretch to meat dishes too. The fixed-price lunch menus at this elegant restaurant in the Majestic hotel (see p170) are good value; dinner is more formal.

6 Assagia Roma
MAP D2 ▪ Via Margutta 19 ▪ 06 9779 7980 ▪ €€
Star chef Angelo Troiani creates tapas-style dishes, allowing diners to experience a range of flavours, from raw fish to Italian cuisine staples.

Casina Valadier, offering great views

7 Casina Valadier
MAP D2 ▪ Piazza Bucarest ▪ 06 6992 2090 ▪ Closed Mon ▪ €€€
Housed in an 18th-century villa with a splendid view of the city, this elegant restaurant serves gourmet Italian cuisine paired with great wines. It is perfect for special occassions.

8 Al 34
MAP D2 ▪ Via Mario de' Fiori 34 ▪ 06 679 5091 ▪ Closed Mon L ▪ €€
Excellently priced menus here feature inventive Italian cooking.

9 Hamasei
MAP N1 ▪ Via della Mercede 35/36 ▪ 06 679 2134 ▪ €€
This popular, minimalist Japanese restaurant has a sushi bar and also offers more substantial dishes.

10 Dal Pollarolo
MAP D2 ▪ Via di Ripetta 4-5 ▪ 06 361 0276 ▪ Closed Thu ▪ €
Pasta dishes here include the local *pasta alla checca*, with raw tomatoes, fennel seeds, olives and capers.

See map on pp114–15

⏍ Ancient Rome

This area has always been a study in contrasts. In ancient times, the emperor's palaces were built on the Palatine, not far from the docks where roustabouts heaved goods imported from around the world. Today, the area is again an enclave of smart houses and greenery, studded with hidden art treasures and some of the world's finest ancient monuments and priceless archaeological finds.

Detail, Baths of Caracalla

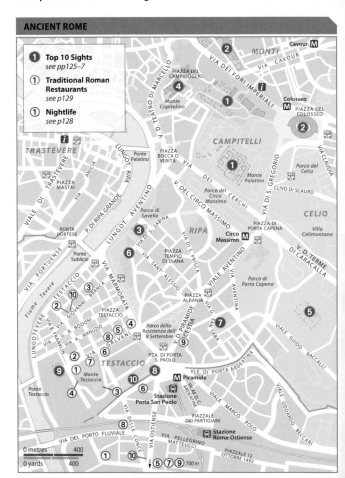

ANCIENT ROME

1 **Top 10 Sights**
see pp125–7

1 **Traditional Roman Restaurants**
see p129

1 **Nightlife**
see p128

0 metres 400
0 yards 400

1 Roman Forum and Palatine Hill

Once the heart of the Roman empire, these ruins are an eerie landscape that seems gripped by the ghosts of an ancient civilization (see pp20–21).

2 The Colosseum and Imperial Fora

These monuments memorialize Imperial supremacy. The Colosseum embodies the Romans' passion for brutal entertainment. Trajan's Forum was called a Wonder of the World by contemporaries; the only remnant is Trajan's Column – Roman sculptural art at its peak (see pp26–7).

3 Santa Sabina

MAP D5 ■ Piazza Pietro d'Illiria 1 ■ 06 579 401■ Open 8:15am–12:30pm & 3:30–6pm daily

This church was built over the Temple of Juno Regina in about 425 to honour a martyred Roman matron. In 1936–8 it was restored almost to its original condition, while retaining 9th-century additions such as the Cosmatesque work and the bell tower. Corinthian columns are surmounted by arcades with marble friezes and light filters through the selenite window panes. The doors are 5th-century carved cypress, with

The elegant nave of Santa Sabina

18 panels of biblical scenes, including the earliest known Crucifixion – strangely without any crosses.

4 Musei Capitolini

The original motivation for these museums was political. When the popes started the first museum here in 1471, it laid claim to Rome's hopes for civic autonomy – the Palazzo dei Conservatori was the seat of hated papal counsellors, who ran the city by "advising" the Senate. Today the museums contain a spectacular collection of art (see pp28–31).

5 Baths of Caracalla

MAP E6 ■ Via delle Terme di Caracalla 52 ■ 06 3996 700 ■ Open 9am–2pm Mon, 9am–1 hr before sunset Tue–Sun ■ Adm (free first Sun of the month)

Inaugurated in 217, these luxurious baths were used by up to 2,000 people at a time until 546, when invading Goths destroyed the aqueducts. In general, Roman baths included social centres, art galleries, libraries, brothels and palestrae (exercise areas). Bathing involved taking a sweat bath, a steam bath, a cool-down, then a cold plunge. The Farnese family's ancient sculpture collection was found here, including Hercules, a signed Greek original. Today, the ruins of individual rooms can be seen.

The ruins of the Baths of Caracalla

6 Piazza of the Knights of Malta

MAP D5

Everyone comes here for the famous bronze keyhole view of St Peter's Basilica, ideally framed by an arbour of perfect trees (see p63). However, it's also worth a look for the piazza's wonderful 18th-century decoration by Giambattista Piranesi, otherwise renowned for his powerful engravings of fantasy-antiquity scenes. To honour the ancient order of crusading knights (founded in 1080), the architect chose to adorn the walls with dwarf obelisks and trophy armour, in the ancient style. Originally based on the island of Rhodes, then Malta, the knights are now centred in Rome.

Pyramid of Caius Cestius

7 San Saba

MAP E6 ■ Piazza Gian Lorenzo Bernini 20 ■ Open 8am–noon, 4–7:10pm Mon–Sat, 9:30am–1pm, 4–7:30pm Sun & public hols

Originally a 7th-century oratory for Palestinian monks fleeing their homeland, the present church is a 10th-century renovation, with many additions. The portico of the 15th-century loggia houses archaeological fragments. Greek style in floorplan, the interior decoration is mostly Cosmatesque. The greatest oddity is a 13th-century fresco showing St Nicholas about to toss a bag of gold to three naked girls lying on a bed, thus saving them from prostitution.

Detail, San Saba

8 Pyramid of Caius Cestius

MAP D6 ■ Piazzale Ostiense ■ 06 3996 7700 ■ Open 1st & 3rd Sun of month by appt only ■ Adm

This 12 BC edifice remains a truly imposing monument to the wealthy Tribune of the People for whom it was built. It is 36 m (118 ft) high and took 330 days to erect, according to an inscription carved upon it. Unlike Egyptian originals, however, it was built of brick then covered with marble, which was the typically pragmatic Roman way of doing things.

Gallery at MACRO Testaccio

9 MACRO Testaccio

MAP C6 ▪ Piazza Orazio Giustiniani 4 ▪ 06 6710 70400 ▪ Open 4–10pm Tue–Sun during exhibitions only ▪ Adm ▪ www.museomacro.org

Originally a working-class quarter that grew up around a slaughterhouse, Testaccio is now a trendy, arty area. The 19th-century former slaughterhouse has been converted into a branch of the dynamic contemporary art gallery, MACRO, which hosts temporary exhibitions of Italian and international art. Monte Testaccio itself – composed entirely of pottery shards – is home to the city's more alternative nightclubs.

10 Protestant Cemetery

MAP D6 ▪ Via Caio Cestio 6 ▪ Open 9am–5pm Mon–Sat, 9am–1pm Sun (closed one week in Aug) ▪ Donation

Also called the Acattolico (Non-Catholic) Cemetery, people of many faiths have been buried here since 1738. The most famous are the English poets Keats and Shelley (see pp48–9). Until 1870, crosses and references to salvation were forbidden.

Keats' tombstone

A MORNING PARKLAND STROLL

▶ The parkland on the other side of the Circus Maximus from the Palatine Hill conceals exquisite early churches and other gems. Start on the south side of the **Circus Maximus**, now a sunken patch of dust and weeds, but once a majestic racecourse until the popes plundered its stones to build their palaces. Head up the hill to the **Roseto Comunale** (see p69). In spring and summer few places in Rome radiate such beauty. Continue along the old wall and enter Parco Savello's **Giardino degli Aranci** (see p69) to take in the view from the parapet. Next door is **Santa Sabina** (see p125). Use a torch and binoculars to scrutinize carved wooden doors and the Crucifixion scene. Stop next at Piranesi's **Piazza of the Knights of Malta** and peer through the celebrated keyhole.

Wind down Via di Sant'Anselmo until Viale Aventino and **San Saba**. Stop to appreciate the notorious St Nicholas fresco on the left wall. In **Parco della Resistenza dell'8 Settembre** you can get a *gelato* in the park's café and admire the 3rd-century Aurelian Wall (see p156).

Cross over to the lovely **Protestant Cemetery**, pay your respects at the graves of Shelley, Keats and friends, pause to reflect on the splendid **Pyramid of Caius Cestius** and leave your donation in the box as you exit.

A five-minute walk north takes you to **Volpetti**, Rome's premier deli, or to **Volpetti Piu**, a *tavola calda* (self-service buffet) around the corner from the deli, both great choices for lunch (see p129).

See map on p124 ←

Nightlife

 Planet Roma
MAP D6 ■ Via del Commercio 36

Housed in a former factory off Via Ostiense, Planet Roma is huge, with three spaces, each of which plays different music. There is live music on Thursdays and Sundays, DJ sets on Fridays and a well-attended gay night on Saturdays, as well as occasional theme nights.

 On the Rox
MAP D6 ■ Via Galvani 54 ■ 347 793 6277

Enjoy great, inexpensive cocktails at this well-established bar. It has a dance floor and a lovely outdoor patio too. Locals come here to start their night out

3 **Radio Londra**
MAP D6 ■ Via di Monte Testaccio 67

One of Rome's perennial favourites for an energetic night out, this is a noisy, buzzing rock-and-roll venue with an air-force theme. It hosts house music DJ sets, discos and occasional up-and-coming live bands. Food is also available.

4 **L'Alibi**
MAP D6 ■ Via di Monte Testaccio 44

The city's largest and most famous gay club has several dance floors, lounges and a huge terrace garden to cool off during the summer months. Note that entrance fees rise after 1am.

5 **Vinile**
Via Libetta 19 ■ 06 5728 8666

Situated in post-industrial Ostiense, this large, trendy nightclub with a barrel roof attracts an older clientele until midnight followed by a younger crowd in the early hours. It hosts artistic performances and evenings where DJs sit on a pedestal over the circular bar while playing retro music. Good food and delicious cocktails are served.

6 **BeBop Music Club**
MAP D6 ■ Via Giuseppe Giulietti 14 ■ 06 575 5582

Set in a bare-brick cellar, this popular venue has a rich jazz programme which includes blues, swing and R&B. It also serves dinner and drinks.

Crowds at a gig at Rashomon Club

7 **Rashomon Club**
Via degli Argonauti 16

This great electronic music and performance space in the hip Ostiense area has an underground vibe. The liveliest night is Thursday.

8 **Porto Fluviale**
Via del Porto Fluviale 22

Set in a former industrial warehouse, this hip, popular trattoria and bar serves great cocktails and tasty, creative Italian staples and pizzas.

9 **Goa**
MAP D6 ■ Via G Libetta 13

One of Rome's hottest nightclubs, Gua attracts fashionable crowds and the DJs who play here are among the most famous in the world.

10 **Doppiozeroo**
MAP D6 ■ Via Ostiense 68

A popular pre-club destination, Doppiozeroo serves great drinks and a huge *aperitivo* buffet.

Traditional Roman Restaurants

 Checchino dal 1887
MAP D6 ▪ Via di Monte
Testaccio 30 ▪ 06 574 3816
▪ Closed Sun D & Mon ▪ €€

Among the great Roman restaurants, this offers offal-based delicacies such as *rigatoni alla pajata* (pasta with calf intestine).

 Agustarello
MAP D6 ▪ Via G Branca 100
▪ 06 574 6585 ▪ No credit cards ▪ €

The Roman-style, rich dishes here include *coda alla vaccinara* (oxtail), *lingua* (tongue) and other rustic fare.

③ Da Remo
MAP D6 ▪ Piazza Santa Maria
Liberatrice 44 ▪ 06 574 6270 ▪ Open
7pm–midnight Mon–Sat ▪ €

This quintessential Roman pizzeria is always packed. It is known for its *scrocchiarella* pizzas, with thin crispy crusts and simple toppings.

④ Volpetti Più
MAP D6 ▪ Via A Volta 8/10
▪ 06 574 4306 ▪ Closed Sun ▪ €

Volpetti Più is an upscale self-service *tavola calda* with dishes to eat in or take away. Around the corner, Rome's top deli, Volpetti, is the ideal place to have a lunchtime sandwich.

⑤ Felice
MAP D6 ▪ Via Mastro Giorgio
29 ▪ 06 574 6800 ▪ Open daily; closed
Aug ▪ €€

This simple trattoria is one of the best places in Rome to try traditional *carciofi alla romana* (see p74).

⑥ Osteria Degli Amici
Via Zabaglia 25 ▪ MAP D6
▪ 06 578 1466 ▪ Closed Tue ▪ €

Founded by two gourmet friends, this traditional *osteria* serves Roman specialities in a friendly setting.

⑦ Angelina
MAP D6 ▪ Via Galvani 24A
▪ 06 5728 3840 ▪ €€

The old butcher's tables and tiled walls are testimony of this restaurant's past as a butcher's store, and this is also reflected in the meaty menu.

⑧ Da Oio a Casa Mia
MAP D6 ▪ Via Galvani 43–45
▪ 06 578 2680 ▪ €

This no-frills trattoria has authentic versions of Roman pasta classics and plenty of offal offerings.

⑨ La Villetta dal 1940
MAP D6 ▪ Viale della Piramide
Cestia 53 ▪ 06 575 0597 ▪ €

Surrealist painter Giorgio de Chirico and other artists frequented this place in the 1960s. The traditional fare includes *saltimbocca alla romana*.

⑩ Trapizzino
MAP D6 ▪ Via Giovanni Branca
88 ▪ 06 4241 9624 ▪ €

Pizza meets sandwich at this popular eatery, resulting in a triangular piece of baked dough filled with Roman staples such as oxtail, tripe or chicken.

Artisanal deli products at Volpetti Più

See map on p124 ←

⭐🔟 The Esquiline and Lateran

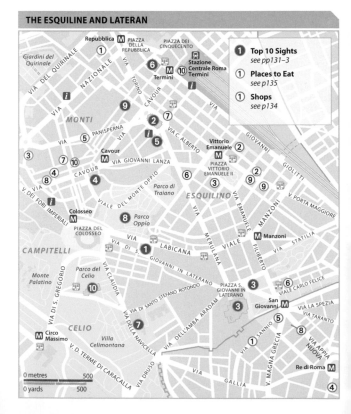

In ancient times the largest of Rome's seven hills was almost entirely an upper-class residential area. The western slope was densely populated and seen as a squalid slum. However, in the 4th century, this zone became central to the growth of Christianity. In supporting it as the official faith, Constantine did not dare step on too many pagan toes, so he set up churches outside town on the sites of holy tombs. The main one was San Giovanni in Laterano. Today, this entire area is still steeped in history and religious mystique.

Moses, San Pietro in Vincoli

THE ESQUILINE AND LATERAN

1	**Top 10 Sights** see pp131–3
1	**Places to Eat** see p135
1	**Shops** see p134

1 San Clemente
MAP F4 ▪ Via di S Giovanni
in Laterano 108 ▪ 06 774 0021
▪ Open 9am–12:30pm, 3–6pm daily
(from noon Sun) ▪ Adm to lower levels

Architectural layers here reveal
Rome's history, from the 2nd century
BC to the 15th century AD *(see p51)*.

2 Santa Maria Maggiore
MAP F3 ▪ Piazza di S Maria
Maggiore ▪ Open 7am–6:45pm daily

This basilica is a unique blend of
architectural styles. The nave and
its mosaics are original 5th century;
the Cosmatesque work, apse
mosaics and Romanesque bell
tower are medieval; the coffered
ceiling (of New-World gold) is
Renaissance; and the domes and
front and back façades are Baroque.
Pope Sixtus V erected the Egyptian
obelisk in 1587 as part of his overall
town-planning, to provide landmarks
for pilgrims. The column in front was
taken from the Basilica of Maxentius
and Constantine in 1615 *(see p51)*.

3 San Giovanni in Laterano and Scala Santa
MAP F5 ▪ Piazza di S Giovanni in
Laterano ▪ Open 7am–6:30pm daily
(cloisters 9am–6pm; baptistry 7am–
12:30pm, 4–6:30pm; museum 10am–
5:30pm); Scala Santa 6:30am–6:30pm
Mon–Sat, 7am–6:30pm Sun & hols (to
7pm in summer) ▪ Adm for cloisters

Founded by Constantine in the
4th century, this is the cathedral
of Rome's bishopric. Popes were
crowned here until the 19th century.

Santa Maria Maggiore

Besides its grandiose Baroque bulk,
the church boasts the world's first
baptistry, its octagonal shape the
model for all those to come. A
building on the piazza houses the
Scala Santa, claimed to be the stairs
to Pontius Pilate's house that Jesus
ascended to face his trial. Tradition
says that St Helena, mother of
Emperor Constantine, brought it
here from Jerusalem.

4 San Pietro in Vincoli
MAP R4 ▪ Piazza di S Pietro
in Vincoli 4A ▪ Open 8am–12:30pm,
3–7pm daily (8am–12:30pm, 3–6pm
Oct–Mar)

Michelangelo's *Moses* is the
unmissable experience here. Weirdly
horned and glaring, the righteously
indignant patriarch is about to smash
the tablets in outrage at his people's
idolatry. This powerful sculpture was
just one of 40 the artist planned, but
never finished, for the tomb of Pope
Julius II *(see p57)*. The original shrine
was built in the 4th century to house
the chains supposedly used to bind
St Peter in prison. It has been rebuilt
since, first in the 8th century and
again in the 15th century.

Devotees climbing the Scala Santa

Depictions of angels and saints at Santa Prassede

5 Santa Prassede
MAP F4 ■ Via di S Prassede 9A
■ Open 7am–noon, 4–6:30pm daily
(from 7:30am Sun)

Built in the 9th century over a 2nd-century oratory, the original design of this basilica is still discernible despite restorations. In the central nave, a stone slab covers the well where St Prassede is said to have buried 2,000 martyrs. Byzantine mosaic artists decorated the apse and the Chapel of St Zeno with jewel-hued, gold-glinting work depicting saints, lambs, palm trees and poppies. There is also a fragment of the column that Christ was said to have been bound to when he was flogged.

6 Palazzo Massimo alle Terme

Housing an extraordinary collection of ancient frescoes, mosaics and

> **ESTABLISHMENT OF THE CHURCH**
>
> This area played a central role in early Christianity. Although Constantine himself was not a firm convert, his mother, St Helena, was untiring in her promotion of the new religion. She convinced her son to found the official seat of the Bishop of Rome on the site of the ancient Laterani family villa, which his wife Fausta had inherited.

sculpture, this branch of the Museo Nazionale Romano is perhaps the most inspiring. The late 19th-century building was built by the Massimo family and later served as a Jesuit college (see pp34–5).

7 Santo Stefano Rotondo
MAP F5 ■ Via di S Stefano
Rotondo 7 ■ Open 10am–1pm &
2:30–5:30pm winter, 10am–1pm
& 3:30–6:30pm summer

The unusual shape of this church (468–83) may mean it was built over Nero's round *Macellum Magnum* (meat market). Or perhaps its form was inspired by Jerusalem's Church of the Holy Sepulchre. Recent digs have found a Mithraeum underneath. The structure is a delightful sanctuary, situated far from urban uproar, although 16th-century frescoes by Niccolò Pomarancio depict martyrdoms in sadistic fashion.

Santo Stefano Rotondo

8 Domus Aurea

MAP E4 ■ Via della Domus Aurea ■ 06 3996 7700 ■ Open by appt Sat & Sun only

After the great fire of Rome in 64 AD, Nero built a new villa decorated with gold and precious stones, giving the villa its name, which means Golden House. Later emperors, embarrassed by his profligacy, tried to undo as much of it as possible. The Flavians drained Nero's lake to build the Colosseum (see p26), and Trajan built Rome's first great public baths over the original house. It was only in 1772 that archaeologists started excavations within the Domus Aurea.

9 Santa Pudenziana

MAP E3 ■ Via Urbana 160 ■ 06 481 4622 ■ Open 8:30am–noon & 3–6pm daily

Converted in the 4th century from a Roman bathhouse, Santa Pudenziana is one of the oldest churches in Rome and now serves the Filipino community. Its simple structure differs from the ornate features of Rome's other churches. The main draw here is the 5th-century apse mosaic, depicting an enthroned Christ surrounded by his disciples and two female figures crowning St Peter and St Paul.

10 Santi Giovanni e Paolo

MAP E5 ■ Piazzale SS Giovanni e Paolo 13 ■ Open 8:30am–noon, 3:30–6pm daily

The home of these 4th-century martyrs is still visible under the 5th-century structure (see p63). Except for the Late Baroque interior, much of the church is medieval. The 45 m (145 ft) bell tower's base is that of the 1st-century Temple of Claudius that once stood here.

Santi Giovanni e Paolo

EXPLORING ROME'S EARLY CHURCHES

Santa Maria Maggiore
Santa Prassede
Panella
Enoteca Cavour
Via dei Santi Quattro Coronati
San Clemente
Cannavota
Santi Quattro Coronati
San Giovanni in Laterano

▶ MORNING

Start with **San Clemente** (see p131), with its fascinating layers. At the lowest level use a torch (flashlight) to appreciate the beautiful fresco of the head of a bearded man. Walk one block over to the **Via dei Santi Quattro Coronati** to glimpse the produce market (see p81), then turn left and walk up the hill to Santi Quattro Coronati, a little-visited 4th-century church with remarkable frescoes in the chapel (1246). Continue on until you reach **San Giovanni in Laterano** (see p131). The 13th-century Cosmatesque cloisters with gorgeously twisted columns and mosaic inlays will make your visit truly memorable.

Then head across the piazza for a hearty lunch at Cannavota (Piazza S Giovanni in Laterano 20) or stop at **Panella** (see p134) on your way to Santa Maria Maggiore.

AFTERNOON

At **Santa Maria Maggiore** (see p131) check out the ancient column in front, then use binoculars inside to examine the 5th-century mosaics lining the upper reaches of the nave. Next, walk over to **Santa Prassede**, where you can take in some of Rome's most radiant Byzantine mosaics and a powerful painting of the Flagellation in the sacristy.

For sustenance after your spiritual journey, walk back past Santa Maria Maggiore and down Via Cavour for some great wines and Modern European dishes at Enoteca Cavour 313 (see p135).

See map on p130 ←

Shops

1 Via Sannio Market
MAP G5

Despite the influx of cheap, made-in-China clothes and designer fakes, this historic flea market still sells good-condition second-hand clothes and paraphernalia (see p81).

2 Nuovo Mercato Esquilino
MAP F4 ■ Via Mamiani and Via Principe Amedeo

Rome's most ethnically diverse market has stalls selling Chinese noodles and soya sauce, African and Asian vegetables, halal meat and spices from all over the world.

3 Oviesse
MAP F4 ■ Piazza Vittorio Emanuele 108–12

Clothing at bargain prices and a large range of cosmetics and toiletries is sold at this store This is the largest of several branches in Rome.

4 Pompi
MAP G6 ■ Via Albalonga 7/9

Known as "the temple of tiramisu", this bar sells the popular dessert in many different varieties, including the must-try banana and strawberry kinds. It also has cakes, pastries, ice cream and many other goodies.

5 Coin
MAP G5 ■ Piazzale Appio 7

A contemporary high-end department store, with reasonable prices, Coin sells clothing, accessories and shoes, as well as kitchenware and more general furnishings.

Panella delicatessen and café

6 Panella
MAP F4 ■ Via Merulana 54

A chic contemporary deli-café, Panella has fantastic freshly baked artisan breads, pizzas, savoury pies and salads to eat in or take away, and shelves of upscale grocery products that make great presents.

7 UPIM
MAP F3 ■ Via Gioberti 64

This trendy and more expensive branch of the mid-range department store chain stocks popular clothing brands and designer homeware.

8 Leam
MAP G5 ■ Via Appia Nuova 26

Prada and D&G are some of the designer brands sold at this extremely trendy clothing emporium. It also has a huge online store.

9 Pacific Trading
MAP F4
■ Via Principe Eugenio 17

Rome's biggest, longest established Asian supermarket has Thai pastes, Indian spices and Filipino ice cream.

10 Borri Books
MAP F3 ■ Inside Termini Station, Plazza dei Cinquecento

This bookshop across three floors has a large English-language section.

Coin department store

Places to Eat

PRICE CATEGORIES

For a three-course meal for one with half a bottle of wine (or equivalent meal), taxes and extra charges.

€ under €40   €€ €40–60   €€€ over €60

① Rosemary – Terra e Sapori
MAP R2 ■ Via Modena 16 ■ 06 4891 3645 ■ €

This eco-friendly bistro serves Italian specialties made with local seasonal produce. The menu includes soups, salads, sandwiches, and homemade cakes and biscuits.

② Himalaya's Kashmir
MAP F4 ■ Via Principe Amedeo 325-327 ■ 06 446 1072 ■ €

Samosas, tandoori, thali and all the usual accompaniments feature at this popular Indian restaurant.

Italian dessert tiramisu

③ Corte del Grillo Osteria
MAP Q4 ■ Salita del Grillo 6B ■ 06 6992 2183 ■ Closed Aug ■ €€€

Super-fresh fish is served either raw or cooked. Select a fish from the cool counter and order it baked in a salt crust, poached, roasted or grilled. Finish with a delicious tiramisu.

④ Taverna Romana
MAP Q4 ■ Via Madonna dei Monti 79 ■ 06 474 53253 ■ Closed Sun D, Aug ■ €€

Enjoy traditional, inexpensive lunches and dinners at this popular taverna. Try soupy pasta with *ceci* (chickpeas) or *fagioli* (beans), *maltagliati* pasta with fresh ricotta or marvellous slow-cooked guinea fowl.

⑤ La Carbonara
MAP R3 ■ Via Panisperma 214 ■ 06 482 5176 ■ Closed Aug, Sun ■ €

Organic produce is used in traditional Roman dishes at this cosy *osteria*.

⑥ Pinsa e Buoi
MAP G5 ■ Via Carlo Felice 51 ■ 06 7720 1760 ■ €€

This intimate trattoria serves Roman staples, including offal dishes, delicious pasta and *pinsa* pizzas.

⑦ Daruma Sushi
MAP R4 ■ Via dei Serpenti 1 ■ 06 4893 1003 ■ €€

Sushi, sashimi, miso soup and fresh noodles are on the menu at this lively Japanese fast-food and take-away place. It offers a free delivery service to local hotels.

⑧ Enoteca Cavour 313
MAP R4 ■ Via Cavour 313 ■ 06 678 5496 ■ Closed Sun in summer ■ €

One of Rome's most appealing restaurants has an inventive Modern European menu and uses carefully sourced ingredients. The cannelloni with wild chicory, ricotta, and anchovies is a highlight.

⑨ Palazzo del Freddo
MAP G4 ■ Via Principe Eugenio 65 ■ 06 446 4740 ■ Closed Mon ■ €

A historic *gelateria* with an Art Deco interior, Palazzo del Freddo is famous for its superb ice creams, *granitas* and bite-sized *sanpietrini*.

⑩ La Bottega del Caffè
MAP R4 ■ Piazza Madonna dei Monti 5 ■ 06 474 1578 ■ €

This bustling bistro and bar is the life and soul of Monti. Come for breakfast, a drink or a light meal.

See map on p130

TOP 10 The Quirinal and Via Veneto

The original hill of Rome, the Quirinal was mainly residential in Imperial times, noted for its grand baths and temples. In the Middle Ages, it reverted to open countryside and it wasn't until the 16th century that it again became important, when the crest

Mosaic detail, Baths of Diocletian

of the hill was claimed for the pope's new palace. Following that, important papal families built their large estates all around the area, including the Barberini, the Corsini and the Ludovisi. The Quirinal Palace has passed through many metamorphoses but the biggest change to the area came after 1870. The Ludovisi sold off their huge villa to developers, and Via Veneto and the smart area around it became an instant success with the wealthy classes of the newly unified country. This quarter speaks of elegance and power throughout all its ages.

THE QUIRINAL AND VIA VENETO

1 Top 10 Sights
see pp137–9

1 Places to Eat
see p141

1 La Dolce Vita Venues
see p140

0 metres 500
0 yards 500

1 Baths of Diocletian

MAP F3 ■ Baths of Diocletian: Viale Enrico de Nicola 79 ■ Open 9am–7:30pm Tue–Sun ■ Adm (free first Sun of the month) ■ Aula Ottagona: Via Romita, Piazza della Repubblica ■ Open during exhibitions only

One of the ancient world's largest *thermae*, these public baths were completed in 306. A large section is now part of the Museo Nazionale Romano and holds a collection of epigraphs, *stele* and statues. The Aula Ottagona has two 2nd-century BC bronze sculptures, found hidden in a trench 6 m (20 ft) below the floor of the Temple of the Sun on the Quirinal hillside *(see pp34–7)*.

2 Santa Maria degli Angeli

MAP F3 ■ Piazza della Repubblica ■ Open 7am–6:30pm Mon–Sat, 7am–7pm Sun

In 1561 the pope commissioned Michelangelo to transform the central hall of Diocletian's Baths, the *frigidarium* (cold plunge room), into a church. The result is this vast, overwhelming space. Even so, the finished church takes up only half of the space of the original baths. Michelangelo had to raise the floor 2 m (6 ft) in order to use the ancient 15 m (50 ft) rose-red granite columns the way he wanted to.

Santa Maria degli Angeli

3 Santa Maria della Vittoria

MAP E2 ■ Via XX Settembre 17 ■ Open 8:30am–noon, 3:30–6pm daily

This 17th-century Baroque church has perhaps Rome's most ornate decor, most of it by Bernini. The most indulgent corner is the Cornaro Chapel, home to Bernini's shocking *Ecstasy of St Teresa (see p57)*.

4 Palazzo Barberini

MAP Q1 ■ Via delle Quattro Fontane 13 ■ 06 482 4184 ■ Open 8:30am–7pm Tue–Sun ■ Adm (free first Sun of the month)

The Barberini sold their palace to the state in 1949 to house part of the National Gallery, which was founded in 1893 with the purchase of the Corsini Palace. Among the famous works is the controversial *La Fornarina*, supposedly Raphael's mistress, probably painted by his pupil Giulio Romano.

A ruined section of the Baths of Diocletian

POWER AND ELEGANCE

Since the 16th century, the Quirinal Hill has been the elemental expression of temporal power and dominion in Rome: first the popes, then the kings, and now the presidents of the Republic. Since the late 1800s, Via Veneto has complemented that raw clout with the charisma and glamour of great wealth and all that money can buy.

5 Piazza Barberini
MAP Q1

This could be called the piazza of the bees, the Barberini family symbol (judiciously upgraded from horseflies when their fortunes improved). Both of the piazza's Bernini fountains have large bees carved onto them to let everyone know who sponsored their creation. The central figure of a triton blowing his conch

Fountain, Piazza Barberini

is one of Rome's most appealing and memorable. The other fountain is a simple scallop shell (see p61).

6 Via Veneto
MAP E2

This street boasts a number of *belle époque* grand hotels and pavement cafés. It enjoyed its famous *dolce vita* heyday in the 1950–60s, when movie stars posed here for the paparazzi. Today, the allure is sadly limited for anybody other than tourists, but every visitor to Rome should come at least once to take a stroll here.

7 Capuchin Crypt and Museum
MAP E2 ▪ Via Veneto 27 ▪ Open 9am–7pm daily ▪ Adm

A taste for the macabre may be all you need to enjoy this *memento mori*. Fantastically creepy chapels are decorated with mosaics made from the bones of dead monks, a few of whose cowled skeletons remain propped up in bone-built niches.

8 Palazzo del Quirinale
MAP P2 ▪ Piazza del Quirinale ▪ Open 9:30am–4pm Tue, Wed, Fri, Sat & Sun (gardens open 2 Jun) ▪ Adm ▪ Scuderie del Quirinale: Via XXIV Maggio 16 ▪ 06 3996 7500 ▪ Open 9am–1pm Tue, Wed, Fri–Sun during exhibitions only ▪ Adm ▪ www.scuderiequirinale.it

The highest of the original seven hills, the Quirinal was also the enclave of the ancient Sabines in early Rome. Today, it is graced by 5.5-m (18-ft) Roman copies of 5th-century BC Greek originals of the Dioscuri and their prancing horses. The hill's stark, imposing palace, Rome's largest, was built in 1574 as a summer papal residence, to escape the endemic malaria around the Vatican. In 1870 it became the residence of the kings of Italy and, since 1947, Italy's presidents have resided and held official functions here. Across the piazza, the Scuderie del Quirinale is the former stables of the palace,

Skulls and skeletons, Capuchin Crypt

Fountain, Quattro Fontane

EXPLORING THE QUIRINAL

Café Doney
Regina Baglioni — Excelsior Hotel
Via
Veneto
Capuchin
Crypt and
Museum — Aula
Piazza Ottagona
Barberini
San Carlo alle
Quattro Fontane
Quirinale
Hill Sant'Andrea
al Quirinale
Scuderie del Quirinale

used for horses, carriages and, eventually, motor vehicles until 1938. In the 1990s the building was restored and converted into Rome's prime art exhibition space by architect Gae Aulenti.

⑨ Sant'Andrea al Quirinale
MAP Q2 ■ Via del Quirinale 29
■ Open 9am–noon, 3–6pm Tue–Sun
■ Donation

Built between 1658 and 1670, this was the only construction over which Bernini was able to exercise total artistic control and may represent his architectural peak. The shallow, wide space needed an oval plan, counterpoised in the concave curving entrance. The eye is drawn around the elliptical interior, where canonical elements blend with sculptural decoration to produce an elegant harmony. For so small a church, the impact is surprisingly grand.

⑩ San Carlo alle Quattro Fontane
MAP R2 ■ Via del Quirinale 23
■ Open 10am–1pm, 3–6pm Mon–Fri, 10am–1pm Sat & Sun. Mornings only Jul–Aug

Borromini's masterpiece appears about as radically freeform as architecture could be in the 17th century. He filled this small space with fluid undulations, which have complex geometrical relationships. He succeeded in blurring the line between architecture and sculpture, resulting in a homogeneous interior topped by an oval dome.

▶ **MORNING**

Start on Quirinal Hill (or Monte Cavallo after the horse sculptures). Walk across Piazza del Quirinale to the **Scuderie del Quirinale** to see an art exhibition. Then walk halfway down Via del Quirinale and find Bernini's architectural tour de force, the church of **Sant'Andrea al Quirinale**. Inside, note the maritime motifs, symbolic of Andrew the fisherman.

Continue on to Borromini's **San Carlo alle Quattro Fontane**. Don't miss the masterful crypt and the exquisite cloister. Just outside are the eponymous four fountains, said to represent rivers. Two blocks along, take a right to the **Aula Ottagona** (see p137). The ancient bronzes of the Prince and the Boxer are amazing expressions of controlled power.

Take Via Bissolati to **Via Veneto**. Check out the shops before enjoying lunch at the elegant **Café Doney** (see p140).

AFTERNOON

Admire the *belle époque* **Westin Excelsior** hotel (see p172), especially its cupola and sexually ambiguous caryatids. Don't miss the public rooms of the sublime **Regina Baglioni** (see p171), which positively reek of luxury.

After soaking up all the opulence, walk down to visit the **Capuchin Crypt and Museum** to put things back in perspective. End your tour at **Piazza Barberini** and Bernini's marvellously life-affirming Triton Fountain.

See map on p136 ←

La Dolce Vita Venues

1 Café Doney

MAP E2 ▪ Via Veneto 141

Although it has had a contemporary makeover, this historical café is still a great place to sip a cappuccino under the magnolias and watch passers-by (see pp78–9).

2 Crispy
MAP E2 ▪ Via Francesco Crispi 80

An organic market and bio takeaway, Crispy is great for organic products and fruit and veg, or a vegan meal to eat there or take home. They also serve energy drinks and fruit shakes.

3 Gioielleria Capuano
MAP E2 ▪ Via Veneto 195

This luxury store has been selling sophisticated jewellery from its own collection as well as pieces made by other Italian brands since the 1930s.

La Terrazza

4 La Terrazza
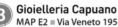
MAP E2 ▪ Via Ludovisi 49

At the top of the premier celebrity Eden hotel (see p170), this bar-restaurant has fabulous views of Rome. It's perfect for a romantic tête-à-tête or any special do.

5 Gran Caffè Roma
MAP E2 ▪ Via Veneto 32

Located in an elegant curve of the street, with outdoor tables at the bottom of a broad staircase, Gran Caffè Roma is a great spot to linger over your cappuccino and newspaper.

Harry's Bar

6 Harry's Bar
MAP E2 ▪ Via Veneto 150

Noted for its American style and Bellini cocktails, this glamorous venue is still frequented by celebrities. It features a piano bar, a restaurant with gourmet Italian cuisine and a café with tables outside.

7 Brunello

MAP E2 ▪ Via Veneto 72

Sumptuous interiors and a chic clientele make this hotel-restaurant a great place for watching the city's rich and beautiful crowd.

8 Jackie O'
MAP E2 ▪ Via Boncompagni 11

A leading watering-hole since the 1960s, this sophisticated club still attracts international stars. It has a piano bar and serves great cocktails and food.

9 Hard Rock Café

MAP E2 ▪ Via Veneto 62/A/B

Great for people-watching, this chain café serving classic American fare, including great burgers and cocktails, has become somewhat of a landmark.

10 Second Chance

MAP E2 ▪ Via Sardegna 57

This vintage store sells near-perfect, second-hand accessories by major names such as Gucci and Chanel.

Places to Eat

1 **Café Veneto**
MAP E2 ■ Via Veneto 120
■ 06 9594 5956 ■ €€€

The carefully prepared dishes at this elegant eatery right in the heart of Via Veneto include game and truffles.

2 **W.O.K**
MAP F3 ■ Stazione Centrale Roma Termini, Via Marsala SNC
■ 06 474 3777 ■ Open daily ■ €

Noodles, rice and Thai curries are wok-fried to order at this restaurant within the atrium of Termini station.

3 **Colline Emiliane**
MAP E2 ■ Via degli Avignonesi 22 ■ 06 481 7538 ■ Closed Sun D, Mon ■ €€

Emilia-Romagna cuisine, consisting of a variety of *prosciutto* (ham) dishes and *tortellini in brodo* (meat-filled pasta in broth), is the speciality here.

4 **Trimani Wine Bar**
MAP F2 ■ Via Cernaia 37/B ■ 06 446 9630 ■ Closed Sun ■ €€

A full menu of soups, pastas and cured meats is available at this classy wine bar.

5 **Dagnino**
MAP E3 ■ Via Vittorio Emanuele Orlando 75 & Via Torino 95
■ 06 481 8660 ■ €

This is Rome's best spot for Sicilian pastries such as *cassata* (iced cake).

6 **Andrea**
MAP E2 ■ Via Sardegna 28
■ 06 482 1819/474 0557 ■ Closed Sat L, Sun ■ €€

Risotto and *suppli* (rice croquette) are classic dishes at this congenial eatery with a wide-ranging menu.

7 **La Giara**
MAP E2 ■ Via Toscana 46, at Via Sardegna ■ 06 4274 5421
■ Closed Sun L in summer, L and D in winter, Aug ■ €€€

This traditional *trattoria* with an unpretentious charm focuses on fish and seafood dishes.

Conservatory, Open Colonna

8 **Open Colonna**
MAP Q2 ■ Palazzo Delle Esposizioni, Via Milano 9A
■ 06 4782 2641 ■ €€€

Housed in the glass conservatory of Palazzo delle Esposizioni, this contemporary restaurant serves modern European cooking by famed chef Antonello Colonna. The weekend family brunches are very good value.

9 **Sapori Sardi**
MAP E2 ■ Via Piemonte 79
■ 06 474 5256 ■ €€

Enjoy fine Sardinian dishes and mirto liqueur at this friendly restaurant.

10 **Africa**
MAP F2 ■ Via Gaeta 26
■ 06 494 1077 ■ Closed Mon ■ €

Spicy vegetables and meats are served with spongy bread here.

Risotto at Andrea

See map on p136

TOP 10 Trastevere and Prati

The Bohemian neighbourhood of Trastevere ("across the Tiber"), a former working-class area, has retained its medieval essence despite now being one of the most restaurant- and nightlife-packed zones of the city. The Borgo is Vatican turf, with kitsch religious souvenir shops and tourist-orientated cafés, while Prati to the north is one of Rome's most genuine, non-touristy, middle-class districts.

Statue, Ponte Sant'Angelo

TRASTEVERE AND PRATI

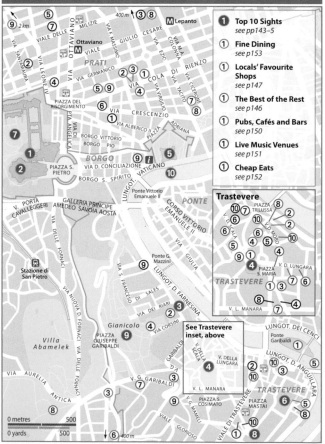

- 1 **Top 10 Sights**
  see pp143–5
- 1 **Fine Dining**
  see p153
- 1 **Locals' Favourite Shops**
  see p147
- 1 **The Best of the Rest**
  see p146
- 1 **Pubs, Cafés and Bars**
  see p150
- 1 **Live Music Venues**
  see p151
- 1 **Cheap Eats**
  see p152

The magnificent St Peter's Square in front of the basilica, Vatican City

1 Vatican City

One of the great museum complexes of the world includes Michelangelo's famous Sistine Chapel and the extensive Raphael Rooms *(see pp12–15)*.

2 St Peter's Basilica

The capital of Christendom is packed with works by Bernini and statues by Michelangelo. The panoramic views from the dome are breathtaking *(see pp16–17)*.

3 Villa Farnesina

MAP J5 ▪ Via della Lungara 230 ▪ Open 9am–2pm Mon–Sat (9am–5pm every second Sun of month) ▪ Adm

Peruzzi's sumptuous villa (1508–11) was built for papal banker Agostino Chigi, whose parties were legendary – he would toss silver platters into the Tiber after each course. In a downstairs room, Peruzzi painted Chigi's horoscope on the ceiling, Sebastiano del Piombo painted scenes from Ovid's *Metamorphoses*, and Raphael painted the sensual *Galatea*. Peruzzi's upstairs hall features a *trompe-l'oeil* balustrade overlooking hills. The 1527 graffiti by Charles V's troops is now protected as historic vandalism. The bedroom contains Sodoma's 1517 *Wedding Night of Alexander the Great (see p58)*.

4 Santa Maria in Trastevere

MAP K6 ▪ Piazza S Maria in Trastevere ▪ Open 7:30am–9pm daily

Rome's oldest church dedicated to the Virgin was founded on the site where a font of oil spouted the day Christ was born. The miracle is depicted in the stupendous *Life of the Virgin* mosaics (1291) by Pietro Cavallini in the apse. The current 12th-century church has ancient mismatched columns, 13th-century mosaics, a Cosmatesque pavement and a rare 7th-century panel painting of the *Madonna della Clemenza* in the chapel left of the altar *(see p51)*.

Santa Maria in Trastevere

Museo di Castel Sant'Angelo

⑤ Museo di Castel Sant'Angelo

MAP J1 ■ Lungotevere Castello 50
■ Open 9am–7:30pm daily ■ Adm
(free first Sun of the month)

Rising above the river, Hadrian designed his massive circular tomb in 123–39. Aurelian fortified it in 271 as part of his city walls (see p156). It was the papal castle for 1,000 years – a viaduct from the Vatican let the popes scurry here in times of crisis. Gregory the Great named it in 590 after a vision of

St Michael announced the end of a plague from its tower, marked by the bronze statue of a sword-bearing archangel. There are frescoed Renaissance papal apartments and a small arms and armour collection, plus stunning panoramas of the city from the ramparts.

⑥ Santa Cecilia in Trastevere

MAP D5 ■ Piazza di S Cecilia 22
■ Open 10am–1pm, 4–7pm daily;
frescoes open 10am–12:30pm
■ Adm for crypt and frescoes

This church is reputedly built over the house of the martyred Cecilia. Look for the Guido Reni painting of her decapitation. Under the apse's glittering 9th-century mosaics rests a 1293 *baldacchino* by Arnolfo di Cambio and Stefano Maderno's 1600 statue of the saint (he saw her incorrupt body when her tomb was opened in 1599). Ring the bell on the left aisle to see the top half of Pietro Cavallini's *Last Judgement* (1289–93), his only remaining fresco in Rome.

⑦ Vatican Gardens

MAP A2 ■ Viale Vaticano
■ Tours daily except Wed and Sun
(06 6988 4676, www.vatican.va)
■ Adm (includes entry to Vatican museums)

Typical 16th-century Italianate gardens of lawns, woods, grottoes and fountains. Structures include the first Vatican radio tower, designed by Marconi in 1931, Pier Luigi Nervi's

The serene lawns of the Vatican Gardens

shell-shaped audience hall (1971)
and the Mannerist Casina of Pius IV
(1558–61), home to the Pontifical
Academy of Sciences.

8 San Francesco a Ripa

MAP C5 ■ Piazza di S Francesco
d'Assisi 88 ■ Open 7am–1pm,
2–7:30pm daily

Though altered during the
Renaissance and Baroque eras,
the church was built just 12
years after St Francis stayed at this
hospice in 1219. Ask the sacristan's
permission to visit the cell in which
St Francis stayed, which contains
a copy of his portrait by Margaritone
d'Arezzo. The last chapel on the
left houses Bernini's *Beata Ludovica
Albertoni* (1671–4) shown in a state
of religious ecstasy.

Bernini's *Beata Ludovica Albertoni*

9 Gianicolo

MAP B4

This long ridge separating Trastevere
from the Vatican offers some of the
best views of Rome (see p63). Its two
equestrian monuments celebrate
Garibaldi and his wife Anita, who
is buried underneath hers.

10 Ponte Sant'Angelo

MAP J2

Hadrian built this bridge in 133–4 to
access his mausoleum, but only the
three central arches of that span
remain. Clement VII had the statues
of St Peter (by Lorenzetto) and St Paul
(by Paolo Taccone) installed in 1534.
Clement IX hired Bernini in 1688 to
design the statues of 10 angels
holding symbols of the Passion.

A TOUR OF TRASTEVERE

Villa Farnesina
Pizzeria Dar Poeta
Orto Botanico
Museo di Roma in Trastevere
Piazza Santa Maria
San Pietro in Montorio
Santa Maria in Trastevere
San Crisogono
Santa Cecilia
San Francesco a Ripa

▶ MORNING

Begin at **San Crisogono** (see p146);
ask the custodian to let you into
the excavations downstairs. By
10am be at **San Francesco a Ripa**
for the five minutes it takes to see
Bernini's sculpture. Head down
Via Anicia Antica, right on Via
Madonna dell'Orto, and left on
Via di S Michele to reach **Santa
Cecilia**. Explore the crypt and pay
the nuns a small donation to get
up to see the Cavallini frescoes.
Head out of the courtyard left
onto Via di Genovesi, which leads
to Viale Trastevere.

Crossing Piazza S Maria in
Trastevere, bear right into Piazza
S Egidio and fork left onto Via
della Scala. Continue past Santa
Maria della Scala and up Via della
Lungara to **Villa Farnesina** (see
p143). You'll be here before noon,
time enough to spend 30 minutes
admiring the frescoes. Take a
breather amid the greenery of the
Orto Botanico (see p146), then
return to the heart of Trastevere
to enjoy a pizza at **Pizzeria Dar
Poeta** (see p152).

AFTERNOON

Peruse the collections of the
Museo di Roma in Trastevere
(see p146), visit the marvellous
medieval church of **Santa Maria
in Trastevere** (see p143) and
walk up Via Garibaldi to peek
through the grille at Bramante's
Tempietto in the courtyard of
San Pietro in Montorio (see p146).
Or simply spend the afternoon
wandering the medieval streets,
awaiting the dinner hour when
Trastevere comes to life.

See map on p142 ←

The Best of the Rest

The small Tiber Island, associated with medicine and healing

1 Tiber Island
MAP M6

It is said that the serpent of medical god Aesculapius jumped ship and swam ashore here in 293 BC. Rome's maternity hospital is still here.

2 Palazzo Corsini
MAP J5 ▪ Via della Lungara 10 ▪ Open 8:30am–7pm Mon, Wed–Sun ▪ Adm (free first Sun of the month)

This small painting collection features works by Fra Angelico, Van Dyck, Titian, Rubens and Caravaggio.

3 San Pietro in Montorio
MAP C4 ▪ Piazza San Pietro in Montorio 2 ▪ Church: Open 8am–noon, 3–4pm daily. Temple: Open 10am–6pm Tue–Sun

Bramante designed this mini-temple to mark the spot where St Peter was supposedly crucified.

4 Orto Botanico
MAP J5 ▪ Largo Cristina di Svezia 24 ▪ Open Apr–Sep: 9am–6:30pm; Oct–Mar: 9am–5:30pm Mon–Sat ▪ Adm

Palazzo Corsini's gardens are now Rome University's botanical museum.

5 Ponte Rotto
MAP N6

Rome's first stone bridge (181–142 BC) was ruined in 1598. Three arches were retained until 1886, when two were destroyed to make way for Ponte Palatino (*rotto* is Italian for broken).

6 Santa Maria della Scala
MAP K6 ▪ Piazza S Maria della Scala 23 ▪ Open 10am–1pm, 4–5:30pm daily

A charming Renaissance church, whose claim to fame is a *Virgin and Child* by Cavalier d'Arpino, who was Caravaggio's teacher.

7 Fontana Paola
MAP B5

This wide basin at the end of the Paola aqueduct is a favourite backdrop for wedding photos.

8 Villa Doria Pamphilj
MAP B5 ▪ Via di S Pancrazio ▪ Open 7am–sunset daily

Rome's largest public park was established in 1644–52 by Camillo Pamphilj. It is a great place for picnics (see p68).

9 Museo di Roma in Trastevere
MAP K6 ▪ Piazza di S Egidio 1b ▪ Open 10am–8pm Tue–Sun ▪ Adm

Housed in a beautifully restored former convent, this museum includes life-size dioramas of Ancient Roman rooms and shops.

10 San Crisogono
MAP L6 ▪ Piazza S Sonnino 44 ▪ Open 7–11:30am, 4–7:30pm Mon–Sat, 8am–1pm, 4–7:30pm Sun ▪ Adm

The 1626 façade copies the medieval one. Inside are 22 ancient columns and excavations of the original 5th-century basilica.

Locals' Favourite Shops

1 Coin Excelsior
MAP C2 ■ Via Cola di Rienzo 173

The flagship of the Coin department store specialises in famous international brands. Housed in an Art Nouveau building redesigned with contemporary touches, it offers high-end shopping, from beauty products and jewellery to shoes and fashion.

2 Franchi
MAP C2 ■ Via Cola di Rienzo 200

One of the best grocers in the city, Franchi is extremely popular at lunchtime for its hot dishes and in the evening for its fried, baked and stuffed pizza pockets. Locals start queueing up at 5pm.

Speciality foods at Castroni

3 Castroni
MAP C2 ■ Via Cola di Rienzo 196

The gastronomic temple of Rome since 1932, this shop is piled high with packaged and prepared speciality foods from countries the world over, such as Japan, Greece, India, China and the Middle East.

4 Boutique Gallo
MAP C2 ■ Via Ovidio 18

Selling high-quality knitwear, this shop specialises in colourful socks and stockings, and also has clothes for women and children.

5 Peroni snc
Piazza dell'Unità 29

From baking pans to chocolate thermometers, Peroni sells an amazing range of baking equipment plus other kitchen goods.

6 L'Artigianino
MAP C4 ■ Vicolo del Cinque 49

Prices for L'Artigianino's pure-leather wallets, bags, purses and belts range from €10 to €250. Styles are mostly colourful and cute but there are classic designs, too.

7 Ottimomassimo
MAP C5 ■ Via Manara 16/17

Superb illustrated books for children, including guidebooks, in Italian, English, French and Spanish, can be found at this bookshop. It also hosts activities and bookclubs.

8 Costantini
MAP C2 ■ Piazza Cavour 16

This fine wine cellar has an excellent selection at reasonable prices.

9 Sabon
MAP C2 ■ Via Cola di Rienzo 241

Luxurious soaps, toiletries and candles made with natural ingredients are sold here.

10 Polvere di Tempo
MAP L6 ■ Via del Moro 59

The non-mechanical timepieces at this shop, including hour glasses, sundials, candle clocks and astrolabes, are all made by the owner.

Timepieces at Polvere di Tempo

See map on p142

Pubs, Cafés and Bars

 Ombre Rosse
MAP K6
■ Piazza S Egidio 12–13

This laid-back pub is a staple of Trastevere nightlife. The atmosphere is always lively, with tables on the piazza in summer.

 Freni e Frizioni
MAP K5 ■ Via del Politeama 4

A former mechanic's garage has been transformed into a hip *aperitivo* spot serving a buffet during the summer. The bar overflows into a pretty outdoor courtyard.

Cool *aperitivo* bar Freni e Frizioni

Bar San Calisto
MAP K6 ■ Piazza San Calisto 3

This quiet neighbourhood bar is the antithesis of the trendy Trastevere scene. Locals come here to play cards, read papers and catch up on the day's gossip. There is a welcoming atmosphere and drinks are reasonably priced.

Caffè di Marzio
MAP K6 ■ Piazza di Santa Maria in Trastevere 15

This café is a perfect place to sit and admire the façade of the basilica of Santa Maria in Trastevere – one of Rome's oldest – and watch life unfold in the lively piazza. They have good coffees, pastries and hot chocolate.

 Caffè della Scala
MAP K6 ■ Via della Scala 4

Highly recommended for when a lazy evening *aperitivo* is called for, this pretty, Bohemian café has seats outside for people watching.

 Ditta Trinchetti
MAP L6 ■ Via della Lungaretta 76

This is a wonderful *tavola calda* (self-service buffet) and delicatessen – try the Puglian *burrata* (fresh cheese made from mozzarella and cream), superior sandwiches, and hot dishes that include great bean soup in winter.

 Enoteca Trastevere
MAP L6 ■ Via della Lungaretta 86

With a pleasingly dark wood interior and plenty of seating out front on the cobblestones, this thriving wine bar also serves light snacks and cocktails.

Enoteca Ferrara
MAP K5 ■ Piazza Trilussa 41

This bustling wine bar has a very loyal following of conoisseurs, which is not surprising as it is known for serving some of the best wines by the glass in the city. There's an in-house deli, and a lovely back garden for when the weather is good.

 Il Baretto
MAP C4 ■ Via Garibaldi 27G

There's an appealingly vintage atmosphere at this informal *aperitivo* bar. Great drinks and the occasional live concert make it a popular nightspot for locals.

Forno la Renella
MAP K6 ■ Via del Moro 15–16

Romans flock here from all over the city for the high-quality bread, pizza, focaccia and biscuits. Try it and you'll understand why. Everything is baked in wood-fired ovens, and the toppings and fillings change according to season.

***Previous pages** the Vatican City from the Ponte Umberto*

Live Music Venues

Blues venue Big Mama

1 Big Mama
MAP C5 ■ Vicolo S Francesco a Ripa 18
Rome's house of blues attracts both big names and smaller acts. There are live performances by established and upcoming artists daily.

2 Alexanderplatz
MAP B1 ■ Via Ostia 9
It may be a little bit off the beaten track, in Prati, but this is the best jazz club in Rome bar none – Winton Marsalis, Lionel Hampton, George Coleman and many other international jazz stars have played here.

3 Alembic # Ak Bar
MAP M6 ■ Piazza in Piscinula 51
The non-matching furniture and colourful decor reflect this bar's bohemian spirit. Cappuccinos are served in refined china cups. It is open all day, with live music at weekends.

4 Saxophone Pub
MAP B1 ■ Via Germanico 26
This warm, cosy spot, close to the Vatican, serves simple pub fare including salads and sandwiches. There is always a friendly atmosphere, with jazz and blues on the stereo and local bands that come here to jam.

5 Four Green Fields
MAP B1 ■ Via C Morin 42
Upstairs is a vaguely British-style pub, while in the basement live music is played nightly.

6 Fonclea
MAP B2 ■ Via Crescenzio 82
Established in 1977, this historic music venue is located close to Piazza del Risorgimento and features a variety of live music including jazz, soul, funk and rock. Punters can either drink at the bar or eat in the buffet restaurant.

7 Birreria Trilussa
MAP K6 ■ Via Benedetta 18
Beer and simple dishes are served until the early hours, with live music some nights. There's a cosy, traditional atmosphere.

8 Da Meo Patacca
MAP D5 ■ Piazza dei Mercanti 30
Local singers perform *stornelli* (street poetry) and Roman songs at this eatery famous for its music nights.

Auditorium Conciliazione

9 Auditorium Conciliazione
MAP B3 ■ Via della Conciliazione 4
On the road to St Peter's Basilica, this auditorium hosts classical and contemporary concerts, dance spectacles, film screenings and art exhibitions.

10 Lettere Caffè
MAP C5 ■ Via S. Francesco a Ripa 100
The focus here is usually on books, but a couple of nights a week are devoted to live roots music.

See map on p142

Cheap Eats

(1) Sorpasso
MAP B2 ▪ Via Properzio 31–33
▪ 06 890 24554 ▪ Closed Sun ▪ €

Enjoy Mediterranean cuisine in a laid-back atmosphere here. There is also a deli counter selling delights to take away for a picnic.

(2) Il Rugantino
MAP K6 ▪ Via della Lungaretta 54 ▪ 06 581 8517 ▪ €

One of the oldest trattorias in Trastevere, Il Rugantino serves traditional Roman cuisine and has an outdoor area overlooking the piazza.

(3) Settembrini Libri e Cucina
MAP C1 ▪ Piazza Martiri di Belfiore 12 ▪ 06 9727 7242 ▪ €

This Bohemian cook book shop owned by the prestigious Settembrini restaurant across the road (see p153) serves excellent-value buffet eats and drinks at lunchtime.

(4) Pizzeria da Ivo
MAP C5 ▪ Via S Francesco a Ripa 158 ▪ 06 581 7082 ▪ Closed L, Tue ▪ €

A lively football theme and ever-present crowds are the features of Rome's favourite pizzeria.

(5) Da Augusto
MAP K6 ▪ Piazza de' Renzi 15 ▪ 06 580 3798 ▪ No credit cards ▪ €

Complete with wooden tables and great traditional Roman food, this is a die-hard, no-frills Trastevere *osteria*.

Outdoor tables at Da Augusto

(6) Pizzeria Dar Poeta
MAP K6 ▪ Vicolo del Bologna 45–6 ▪ 06 588 0516 ▪ €

Innovative pizzas are made in a wood-fired oven here – Roman-style, but with a thick crust.

(7) Osteria dell'Angelo
MAP B1 ▪ Via G Bettolo 24 ▪ 06 372 9470 ▪ Closed Sun ▪ €€

Angelo prepares excellent traditional Roman cooking at equally admirable prices. The service charge is 15 per cent. Book ahead.

(8) Pizzeria da Vittorio
MAP K6 ▪ Via S Cosimato 14A ▪ 06 580 0353 ▪ €

Good Neapolitan-style pizza and *antipasti* are offered at this local favourite. A pleasant fan-cooled interior plastered with photos of famous patrons makes this one of Rome's most enjoyable pizzerias.

(9) Da Giovanni
MAP J4 ▪ Via della Lungara 41 ▪ 06 686 1514 ▪ Closed Sun ▪ €

This cosy, friendly trattoria serves a variety of authentic Roman dishes prepared with fresh ingredients, and fantastic desserts. It is small, so book ahead (see p77).

(10) La Boccaccia
MAP K5 ▪ Via di Santa Dorotea 2 ▪ 32 0775 6277 ▪ Closed Mon ▪ €

Serving supremely delicious *pizza a taglio* (pizza by the slice), La Boccaccia is great for a snack on the go. It also has a few seats inside and a bench to squeeze onto outside.

Fine Dining

1 Sabatini
MAP K6 ▪ Piazza di Santa Maria in Trastevere 13 ▪ 06 581 2026 ▪ €€€

Roman cuisine and seafood are served at Sabatini. Book ahead for a table out on the main square.

2 Ferrara
MAP K6 ▪ Via del Moro 1a ▪ 06 580 3769 ▪ Closed L (except Sun) ▪ €€

The creative food is as good as the wine at this restaurant belonging to the superb Enoteca Ferrara.

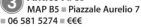

The laid-back Antico Arco

3 Antico Arco
MAP B5 ▪ Piazzale Aurelio 7 ▪ 06 581 5274 ▪ €€€

Try the signature risotto with Castelmagno cheese in Nebbiolo wine sauce at this easy-going, contemporary Italian restaurant. Book ahead for an outdoor table.

4 Glass Hostaria
MAP K2 ▪ Vicolo del Cinque 58 ▪ 06 5833 5903 ▪ Closed Mon, L ▪ No credit cards ▪ €€€

This ultra-modern restaurant offers inventive Italian fusion cuisine and a great wine list (see p73).

5 Roma Sparita
Piazza di Santa Cecilia 24 ▪ 06 580 0757 ▪ Closed Sun D, Mon ▪ €

Set on a picturesque, quiet piazza far from the crowds of central Trastevere, Roma Sparita serves simple Roman fare, brilliantly executed.

6 Il Vascello dai Sardi
MAP B5 ▪ Via G Massari 8 ▪ 06 580 6517 ▪ Closed Tue ▪ €€

This Sardinian jewel's specialities include giant ravioli with ricotta and lemon zest, and spaghetti with *bottarga* (cured fish roe). The homemade *torta di ricotta* is divine.

7 L'Arcangelo
MAP C2 ▪ Via Giuseppe Gioacchino Belli 59 ▪ 06 321 0992 ▪ Closed Sat L, Sun ▪ €€

High-quality ingredients are used in the classic Roman trattoria food here. After a meal guests are given a complementary zabaglione liqueur with sweet biscuits. There are very good fixed-menu deals at lunchtime.

8 Settembrini
MAP C1 ▪ Via Settembrini 25 ▪ 06 9761 0325 ▪ Closed Sat L, Sun ▪ €€€

Well-regarded for both its traditional and more inventive dishes, this restaurant has three tasting menus and an adventurous, intelligently researched wine list.

9 La Pergola
Rome Cavalieri Hotel, Via Alberto Cadlolo 101 ▪ 06 3509 2152 ▪ Closed L, Sun & Mon ▪ €€€

Offering the finest dining experience in Rome, this is the only restaurant in the city with three Michelin stars. Elegant dress code (see p72).

10 Fish Market
MAP M6 ▪ Vicolo della Luce 2–3 ▪ 366 9144 157 ▪ €

This spartan chic place is a must for fish lovers more interested in the fabulous fish (bought direct from fishermen in Anzio) than fancy service.

See map on p142

🔟 Beyond the City Walls

The 3rd-century Aurelian Walls are still largely intact and served as the defence of the city for 1,600 years until Italian Unification in 1870. After that, the walls were pierced in several places so that traffic could bypass the old gates and the modern city quickly sprawled far and wide in every direction. It is undeniable that Rome's most dazzling sights lie within the walls, but venturing outside them can have spectacular rewards. Ancient roads, an entire ancient town, some of Rome's oldest churches, the mystical catacombs and even Mussolini's pretentious contributions to modern architecture are all must-sees away from the city centre.

Sarcophagus, Via Appia Antica

BEYOND THE CITY WALLS

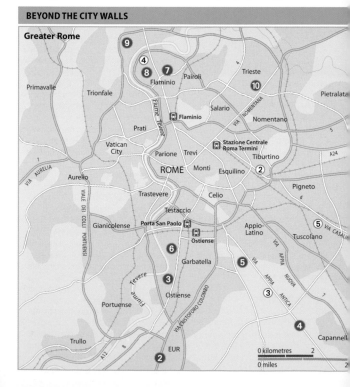

1 Ostia Antica

Ancient Rome's trading heart has a wealth of fascinating ruins that evoke the city's earliest days, and a lovely rural site (see pp42–3).

2 EUR
Metro EUR Palasport and EUR Fermi

Built by Mussolini as a showcase to the world of the ideal Fascist metropolis, the EUR (l'Esposizione Universale di Roma) is disturbing to many visitors. The critic Robert Hughes described the Square Colosseum as "the most frightening building in the world", yet the aesthetic inspired many post-war architects. Today the area is largely a residential and business district. There's also a park with a lake, and Rome's aquarium, boasting sealed glass windows that face the lake.

San Paolo fuori le Mura

3 San Paolo fuori le Mura
Via Ostiense 190 ▪ Metro Basilica S Paolo ▪ Open 7am–6:30pm daily

Rome's second largest church has had a history of violent ups and downs. It was built by Constantine in the 4th century, over the spot where St Paul was buried, and for about 400 years it was the largest church in Europe, until it was sacked by the Saracens in 846. It was rebuilt and fortified, but its position outside the walls left it mostly ignored until the mid-11th century, when it underwent a renewal. A fire in 1823 led to the reworking we see today. Fortunately, the cloisters, considered Rome's most beautiful, escaped the flames.

4 Via Appia Antica
Buses 118, 218

"The Queen of Roads" was completed in 312 BC by Appius Claudius, also the architect of Rome's first aqueduct. The most pastoral part begins at the circular Tomb of Cecilia Metella, which was made into a fortification in the Middle Ages. Starting here, you'll see more tombs and fragments of tombs, as well as grazing sheep and the private gates to fabulous modern villas. As you walk along, look to the east to see the arches of an ancient aqueduct marching towards the city.

Concert halls of the Auditorium Parco della Musica

THE AURELIAN WALL

This ancient wall was begun by Emperor Aurelian (AD 270–75) and completed by his successor Probus (AD 276–82). It stretches 18 km (11 miles) around the city, with 18 gates and 381 towers, enclosing all seven of Rome's hills. In the 4th century, Emperor Maxentius raised it to almost twice its original height. To this day, most of the wall survives.

---

⑤ Appian Way Catacombs

San Sebastiano: Via Appia Antica 136; Open 10am–5pm Mon–Sat; Adm ■ San Callisto: Via Appia Antica 110; Open 9am–noon & 2–5pm Tue–Thu; Closed 1 Jan, Easter, 25 Dec & around 29 Jan–25 Feb; Domitilla: Via delle Sette Chiese 282; Open Feb–Dec: 9am–noon & 2–5pm daily; Adm

The burial tunnels of Rome's early Christians are like a honeycomb beneath the consular roads out of Rome, especially along Via Appia Antica. Grave niches stacked like shelving are carved into the tufa. The soft volcanic rock is suitable for tunnelling, as it is softer when first exposed to air, hardening afterwards. There are some precious remnants of fresco and engraved marble slabs.

⑥ Centrale Montemartini

Via Ostiense 106 ■ 06 0608 ■ Open 9am–7pm Tue–Sun ■ Adm ■ www.centralemontemartini.org

Rome's first power station has been transformed into a stunning showcase for Greek and Roman art – parts of the Musei Capitolini collection (see pp28–9)

that, until now, were kept in storage. The effect is extraordinary, playing off the might of modern technology against the human vulnerability of these ancient masterpieces (see p67).

⑦ Auditorium Parco della Musica

Viale Pietro de Coubertin 30 ■ 06 802 41281 ■ Open 11am–8pm daily, to 6pm winter (closed Aug) ■ Adm to concerts ■ www.auditorium.com

Italian architect Renzo Piano's "city of music" is the heart of Rome's cultural life, with three whale-shaped concert halls hosting daily classical, rock, pop and jazz performances. The "theatre hall" is for dance shows and electronic nights, while revolving art exhibitions adorn the complex's hallways. There is also a café, bookshop and playground.

⑧ MAXXI

Via Guido Reni, 4A ■ 06 320 1954 ■ Open 11am–7pm Tue–Sun (until 10pm on Sat) ■ Adm ■ www.maxxi.art

Opened in 2010, MAXXI (Museo delle Arti del XXI secolo), Rome's first contemporary art centre, was designed by the English-Iraqi architect Zaha

Futuristic buildings of MAXXI

Hadid and is a jewel of modern architecture. The galleries are a series of long intertwining bands. The permanent collection contains more than 350 works, and the museum has two sections, one for visual arts and one for architecture *(see p55)*.

9 Foro Italico and Stadio dei Marmi

Viale del Foro Italico

Originally called the Foro Mussolini, this sports complex was under-standably renamed in the late 1940s, even though the 16-m (55-ft) obelisk still shouts out "Mussolini Dux" ("Mussolini the Leader"). In imitation of every mad Roman emperor, there was supposed to have been a 75-m (250-ft) statue of Il Duce as Hercules. The Classical-style statues of the Stadio dei Marmi, 60 colossal young Fascist athletes, are worth a look.

Apse mosaic at Sant'Agnese

10 Sant'Agnese fuori le Mura and Santa Costanza

Via Nomentana 349 ■ Buses 36, 60, 62, 84, 90 ■ Open Sant'Agnese 8am–7pm Mon–Sat; Santa Costanza 9am–noon, 3–6pm Mon–Sat, 3–6pm daily

These 4th-century churches are located in the same Early Christian complex. Both are decorated with mosaics. Sant'Agnese depicts the martyred St Agnes as she appeared in a vision eight days after her death. The ambulatory around the circular Santa Costanza has detailed scenes of an ancient Roman grape harvest.

A MORNING WALK ON THE VIA APPIA ANTICA

Museo delle Mura — Porta San Sebastiano
Via Appia Antica
Domine Quo Vadis?
Parco della Caffarella
Catacombs of San Sebastiano
Ristorante l'Archeologia
Tomb of Cecilia Metella
Circus of Maxentius

▶ Start at the Porta San Sebastiano, the grandest city gate of them all, where you can visit the **Museo delle Mura** *(see p67)*, which illustrates the history of the Aurelian Wall. Climb the stairs for great views. From here, continue straight on along the **Via Appia Antica** *(see p155)*. One of the first sights you'll come to, on the left at a crossroads, is the small Domine Quo Vadis? church – this marks the spot where Peter, flee-ing persecution, encountered Christ and decided to return to Rome and face his martyrdom like a saint. The church contains a replica of footprints in stone, said to be those of Christ, but it is actually an ancient pagan *ex voto*.

Quite a bit further ahead, you'll come to the **Catacombs of San Sebastiano** *(see p62)*. Take the guided tour, and don't miss the curious fresco of a bowl of fruit and a partridge, which, according to some ancient writers, was the most lascivious of all creatures. Continuing on, past a mobile bar where you can buy snacks and drinks, visit the **Circus of Maxentius**, an ancient racetrack. Note how *amphorae* were embedded in the bricks to lighten the construction of the upper grandstands. Your last stop will be the 1st-century BC Tomb of Cecilia Metella. The frieze of bulls' skulls and garlands is beautiful and the cone-shaped sanctum is peaceful.

🍴 For lunch, walk back to the **Ristorante l'Archeologia** *(see p159)* for a hearty meal. Then backtrack a few hundred metres to the bus stop to catch the No. 118 into town.

See map on pp154–5

Day Trips from Rome

1 Villa d'Este
Piazza Trento, Tivoli ▪ 07 7433 2920/07 7433 312070 ▪ COTRAL bus from Ponte Mammolo ▪ Open 8:30am–1hr before sunset Tue–Sun ▪ Adm (free first Sun of the month)

Built in the 16th century, Villa d'Este is renowned for its gardens and features 100 fountains.

Canopus Pool, Hadrian's Villa

2 Hadrian's Villa
Via Tiburtina, 6 km (4 miles) southwest of Tivoli ▪ 07 7438 2733 ▪ COTRAL bus from Ponte Mammolo ▪ Open 9am–1hr before sunset daily ▪ Adm (free first Sun of the month)

Built as Hadrian's summer retreat between AD 118 and 34, this vast area contained full-scale reproductions of the emperor's favourite buildings from Greece and Egypt. The ruins include temples and theatres.

3 Tarquinia Necropolis
Train from Termini or Ostiense or COTRAL bus from Lepanto ▪ 07 6685 0080 ▪ Open 8:30am–dusk Tue–Sun ▪ Adm

The museum of Etruscan artifacts housed within this large necropolis is famous for its 4th-century BC terracotta horses.

4 Cerveteri Necropolis
Train from Termini to Cerveteri-Ladispoli ▪ 06 994 0651 ▪ Open 8:30am–1 hour before sunset Tue–Sun ▪ Adm

Established in the 6th century BC, this town's necropolis has intact streets, houses and frescoes.

5 Castelli Romani
Metro Anagnina, then COTRAL buses ▪ Palazzo Chigi Ariccia: Piazza di Corte 14, Ariccia ▪ 06 933 0053 ▪ Open 10am–7pm Tue–Sun; tours at 11am, 4pm, 5:30pm Tue–Fri & all day weekends (gardens Apr–Sep) ▪ Adm

There is much to attract in this area of the Alban Hills. Swim in Lago di Albano, or visit Ariccia's Palazzo Chigi, a Baroque complex designed by Bernini in the 17th century.

6 Frascati
Metro Anagnina, then COTRAL bus ▪ Villa Aldobrandini: Via Cardinale Massaia 18 ▪ 06 683 3785 ▪ Open 9am–5:30pm Mon–Fri

This small town is home to Villa Aldobrandini, whose gardens offer magnificent panoramas of Rome.

7 Palestrina
Metro Anagnina, then COTRAL bus ▪ Museum: Palazzo Barberini ▪ Open 9am–8pm daily ▪ Adm

This town boasts Italy's greatest Hellenistic temple. Among its treasures is a 2nd-century BC mosaic.

8 Rome's Beaches
Trains depart from Porta San Paolo; ATAC bus or metro ticket required

The Ostia sea strip to the city's south is dotted with beach clubs and free beaches (spiaggia libera).

9 Viterbo
Most sights: Open 8:30am–6:30pm Tue–Sat ▪ Adm

Visit this medieval town's Papal Palace, Fontana Grande and Archaeological Museum.

10 Pompeii
Train from Termini to Naples, then Circumvesuviana train ▪ 08 1857 5111 ▪ Open 9am–5pm (to 7:30pm in summer) ▪ Adm

Now a UNESCO World Heritage Site, this city was buried and preserved by the eruption of Vesuvius in AD 79.

Places to Eat

1 Allo Sbarco di Enea, Ostia Antica

Via dei Romagnoli 675 ■ Metro Piramide then local train ■ 06 565 0034 ■ Closed Mon L ■ €€

The waiters dress up in Ancient Roman gear and the decor is like a low-budget epic movie at this kitsch but fun restaurant. The speciality is fish; try the *spaghetti alle vongole* (clams).

2 Pizzeria Formula Uno

MAP G4 ■ Via Degli Equi 13 ■ 06 445 3866 ■ Closed Sun ■ €

A San Lorenzo institution, this lively, no-frills pizzeria has been serving thin-crusted, scrumptious pizzas with top-quality toppings for decades. The carciofi alla giudia and anchovies *(see p74)* are an absolute must, too.

Ristorante l'Archeologia

3 Ristorante l'Archeologia, Via Appia Antica

Via Appia Antica 139 ■ Bus 118 ■ 06 788 0494 ■ €€

Dine around the fireplace in winter and in the garden in summer at this restaurant in an elegant converted farmhouse. It serves rustic regional fare, such as roast lamb and home-made pasta dishes.

4 Trentino

Via Giuseppe Sacconi 21-31 ■ 06 323 6806 ■ Closed Sat ■ €

Handy for when you're visiting MAXXI *(see p156)*, this excellent, bustling, great-value self-service restaurant has an abundant *tavola calda* and pizzas made in a wood-fired oven.

PRICE CATEGORIES

For a three-course meal for one with half a bottle of wine (or equivalent meal), taxes and extra charges.

€ under €40 ■ €€ €40–60 ■ €€€ over €60

5 Osteria Bonelli

Viale dell'Acquedotto Alessandrino, 172/174 ■ 329 863 3077 ■ Closed Sun ■ €€

Classic dishes at this friendly, lively *osteria* include pasta, lamb and fabulous roasted beef cheeks.

6 La Sibilla, Tivoli

Via della Sibilla 50 ■ COTRAL bus from Ponte Mammolo ■ 07 7433 5281 ■ Closed Mon ■ €€

Overlooking Villa Gregoriana, this restaurant is in a spectacular location.

7 Ambaradam, Tarquinia

Piazza Matteotti 14 ■ 07 6685 7073 ■ Closed Wed L ■ €

Conveniently located on the main piazza, this homely and authentic trattoria is known for its delicious ravioli and attentive service.

8 Pinocchio, Frascati

Piazza del Mercato 21 ■ Metro Anagnina, then COTRAL bus ■ 06 941 7883 ■ Closed Mon–Sat L ■ €

Pinocchio (also a hotel) specializes, as does this entire area, in the celebrated *porchetta* (pork roast).

9 Scylla, Sperlonga

Via San Rocco 26 ■ Train from Termini to Fondi, then bus ■ 07 7154 9652 ■ Closed Tue (winter) ■ €€

Great for seafood, this popular spot on the beach has pleasant deck seating.

10 Piccola Trattoria da Patrizio, Viterbo

Via della Cava 50 ■ Train from Roma Ostiense or COTRAL bus from Saxa Rubra ■ 07 6117 31036 ■ €

This family-run, cosy trattoria offers reasonably priced delicious food in generous portions.

See map on pp154–5

Streetsmart

Roman street scene

Getting To and Around Rome

Arriving by Air

Rome has two airports, Fiumicino and Ciampino, both served by international flights and with excellent transport links to the city centre.

Fiumicino (FCO), 30 km (19 miles) southwest of Rome, is the main hub. From here, the **Leonardo Express**, run by Trenitalia, takes 32 minutes non-stop to Termini station in the city. There is also a slower train to Tiburtina station (48 minutes), stopping at Trastevere and Ostiense. Buy tickets at the station or online.

Several bus companies, including **Terravision** and **Sit Bus Shuttle**, run services to Termini station, taking about an hour. Touts will usually approach you with their latest ticket offer.

Taxis charge a flat fare from Fiumicino to the city centre and can be booked online. Minibus taxis, such as **AirportShuttle**, charge per person.

Ciampino (CIA) is 15 km (9 miles) southeast of the city. The fastest way to Rome is by bus to Termini station (40 minutes). Bus companies include **Atral**. Taxis charge a flat fare to the city centre.

Arriving by Rail

Italy's main train operator, **Trenitalia**, runs two high-speed connections (Frecciarossa and Frecciargento) between major cities. Rome's main stations are **Termini** and **Tiburtina**. **Italo Treno**, offers fast links to Milan and Naples.

Arriving by Road

Coaches from European destinations arrive at Tiburtina, the city's main bus station, with **Eurolines** being one of most popular services. Tiburtina is in metro Line B, with rapid connections to the centre.

Those arriving by car are advised to leave their vehicle in a car park outside the city centre. Driving in Rome is not recommended – roads are congested and parking is extremely difficult.

Getting Around by Metro

Rome Metro, run by **ATAC**, has two lines, A and B, with a third under construction. Line A runs from west to southeast, while Line B runs from northeast to south. They cross at Termini. Trains run every 4 to 10 minutes from 5:30am to 11:30pm, and until 1:30am on Friday and Saturday.

Getting Around by Bus and Tram

Run by ATAC, bus and tram services are reliable, cheap and comprehensive, but progress can be slow in the city centre. Routes are listed on stops. After 11:30pm there is a good night bus service. The most useful tram lines are No. 2 (to MAXXI) and No. 19 (connecting Vatican City with Villa Borghese).

For day trips, **COTRAL** blue buses run from several Rome terminals into the suburbs and surrounding countryside.

Getting Around by Local Train

There is a useful city line to Ostia Antica and Ostia Lido from Stazione Porta San Paolo, next to the Piramide metro station. Regular ATAC bus and metro tickets are valid on local train services.

Tickets

The same tickets are valid on buses, trams, metro and local train lines. They are sold at shops with an ATAC sticker in the window; at booths at major terminals; and from machines at smaller hubs. There are regular tickets valid for 100 minutes (BIT), day tickets (ROMA 24H), 2-day tickets (ROMA 48H), 3-day tickets (ROMA 72H) and weekly passes (CIS). Tickets need to be validated on board buses the first time they are used. Children under 10 years travel free if with an adult.

Getting Around by Taxi

Official taxis are white and cannot be hailed on the street. There are taxi ranks across the city centre, including at Termini, Piazza del Popolo, Piazza di Spagna, Piazza Venezia and Piazza Barberini. You can also book online or by phone through **Radiotaxi**. This is more costly than boarding at a taxi rank as the meter is switched on as soon as the driver sets off. Municipal regulation fares must be displayed. Luggage over the specified size incurs an extra fee.

Getting Around by Car

City centre streets are designated ZTL (Zona a Traffico Limitato) which means that only official residents can drive and park. It is best to leave your car at the underground car park at Villa Borghese (entrance in Viale del Galoppatoio), which is connected by an underground walkway to the Piazza di Spagna metro station. There are several free car parks on the city periphery. You can locate one at **06 0608** (the city information service) and **Saba**.

Getting Around by Bicycle

Cycling in Rome can be challenging due to the city's hilly nature, its heavy traffic, and the near absence of cycle paths. However, it can be a nice way to explore the city centre. **Bici & Baci** and **Roma Rent Bike** rent bikes and scooters by the hour and by the day.

Rome by Segway offers themed Segway tours, complete with a map, iPod and helmet. Unless you are an experienced moped or scooter rider, it is wiser not to ride in Rome.

Getting Around on Foot

Rome is a fabulously walkable city – everything from St Peter's and the Janiculum to Villa Borghese and beyond can be seen without having to use public transport.

Guided Bus Tours

City Sightseeing Roma and **Big Bus Tours** offer hop-on-hop-off tours of the city aboard double-decker buses with audio guides in eight languages. Tours run daily with a first departure from 9pm until 7pm. The two companies offer similar services, with a full tour lasting about 1 hour 40 minutes, and buses run with a frequency of 15 to 20 minutes. Buses can be boarded at any of the eight stops, including the Colosseum, Trevi Fountain, Piazza Barberini and the Vatican. Check the website for "combo" ticket offers that include the Colosseum and the Vatican, the Appian Way, or a river cruise.

The **Roma Cristiana** bus is a tour with a Christian emphasis. It runs from Termini to Piazza San Pietro with stops close to religious sights.

Boat Tours

Battelli di Roma runs hop-on-hop-off cruise trips on the Tiber between Isola Tiberina and Ponte Nenni. Boats leave hourly from 10am to 2pm and 4pm to 8pm (summer only). Ponte Sant' Angelo and Isola Tiberina are the boarding points. Tickets are valid 24 hours.

DIRECTORY

ARRIVING BY AIR

AirportShuttle
☒ airportshuttle.it

Atral
☒ atral-lazio.com

Ciampino and Fiumicino
☒ adr.it

Leonardo Express
☒ trenitalia.com

Sit Bus Shuttle
☒ sitbusshuttle.com

Terravision
☒ terravision.eu

ARRIVING BY RAIL

Italo Treno
☒ italotreno.it

Termini
MAP F3 ▪ Piazza dei Cinquecento
☒ romatermini.com

Tiburtina
MAP H2 ▪ Piazzale della Stazione Tiburtina

Trenitalia
☒ trenitalia.com

ARRIVING BY ROAD

Eurolines
☒ eurolines.com

METRO, BUS AND TRAM

ATAC
☒ atac.roma.i

COTRAL
☒ cotralspa.it

TAXIS

Radiotaxi
06 3570 or 06 0609
☒ 3570.it

CAR

06 0608
☒ 060608.it

Saba
☒ sabait.it

BICYCLE

Bici & Baci
☒ bicibaci.com/en

Roma Rent Bike
☒ romarentbike.com

Rome by Segway
☒ romebysegway.com

GUIDED BUS TOURS

Big Bus Tours
☒ bigbustours.com

City Sightseeing Roma
☒ roma.city-sightseeing.it

Roma Cristiana
☒ operaromana pellegrinaggi.org

BOAT TOURS

Battelli di Roma
☒ batellidiroma.it

Practical Information

Passports and Visas

Visitors from outside the European Economic Area (EEA), European Union (EU) and Switzerland need a valid passport to enter Italy. EEA, EU and Swiss nationals can use identity cards instead. Those from Canada, the US, Australia and New Zealand can stay for up to 3 months without a visa as long as their passport is valid for 6 months beyond the date of entry.

All other nationals need a valid passport and visa, and should consult the **Ministero degli Esteri** website. Schengen visas are valid for Italy.

Travel Safety Advice

Visitors can get up-to-date travel safety information from the **UK Foreign and Commonwealth Office**, the **US Department of State** and the **Australian Department of Foreign Affairs and Trade**.

Customs Information

For EU citizens there are no limits on most goods taken in or out of Italy provided they are for personal use only. Exceptions include firearms and weapons, endangered species and some types of food and plants. Non-EU residents can claim back sales tax on purchases over €155.

Travel Insurance

It is advisable to take out insurance against medical emergencies, travel cancellations or delays, emergency expatriation, theft or loss. Italy has a reciprocal health agreement with other EU countries, and EU citizens are entitled to free emergency treatment under Italy's public healthcare system if they have with them a valid European Health Insurance Card (EHIC). However, you will have to pay for any prescriptions upfront. Italy also has a reciprocal agreement with Australian Medicare, but all other nationals should check before travelling.

Health

There are no vaccinations necessary or recommended for visiting Italy, and there are few health hazards in Rome. In summer, you should wear hats and sunscreen, stay out of the sun, and drink plenty of water. Tap water is drinkable.

Mosquitoes can be a pest, but are not malarial. Spray exposed skin (especially ankles) with mosquito repellent when going out in the evenings and keep windows closed when the lights are on in your hotel room. Calamine lotion – the best way to stop the itching – is not widely available in Italy, so bring your own. If you don't, most pharmacies will recommend the use of an antihistamine.

Pharmacies are indicated by a green cross. Many will sell common drugs such as antibiotics without a prescription. If you run out of medicine you take regularly, most pharmacists will be happy to sell replacements, especially if you have the packaging.

There are two 24-hour clinics aimed at tourists, the **Guardia Medica Turistica**. English is spoken in both. Hospitals with accident and emergency departments include **Fatebenefratelli** on Isola Tiberina and **Policlinico Universitario** in northwest Rome. Your hotel will usually also be able to suggest local doctors and dentists.

Emergency Services

For **emergency police, ambulance or fire brigade services** dial 112 – the operator will ask which service you require. You can call from landlines, mobiles and pay phones, and calls are free. For **ambulance** emergencies you can also dial 118 and for the **fire brigade** the direct number is 115.

Personal Security

Italy is relatively safe, and even in a big city like Rome street violence is rare. Drinking in excess is not a cultural norm, although parts of the historic centre such as Campo de' Fiori and Trastevere can be rowdy at night. The historic centre is well policed, but pickpocketing is common, particularly on crowded buses and at popular tourist sites.

There are two police forces, the **Carabinieri**,

the military branch, and the **Polizia di Stato**, the civil branch. They fulfill much the same functions. Crimes can be reported to either, and both can issue the crime or loss reports (denuncia di furto o smarrimento) that you will need when making an insurance claim for theft or loss. Central carabinieri stations include **Janiculum**, **Centro Storico**, **Termini** and **Prati**. The **Polizia di Stato Questura** (headquarters) is also centrally located. Dial 112 for the carabinieri and 113 for the polizia di stato.

Women may receive much more attention than at home, especially around tourist areas. Open staring and verbal flirtation is not uncommon. Most of this is harmless, but can be annoying and unwelcome.

Lost property handed in to the police ends up at the **Oggetti Smarriti** near the Piramide metro. ID will be required to reclaim anything, plus a crime report unless the object is clearly identifiable. There is a small administrative fee. **Oggetti Smarriti Metro Lines A and B** have their own lost property offices.

Travellers with Specific Needs

Rome isn't yet fully accessible largely because conservation laws prevent alterations to very old buildings to accommodate wheelchairs. The cobbled streets can make for some bone-shaking journeys.

Major museums have disabled facilities and many hotels have converted a few rooms. Some metro stops (but not Colosseo) are wheelchair accessible. **RADAR** and **Roma per Tutti** have useful information.

DIRECTORY

PASSPORTS AND VISAS

Ministero degli Esteri (Foreign Ministry)
w esteri.it/visti/index_eng.asp

TRAVEL SAFETY ADVICE

Australian Department of Foreign Affairs and Trade
w dfat.gov.au
w smartraveller.gov.au

UK Foreign and Commonwealth Office
w gov.uk/foreign-travel-advice

US Department of State
w travel.state.gov

EMBASSIES AND CONSULATES

Australia
Via Antonio Bosio 5
w italy.embassy.gov.au

UK
MAP F2
■ Via XX Settembre 80A
w ukinitaly.fco.gov.uk

USA
MAP E2
■ Via Vittorio Veneto 121
w it.usembassy.gov

HEALTH

Fatebenefratelli
MAP M6
■ Isola Tiberina, Via di Ponte 4 Capi 39
[06 68371

Guardia Medica Turistica
MAP D2 & C5
■ Via Canova 19 and Via Morosini 30
[06 7730 6112

Policlinico Universitario
Largo Agostino Gemelli 8
[06 30151

EMERGENCY SERVICES

Police, Ambulance and Fire Brigade
[112

Ambulance
[118

Fire Brigade
[115

PERSONAL SECURITY

Carabinieri
[112
w carabinieri.it

Carabinieri Centro Storico
MAP M1
■ Piazza di San Lorenzo in Lucina 6
[06 6959 4538

Carabinieri Janiculum
MAP C4 ■ Via Garibaldi 41
[06 58591

Carabinieri Termini
MAP F3 ■ Via Marsala s/n
[06 4730 6040

Carabinieri Prati
MAP C5 ■ Via del Crocifisso 46 [06 6959 4538

Oggetti Smarriti
Circ.ne Ostiense 191
[06 6769 3214/15/16/17

Oggetti Smarriti Metro Line A
Stazione Giulio Agricola
[06 4695 7068

Oggetti Smarriti Metro Line B
MAP D6
■ Stazione Piramide
[06 4695 8164/65

Polizia di Stato
[113

Polizia di Stato Questura
MAP R2
■ Via di San Vitale 15
[06 46861

TRAVELLERS WITH SPECIFIC NEEDS

RADAR
w radar.org.uk

Roma per Tutti
w romapertutti.it

Currency and Banking

Italy is one of the 19 European countries using the euro (€), which is divided into 100 cents. Paper notes are in denominations of €5, €10, €20, €50, €100, €200 and €500. Coins are €2, €1, 50c, 20c, 10c, 5c, 2c, 1c.

The easiest way of getting cash is with a debit card from a cash machine (ATM), known in Italy as Bancomat. Most cards allow a maximum daily withdrawal of €250, but most banks charge for withdrawals abroad.

Exchange rates offered by hotels and bureaux de change are rarely good – far better to go to a bank branch. Banks are open 8:30am–1.30pm Monday to Friday and then usually again for an hour sometime between 2.30–4pm.

Pre-paid currency cards (cash passports) are a more secure way of carrying money. They can be preloaded with euros, fixing exchange rates before you leave, and used like a debit card. The maximum daily withdrawal is usually €700. **Thomas Cook** offers these, as do most banks.

Many shops accept chip and pin cards, and most hotels and restaurants accept credit cards.

Internet and Telephone

Fast speed internet and Wi-Fi is available in cafés and hotels all over the city. The city council also provides free Wi-Fi in many piazzas throughout the city – all Wi-Fi zones are clearly marked.

Registration is done online, and it is essential to have an Italian mobile number, as accounts are validated by asking users to dial a free number.

In Italy the regional phone code is an integral part of every number, and always has to be dialled. Rome's area code is 06 and Italy's code is 39.

European mobile phones work in Italy, but Americans will need a triband phone. Your home provider will have roaming options, but check rates carefully. A cheaper alternative may be to purchase an Italian SIM card (you will need ID). The main mobile operators are TIM, Vodafone, 3 and Wind. Rechargeable SIM cards can be bought for €10, including €5 of credit. They can be topped up at tobacconists with a SISAL terminal (used for registering lottery numbers), by buying a scratch card (from newsagents and tobacconists or online) or by going into the phone company's own shops.

There are virtually no public phones that take coins, but some, especially at the airport and train stations, accept credit cards. However, the fares are exceptionally high. Several kinds of phone card are available for international calls – the best value is the EDICARD.

Postal Services

The Italian postal system, **Poste Italiane**, can be appallingly slow. If using Poste Italiane, avoid sending registered mail as it tends to accumulate at the collection point before being sent on. If speed is

of the essence for destinations within Italy, use the postal system's courier service, Posta Celere; for international destinations use a private courier such as **DHL**. Stamps (francobolli) are on sale at post offices and tobacconists, and often (unofficially) at any shop selling postcards.

Newspapers and Radio

For information in English about what's on, a good source is the monthly magazine Where Rome, available for free in hotels. TrovaRoma, a supplement of the daily newspaper La Repubblica, is more up-to-date; however it is in Italian only. There is also a bi-weekly magazine produced by and for the Anglophone expat community, **Wanted in Rome**, which also has a website. It is sold at newsstands throughout the city centre.

International magazines and newspapers are easy to find around the centre, but prices can be high and they may be out of date, making online news sources far better value.

To keep in touch with Italian news in English try the **Life In Italy** website or tune into the **Vatican Radio** English news.

Opening Hours

The days when Rome's museums and sights closed for riposo, the long lunch break, or even the entire afternoon are fast becoming history. Most major museums and sights stay open all day, as do an increasing number of supermarkets and international chain stores. Shops, churches and other businesses that still follow tradition will usually open at 8am or 9am, close at 12:30 or 1pm, open again at 3 or 4pm (or 5pm in summer), and close between 6 and 8pm. Many museums, art galleries and archeological sites are closed on Monday. Their opening times vary widely – check before starting out. Last admission to many visitor attractions is an hour before closing time.

Time Difference

Italy operates on Central European Time (CET), which is 1 hour ahead of Greenwich Mean Time (GMT) and 6 hours ahead of US Eastern Standard Time (EST). The clock moves forward 1 hour during daylight saving time from the last Sunday in March until the last Sunday in October.

Electrical Appliances

The electricity supply in Italy is 220 volts. Italian plugs come with two and three round pins, and sometimes an adaptor is necessary – ask as you make a purchase. All non-Italian plugs will also need adaptors.

Driving

To rent a car in Italy you generally need to be over 20 years old and have held a full driving licence for at least one year. When you pick up the vehicle, you will need to show your passport, driving licence and a credit card from which to pay the security deposit. Be sure to inform your insurer before you travel, too.

Weather

Rome has a temperate climate. August heat is oppressive; February snow flurries are possible. Spring's middle ground keeps hotels booked; autumn is less crowded, but prone to downpours. High season is Easter to July and September to October. Rome is deserted and most of the city's shops and restaurants closed through much of August as residents head to the beaches or mountains to escape the heat.

Tourist Information

The first and most convenient port of call is **06 0608**, the internet information service of the city of Rome (available in English and Italian), with everything a tourist needs to know – both practical and cultural. It also lets you make bookings for hotels, exhibitions and concerts. 06 0608 is available in Italian and English on the phone as well, charged at local rates.

The **Italian State Tourism Board** has very useful websites, and there are several **tourist information points** dotted around the city.

The 2- and 3-day **Roma Pass** cards are excellent value for visitors as they include travel on all public transport plus free entrance to two museums as well as discounted entry to many others. For a full list of participating museums and sites, visit their website.

DIRECTORY

CURRENCY AND BANKING

Thomas Cook
w thomascook.com

POSTAL SERVICES

DHL
w dhl.it/en.html

Poste Italiane
w poste.it

NEWSPAPERS AND RADIO

Life in Italy
w lifeinitaly.com

Vatican Radio
w radiovaticana.va

Wanted in Rome
w wantedinrome.com

TOURIST INFORMATION

06 0608
c 06 0608
w 060608.it

Italian State Tourism Board
w italia.it
w enit.it

Roma Pass
w romapass.it

Tourist Information Point Ciampino
International Arrivals Baggage Claim
8:30am–6pm

Tourist Information Point Fiumicino
International Arrivals Terminal B–C
9am–7:30pm

Tourist Information Point Navona
MAP L2 ▪ Piazza delle Cinque Lune
9:30am–6pm

Tourist Information Point Termini
MAP F3 ▪ Via Giovanni Giolitti 34
Inside Office F
Platform 24
8am–6:45pm

Shopping Tips

Rome is full of antiquities, paintings and sculpture from the ancient past to 20th-century collectibles, although buyers should remember that exporting these will require a good deal of paperwork. If your taste is more contemporary, shop for kitchen implements, homeware and lighting systems by top local and international designers. Rome is also home to many fine jewellers, from all the big names to highly-skilled artisans labouring in small boutiques.

High street and designer fashion is rarely cheaper than back home, but fabulous bargains can be found in stock houses and outlets, which sell the previous season's overstock and seconds.

Haggling is expected in markets, but hardly ever in shops. Be ready to go through the full ritual, including acting less and less interested, while the merchant acts ever more offended and claims he can go no lower.

Italy's Value Added Tax (IVA) is a sales tax already added on to the sticker price of every item. If you are a non-EU resident and spend more than €155 in a single shop, you can get the tax refunded. Ask the store to help you fill out the forms, then take these and the receipts to the customs office at the airport of the last EU country you'll be visiting to complete the paperwork. Your refund will be posted but it may take months. Stores marked "Tax-Free Shopping for Tourists" speed up the process, giving you a cheque for the customs office to stamp, which you redeem at the airport's Tax-Free Shopping desk.

Dining

There is no clear difference these days between an *osteria*, a trattoria, a *ristorante* and an *enoteca*. A *ristorante* can be a refined establishment for fine dining, or a joint round the back of Termini station dishing out indifferent pasta at inflated prices to unsuspecting tourists. Osterias and trattorias are pretty much interchangeable – some are old fashioned places serving simple food that haven't changed in years, others chic new establishments where "trattoria osteria" is used to signal that they are revisiting culinary traditions. The original meaning of *enoteca* was simply "wine shop"; these days it is also used by wine shops that serve meals, and by fully-fledged restaurants that want clients to know they have a serious wine cellar.

The traditional Italian meal consists of an *antipasto* (starter), *primo* (pasta, rice or soup), *secondo* (meat or fish), *contorno* (vegetable) and *dolce* (dessert), and until recently, tourists ordering only a plate of pasta would be treated with disdain. But international eating habits have arrived, and most places – especially in the *centro storico* – no longer expect diners to spend two hours over a five-course meal. Menus have freed up, and many places advertise themselves as serving "easy food" meaning that the menus are designed for clients to pick and choose from, whatever the time of day. Only the more traditional restaurants open solely at lunch and dinner – most of the new-wave eateries serve food all day.

Most restaurants charge for bread and cover. If the menu says "*servizio incluso*", the service charge is built in, although it is customary to round up by a few coins. If not, tip a discretionary 10 per cent.

Jacket and tie are almost never required, although in more upmarket places reservations often are. Waiters expect you to linger over your meal, and won't rush you (some mistake this for slow service).

Where to Stay

Rome has a great range of memorable places to stay – opulent grand hotels, chic boutique places, and a huge variety of B&Bs, apartments and hostels (but book well in advance for the latter in peak season). There are also lodgings run by religious organisations.

It is as important to choose a neighbourhood as it is to find the right kind of accommodation. Wonderful as it is to stay in the *centro storico* around Campo de' Fiori, Piazza di Spagna and Piazza Navona, it is not only expensive, but can be touristy, crowded and noisy. The charming, tangled streets of Trastevere are worth considering, although the area does attract a noisy nighttime crowd. The Ghetto and Monti are both delightful, authentic neighbourhoods just off the beaten track, with lots of atmosphere and some lovely places to stay, but are still within walking distance of most sights. There are also several good-value places to stay around MAXXI. The Aventine Hill is peaceful, with some gorgeous hotels, although the reason it is quiet is that there is nowhere to eat and drink nearby. The area behind Termini is packed with budget places, but the streets are unappealing and occasionally unsavoury.

Types of Accommodation

Italian hotels are given an official rating of between one and five stars based on a checklist of facilities. The stars are no guide to the subtler attractions of a hotel, such as the decor or the friendliness of staff. B&Bs and apartments often provide more for your money than cheap one- and two-star hotels. Websites such as **Enjoy Rome**, **TripAdvisor** and **Booking.com** can help with reviews, suggestions and actual bookings.

Over the past decade, since a law was passed to allow ordinary people to offer bed-and-breakfast in their homes, hundreds of "BDs" have opened in Rome. **BBPlanet**, **Venere** and the **B&B Association of Rome** will help you find and book one. The nicest offer excellent value for money, with charming

owners and fantastic breakfasts. Many B&Bs do not have staff on the premises – not necessarily a disadvantage, but be sure to ask how to contact the owner should the need arise, if breakfast is served in the B&B or at a local café, and if there is use of the kitchen.

Sites such as **Airbnb**, **NiceFlatInRome.com** and **Go2Rome** have made it easy for owners to offer their home for short holiday rentals, whether it is a simple, functional city centre crash-pad or a glamorous apartment on the *piano nobile* of a historic palazzo.

Several religious organizations also offer accommodation, not solely to the religious. These may, however, have a curfew and be open only to one gender. Prices are not necessarily low, but they can be a good option for anyone (especially women) nervous about travelling alone.

Rates and Booking

Booking and hotel websites often offer huge discounts on standard rates as it is common for prices to be adjusted according to demand. Shop around before you book. The best deals are usually to be had online and in advance. Smaller hotels' websites are not always secure, and it is unwise to email credit card details to them. Finalize the booking over the phone or use a hotel broking organization with a secure site.

All accommodation in Rome – five-star hotels, rented rooms, flats and

even campsites – is by law obliged to add the city tourist tax to its rates. This varies between €3 and €7 per night – always check if it is included in the rate quoted to you. The tax is charged for a maximum of 10 nights.

Watch out for hidden costs. Some hotels still charge for Wi-Fi, although it is worth using your powers of persuasion to get it waived. Phoning from a hotel room is always expensive, but phone cards usually work from hotels. If the hotel has blocked the free-phone number, there will generally be a local access number on the phone card as well. Most B&Bs do not have phones for guest use (although some offer their guests rechargeable SIM cards).

Places to Stay

PRICE CATEGORIES

For a standard, double room per night (with breakfast if included), taxes and extra charges.

€ under €150   €€ €150–350   €€€ over €350

Bastions of Luxury

Giulio Cesare

MAP B2 ■ Via degli Scipioni 287 ■ 06 321 0751 ■ www.hotelgiulio cesare.com ■ €

Formerly the patrician villa of a countess, this hotel's atmosphere is still aristocratic. Chandeliers, antiques, art, Oriental carpets and a grand piano typify the quiet elegance of the public rooms. Mirror-lined hallways lead to elegant bedrooms with marble baths. You can eat at outdoor tables in a lovely terrace garden. It is located on a quiet street close to the Vatican.

Atlante Star

MAP B2 ■ Via Vitelleschi 34 ■ 06 686 386 ■ www. atlantehotels.com ■ €€

In a grand 19th-century building with old-world charm, this hotel offers its guests attentive service and extras such as a free airport pick-up and Jacuzzis. The rooftop garden and restaurant is famous for its spectacular panorama of the nearby St Peter's Basilica.

De Russie

MAP D2 ■ Via del Babuino 9 ■ 06 328 881 ■ www.roccofortehotels. com ■ €€€

This historic hotel, a favourite of Picasso, has been refurbished in a sumptuous, understated style. Delights include terraced garden cafés; an excellent restaurant; the Stravinskij, one of Rome's most renowned cocktail bars (see p122); a spa and gym and a secret garden on the Pincio. All of its bedrooms are decorated in elegant muted colours and provide sheer comfort.

Eden

MAP E2 ■ Via Ludovisi 49 ■ 06 478 121 ■ www. dorchestercollection. com/en/romehotel-eden ■ €€€

Perhaps Rome's most illustrious defender of the grand tradition, this hotel has been the choice of celebrities for years. One of the city's most exclusive places to stay, it speaks of refinement in every detail and an extensive restoration has made it more splendid than ever. A superb restaurant-bar, La Terrazza, tops the edifice, dominating the city (see p140). With some of the best views in Rome, it is perfect for a special occasion or a romantic meal.

Grand Hotel Flora

MAP E2 ■ Via Veneto 191 ■ 06 489 929 ■ www. marriott.com ■ €€€

Set in a Neo-Classical building, this gracious and elegant hotel has the air of refinement you expect on Via Veneto, combined with efficient service. The decor features marble, antiques and soft colours. The Ailanto Roof Garden restaurant boasts views of the great dome of St Peter's Basilica, the Villa Borghese park and the beautiful skyline of the city. There is also a piano bar. The hotel is part of the Marriott chain.

Hassler

MAP D2 ■ Piazza Trinità dei Monti 6 ■ 06 699 340 ■ www.hotelhassler roma.com ■ €€€

In one of the few genteel hotels that's not yet part of a luxury chain, the honey-coloured tones of the public rooms set the mood of timeless luxury. The sumptuous suites and the terrace restaurant offer some of the most magnificent views in the city. Its elegant restaurant, Imàgo, has been awarded a Michelin star for its imaginative Italian fusion cuisine (see p72).

J.K. Place

MAP L1 ■ Via Monte D'Oro 30 ■ 06 982 634 ■ www.jkroma.com ■ €€€

Providing a truly deluxe experience, J.K. Place has impeccably furnished rooms and suites. The decor combines antiques and modern design pieces to create a "Dolce Vita" retro feel. Service is informal but attentive, and the café, which is open all day, has a great menu of Italian and international classics.

Majestic

MAP E2 ■ Via Veneto 50 ■ 06 421 441 ■ www. hotelmajestic.com ■ €€€

Magnificence is the keynote in the Majestic, the oldest of the Via

Veneto hotels, founded in 1889. This beautiful Neo-Classical property boasts rich decor and antiques throughout, and bathrooms with Jacuzzis. The Majestic Bar is a great place for afternoon tea, and the formal Massimo Riccioli restaurant is one of the top places to eat in the area (see p123). The hotel is within walking distance of major sights, such as the Trevi Fountain and the Spanish Steps.

Regina Baglioni
MAP E2 ▪ Via Veneto 72 ▪ 06 421 111 ▪ www. baglionihotels.com ▪ €€€
A setting fit for a king, which it has been more than once. With extravagant Italian Art Nouveau styling, wall silks, Oriental carpets, paintings, marble floors and antiques, this beautiful hotel is a palace inside and out. A beautiful wrought-iron staircase, watched over by a statue of Neptune, leads up from the reception area. Suites on the seventh floor have panoramic views.

St Regis Grand
MAP E3 ▪ Via V E Orlando 3 ▪ 06 470 91 ▪ www. stregisrome.com ▪ €€€€
The extravagant St Regis Grand was set up by César Ritz in 1894, and continues to live up to the illustrious hotelier's name. Completely restored, it attracts guests drawn from the ranks of royalty, heads of state, captains of industry and celebrities. A world-class restaurant, Vivendo, a business centre and a fitness club complete its offerings.

Romantic Charmers

San Anselmo and Villa San Pio
MAP D5 ▪ Piazza Sant' Anselmo 2 and Via di Santa Melania ▪ 06 570 057 ▪ www.aventino hotels.com ▪ €
Nestled on a tranquil hill, both these adjacent establishments are spacious and pleasant. Rococo decor predominates, and includes elegant tapestries and chandeliers. Shiatsu massages are also available on request.

Caesar House Residenze Romane
MAP R4 ▪ Via Cavour 310 ▪ 06 679 2674 ▪ www. caesarhouse.com ▪ €€
A small boutique hotel housed in an elegant old building with views of the Roman Forum. Each room is decorated with antiques, replicating the atmosphere of a noble apartment. There is a Turkish bath and a massage service is also available.

Farnese
MAP C1 ▪ Via Alessandro Farnese 30 ▪ 06 321 2553 ▪ www.hotelfarnese.com ▪ €€
This belle époque mansion is furnished with period authenticity. Captivating trompe l'oeil fresco decorations and a roof garden are just a few of its attractions. Rich fabrics and high ceilings are typical of the rooms.

Grand Hotel del Gianicolo
MAP B4 ▪ Viale delle Mura Gianicolensi 107 ▪ 06 5833 3405 ▪ www.grand hotelgianicolo.it ▪ €€
Located on the hill above Trastevere, this former convent offers every amenity, including roof gardens, beautiful lawns and a swimming pool. The location is serene, despite nearby traffic. Public rooms feature Venetian glass fixtures.

Lord Byron
MAP B2 ▪ Via G de Notaris 5 ▪ 06 322 0404 ▪ www.lordbyronhotel. com ▪ €€
This refined boutique hotel was originally a monastery, but there is nothing ascetic about it nowadays. The decor is an eclectic mix of styles and periods, but all of it evokes opulence. Its location provides serene solitude that makes a perfect antidote to the hectic life of the centre.

Piranesi
MAP D2 ▪ Via del Babuino 196 ▪ 06 328 041 ▪ www. hotelpiranesi.com ▪ €€
Located just off the Piazza del Popolo, this is a romantic boutique hotel run by a charming family. The bedrooms have wooden floors and are beautifully decorated with brocade. There are fine views of the city from the pretty roof terrace.

Crossing Condotti
MAP N1 ▪ Via Mario de' Fiori 28 ▪ 06 6992 0633 ▪ www.crossingcondotti. com ▪ €€€
This private residence offers the comfort of a wonderful downtown house, complete with a shared kitchenette with tea and coffee-making facilities. The nine rooms are decorated with the owner's art and antiques.

Portrait Roma

MAP D2 ■ Via Bocca di Leone 23 ■ 06 6938 0742 ■ www.lungarno collection.com ■ €€€

The classic Italian home inspired this luxury boutique hotel, created with couples in mind. The suites are elegant and romantic, with designer furnishings and customized service.

Raphael

MAP L3 ■ Largo Febo 2 ■ 06 682 831 ■ www. raphaelhotel.com ■ €€€

Set just behind Piazza Navona in a burnt-siena palazzo, the location could not be more perfect. The foyer is full of unusual art treasures and most of the rooms are originally decorated.

Westin Excelsior

MAP E2 ■ Via Veneto 125 ■ 06 470 81 ■ www. westinrome.com ■ €€€

The grande dame of Rome's hotels, noted for its commanding location and *belle époque* architecture, boasting sculpted balconies with caryatids. Notes of grandeur abound every-where you look, with sumptuous rooms and classic decor. There is a spa with a pool and several fine restaurants.

Rooms with a View

Abruzzi

MAP M3 ■ Piazza della Rotonda 69 ■ 06 9784 1351 ■ www.hotel abruzzi.it ■ €€

Located in the heart of the city centre, this hotel offers large rooms decorated with charming images of ancient Rome. Ask for a room that opens onto the dazzling view of the piazza and Pantheon.

Domus Aventina

MAP D5 ■ Via di Santa Prisca 11B ■ 06 574 6135 ■ www.hoteldomus aventina.com ■ €€

Housed within a former 14th-century convent with a 17th-century façade and located at the bottom of the Aventine Hill, this serene hotel has large, subtly coloured rooms. There are wonderful views from the balconies and terrace. Prints, murals and Classical artifacts decorate the rooms, which lend a timeless elegance.

Homs

MAP D2 ■ Via della Vite 71–2 ■ 06 679 2976 ■ www.hotelhoms.it ■ €€

On a quiet shopping street, this mid-sized hotel is a bit plain, but antique furnishings here and there give it a gracious feel. There are two roof terraces, one of which is indoors for year-round breakfasts, from which you can admire the panorama of Rome's skyline.

Scalinata di Spagna

MAP D2 ■ Piazza Trinità dei Monti 17 ■ 06 458 6150 ■ www.hotel scalinata.com ■ €€

With its coveted location housed in an 18th-century villa at the top of the Spanish Steps, this intimate jewel boasts marvellous views from many of its rooms and from the trellis-covered terrace. The rooms are not large but are beautifully appointed. Book well in advance.

Sofitel Villa Borghese

MAP E2 ■ Via Lombardia 47 ■ 06 478 021 ■ www. accorhotels.com ■ €€

Housed in a renovated palazzo, this luxurious hotel has a classically elegant, modern interior and offers superb views of the Villa Borghese park from its top floor terrace.

Sole al Pantheon

MAP M3 ■ Piazza della Rotonda 63 ■ 06 678 0441 ■ www.soleal pantheonrome.com ■ €€

Noted as an inn since 1467, this distinguished hotel was the choice of Renaissance writer Ariosto. Facing the Pantheon, it has painted period decoration in many of the rooms and modern touches such as Jacuzzis and double-glazing.

Teatro di Pompeo

MAP N6 ■ Largo del Pallaro 8 ■ 06 6830 0170 ■ www.hotelteatrodi pompeo.it ■ €€

Have breakfast under the arches of the first theatre in Rome, built by Pompey the Great in 55 BC and said to be where Caesar met his end. Rooms have wood-beamed ceilings, marble-topped furni ture, and some have great views. This lovely little hotel offers guests the style and many of the amenities of bigger, more expensive places.

Torre Colonna

MAP P4 ■ Via delle Tre Cannelle 18 ■ 06 8360 0192 ■ www.torre colonna.it ■ €€

Housed inside a medieval defensive tower, this boutique hotel sits right on top of the Imperial Fora. Each of the five individually decorated rooms has a Jacuzzi and there's also one on the terrace with views overlooking the Fora.

Victoria

MAP E2 ▪ Via Campania 41 ▪ 06 423 701 ▪ www. hotelvictoriaroma.com ▪ €€

Just off Via Veneto, this lovely boutique hotel displays 18th- and 19th-century paintings of Rome. A terrace bar has spectacular views of the ancient Aurelian Wall and Villa Borghese.

Inn at the Spanish Steps

MAP D2 ▪ Via dei Condotti 85 ▪ 06 6992 5657 ▪ www.atspanish steps.com ▪ €€€

This upmarket hotel is in a 17th-century building once lived in by Danish author Hans Christian Andersen. It offers great views of the Spanish Steps from its attractive rooftop garden. The well-equipped rooms feature an iPod docking station and a coffee machine.

Comfort, Style and Value Hotels

Des Artistes

MAP F3 ▪ Via Villafranca 20 ▪ 06 445 4365 ▪ www. hoteldesartistes.com ▪ €

A cheerful hotel with accommodation to suit all budgets. Warm fabrics, modern art and marble bathrooms create an air of luxury; rooms have data ports. There's a floor set aside for budget travellers, and a pleasant roof terrace. One of the best choices near Termini.

Fori Imperiali Cavalieri

MAP Q5 ▪ Via Frangipane 34 ▪ 06 679 6246 ▪ www.hotelforiimperiali cavalieri.com ▪ €

Just steps away from the ancient centre. Serenity reigns supreme, with service to match. The historic building has been renovated and every room has a data port.

Cesàri

MAP N2 ▪ Via di Pietra 89A ▪ 06 674 9701 ▪ www. albergocesari.it ▪ €€

Close to the Pantheon next to the Temple of Hadrian, this little gem was famous in the 1800s, when French writer Stendhal stayed here. The exterior is little changed. The interior, however, has been kept up to date, set off with antiques and old prints. All rooms have blue marble bathrooms.

Condotti

MAP N1 ▪ Via Mario de' Fiori 37 ▪ 06 679 4661 ▪ www.hotelcondotti. com ▪ €€

Amid the designer boutiques along this street, the Condotti Hotel offers comfort and period furnishings. All rooms are soundproofed, and many feature views over the rooftops; one has a terrace. The staff are unfailingly attentive.

Dei Borgognoni

MAP P1 ▪ Via del Bufalo 126 ▪ 06 6994 1505 ▪ www.hotelborgognoni. it ▪ €€

Although just around the corner from the bustling historic centre, this up-to-date period building feels removed from it all. Subdued lighting and

colours enhance the antique accents, and the hushed garden is very inviting. Some rooms have private patios. Fitness clubs and sports facilities are also available at this hotel.

Mecenate Palace

MAP F3 ▪ Via Carlo Alberto 3 ▪ 06 4470 2024 ▪ www.mecenatepalace. com ▪ €€

With views of Santa Maria Maggiore (see p131), this comfortable hotel's name recalls a great patron of the arts under Augustus Caesar. The terrace café is ideal for small conferences and the meeting hall holds up to 40 people.

Pantheon

MAP M3 ▪ Via dei Pastini 131 ▪ 06 678 7746 ▪ www.hotelpantheon. com ▪ €€

Less than a block from the eponymous temple (see pp18–19), this small, tasteful establishment has public areas boasting stained glass, mosaics and beamed ceilings. The door to each room has an antique print of a Rome obelisk, and inside you'll find fresh flowers. Small pets are welcome.

La Rovere

MAP B3 ▪ Vicolo Sant'Onofrio 4 ▪ 06 6880 6739 ▪ www.hotel larovere.biz ▪ €€

This quiet, family-run hotel is on the lower slopes of the Janiculum, a short walk from the centro storico. The rooms are a charming mix of modern and classic styles (some with wooden-beamed ceilings), and there is a roof terrace in summer. Smoking is prohibited in the hotel.

For a key to hotel price categories see p170

Santa Maria

MAP K6 ▪ Vicolo del Piede 2 ▪ 06 589 4626 ▪ www.hotelsantamaria trastevere.it ▪ €€

Occupying a 16th-century cloister, this is an oasis of calm within the bustling Trastevere area. Ground-floor rooms (one is adapted for disabled guests) surround a charming courtyard garden, which is filled with citrus trees. A wine bar serves snacks and drinks. Single-rate and multiple-occupancy rooms are available.

Teatropace 33

MAP L2 ▪ Via del Teatro Pace 33 ▪ 06 687 9075 ▪ www.hotelteatropace. com ▪ €€

In a quiet street just a few minutes' walk from Piazza Navona, Teatropace 33 occupies a beautiful ochre former cardinal's palazzo, wonderfully restored. Every room in the stylish interior is different. No lift.

Tritone

MAP P1 ▪ Via del Tritone 210 ▪ 06 6992 2575 ▪ www. tritonehotel.com ▪ €€

Near the Trevi Fountain and Piazza Barberini, Tritone has comfortable rooms and good-quality decor. The emphasis is on tranquillity, ensured by double-glazing and wall-to-wall carpeting. The superior rooms feature wood-veneered walls. Breakfast in the roof garden is a joy.

Business Hotels

Dei Consoli

MAP B2 ▪ Via Varrone 2D ▪ 06 6889 2972 ▪ www. hoteldeiconsoli.com ▪ €€

Elegant hotel with all the facilities, including Internet, hydromassage and meeting rooms. Enjoy breakfast on the roof terrace with views of St Peter's.

Forum

MAP P4 ▪ Via Tor de' Conti 25–30 ▪ 06 679 2446 ▪ www.hotelforum rome.com ▪ €€

Set in an 18th-century converted convent, this hotel has a sunny roof garden restaurant and bar which overlooks the Imperial Fora (see pp26–7). The meeting room can seat up to 100 people and is equipped with full facilities.

Grand Hotel Plaza

MAP D2 ▪ Via del Corso 126 ▪ 06 6992 1111 ▪ www.grandhotelplaza. com ▪ €€

Dating from 1860, this is one of Rome's oldest hotels, and is replete with Edwardian lavish-ness. Grand salons with frescoes, stained-glass skylights, chandeliers and antiques combined with modern amenities produce a comfortable ambience. Some of the rooms have their own private terrace, and the two large rooftop terraces offer magnificent views of the city.

Nazionale a Montecitorio

MAP M1 ▪ Piazza Montecitorio 131 ▪ 06 695 001 ▪ www.hotel nazionale.it ▪ €€

Located next to the Italian Parliament, in the heart of the historic city center, this hotel in a 16th-century palace has welcomed many politicos. It has a regal atmosphere, especially in the marble-floored restaurant.

Parco dei Principi

MAP E2 ▪ Via G Frescobaldi 5 ▪ 06 854 421 ▪ www.parcodei principi.com ▪ €€

Just at the edge of Villa Borghese park stands this modern high-rise, yet inside all is over-the-top Italian court decor. Panoramas from every room take in greenery and the city's domes. There's a gym, a pool, patios, lounges and a business centre as well.

Radisson Blu es. Hotel

MAP F3 ▪ Via Filippo Turati 171 ▪ 06 444 841 ▪ www. radissonblu.com/en/ eshotel-rome ▪ €€

Contemporary hotel of glass, wood and steel with high-tech conference facilities, and a trendy rooftop bar and restaurant.

Bernini Bristol

MAP Q1 ▪ Piazza Barberini 23 ▪ 06 488 931 ▪ www. sinahotels.com ▪ €€€

This unprepossessing brick building faces Bernini's Triton fountain (see p138). The decor is also uninspiring, but the hotel has excellent facilities. There's a roof garden, and top rooms have fine views.

Boscolo Exedra

MAP E3 ▪ Piazza della Repubblica 47 ▪ 06 489 381 ▪ www.exedra-roma. boscolohotels.com ▪ €€€

Set in a majestic palazzo overlooking the Baths of Diocletian (see p137), this five-star luxury hotel provides top service and quality. The low lighting, warm colours and fresh flowers recall Neo-Classical elegance and the roof terrace is a perfect place for a business lunch.

Cavalieri Hilton

MAP B1 ■ Via Cadlolo 101 ■ 06 350 91 ■ www.rome-cavalieri.it ■ €€€

Located on a hill across the river, away from the centre, this hotel is possibly the best place in Rome for doing business on a grand scale, thanks to its two restaurants – La Pergola has three Michelin stars and is Rome's finest dining experience (see p72) – four bars, indoor and outdoor pools, beauty salon, spa, fitness centre, tennis courts and parks.

Budget Gems

Al Centro di Roma B&B

MAP L4 ■ Piazza Sant'Andrea della Valle 3 ■ 333 577 3438 ■ www.bbalcentrodiroma.com ■ €

This small B&B with just three rooms is located between the Pantheon and Piazza Navona. It has an excellent reputation for service, cleanliness and value for money.

Columbia

MAP E3 ■ Via del Viminale 15 ■ 06 488 3509 ■ www.hotelcolumbia.com ■ €

Located in Termini, one of Rome's busiest neighbourhoods, this quiet gem of a hotel is close to the Baths of Diocletian and has good transport options for sightseeing. Dark wood and light-coloured fabrics create an airy feel. The breakfast buffet can be enjoyed on the beautiful roof terrace.

Locanda Carmel

MAP K6 ■ Via Goffredo Mameli 11 ■ 06 580 9921 ■ www.hotelcarmel.it ■ €

An old-fashioned pensione-style place

with spartan decor and modest rooms. There's a vine-covered terrace and most rooms have double-glazing. A unique touch is the kosher kitchen for use by Jewish guests.

Alimandi Vaticano

MAP B2 ■ Viale Vaticano 99 ■ 06 3974 5562 ■ www.alimandivaticano hotel.com ■ €€

Close to the Vatican, with an attractive foyer and large rooms. Terraces and a roof garden with great views are outstanding features for this price range. Staff provide quality service. On a fairly quiet shopping street, handy for public transport. Free cable TV and airport shuttle.

Artorius

MAP R4 ■ Via del Boschetto 13 ■ 06 482 1196 ■ www.hotelartorius rome.com ■ €€

On one of Monti's prettiest roads, this two-star family-run hotel offers a relaxing experience at reasonable prices. The rooms are spacious, comfortable and elegant, and there's a pleasant bar.

Buonanotte Garibaldi

MAP C4 ■ Via Garibaldi 83 ■ 06 5833 0733 ■ www.buonanottegaribaldi.com ■ €€

This small, luxury B&B in the heart of Trastevere was carved out of an art studio and is a perfect romantic getaway. Breakfast is served in the elegant dining room or in the lush courtyard. Take a pick from the Rome, Chocolate or Tinto rooms, which have all been decorated by the owner herself.

Campo de' Fiori

MAP L4 ■ Via del Biscione 6 ■ 06 6880 6865 ■ www.hotelcampodefiori.com ■ €€

In a great location, this cosy boutique hotel is housed in a medieval building, which has been restored and decorated with mirrors, frescoes and antique coffered ceilings to highlight its orginal features. The roof terrace offers a panoramic view of the spires and domes of Rome's ancient quarter. Friendly staff provide an excellent service.

San Carlo

MAP D2 ■ Via delle Carrozze 93 ■ 06 678 4548 ■ www.hotel sancarloroma.com ■ €€

The overall decor of this hotel echoes a Classical influence, with marble touches here and there. Located on one of the quieter streets near the Spanish Steps, the rooms at this three-star hotel are light and spacious, and some have roof top views and private terraces. Breakfast is offered in the top-floor garden. Free Internet access is available.

Sant'Anna

MAP B3 ■ Borgo Pio 134 ■ 06 6880 1602 ■ www.santannahotel.net ■ €€

This fashionable small hotel in the medieval Borgo next to St Peter's has frescoes in the breakfast room and a fountain in the courtyard. The rooms are spacious and those at the top have their own tiny balconies. The area is quiet and still has the feel of old Rome.

Smeraldo

MAP M4 ■ Vicolo dei Chiodaroli 9 ■ 06 687 5929 ■ www.smeraldo roma.com ■ €€

An excellent choice for both location and quality. The name honours the emerald-green marble entrance, and there are marble accents throughout. Rooms are clean and simple and some have private balconies. There are two terraces.

Hostels and Religious Institutions

B&B Il Covo

MAP R4 ■ Via del Boschetto 91 ■ 06 484 894 ■ www.bbilcovo.com ■ €

A simple but charming B&B in the heart of Monti, with wooden beams and brick-vaulted ceilings. Breakfast is served downstairs at the café.

The Beehive

MAP K4 ■ Via Marghera 8 ■ 06 4470 4553 ■ www.the-beehive.com ■ €

Run by an American couple, this contemporary hotel-cum-hostel is near Roma Termini but is quiet with a secluded walled garden. It offers free Internet access and national phone calls.

Centro Diffusione Spiritualità

MAP J5 ■ Via dei Riari 44 ■ 06 6880 6122 ■ No credit cards ■ No air conditioning ■ €

This religious house, next to the botanical gardens in Trastevere, is a bit characterless but clean and well organized, and has a lovely garden. There is an 11pm curfew.

Colors

MAP B2 ■ Via Boezio 31 ■ 06 687 4030 ■ www.colorshotel.com ■ €

Run by the experienced Enjoy Rome team (see p169) and handily located in a quiet street near St Peter's, Colors has comfortable rooms and is run by friendly, multilingual staff. It offers free internet access and use of the kitchen and terrace. There is no curfew.

Fraterna Domus

MAP C3 ■ Via di Monte Brianzo 62 ■ 06 6880 2727 ■ www.fraterna-domus.it/english.html ■ €

A small hostel built around a 6th-century church and run by a group of friendly nuns, Fraterna Domus has small, clean and comfortable rooms and offers excellent homemade meals at a fraction of the price of those at other centro storico places. It has well-equipped conference facilites.

Hostel Alessandro and Alessandro Downtown

MAP E2 ■ Via Vicenza 42 and Via Carlo Cattaneo 23 ■ 06 446 1958/44 340 147 ■ www.hostelsalessandro.com ■ €

Friendly staff, a 24-hour reception, no curfew, a shared kitchen, internet access and free coffee, tea and pastries make these two hostels a popular choice. They also offer lockers, free maps and provide tourist information. Hostel Alessandro is situated to the north of Termini, while Alessandro Downtown is on the other side, near Via Cavour.

Hostel Sandy

MAP E3 ■ Via Cavour 136 ■ 06 488 4585 ■ www.sandyhostel.com ■ No credit cards ■ No air conditioning ■ €

The dormitories at this friendly hostel sleep three to eight people. Lockers and free internet access are provided. There is no curfew.

Hotel Panda

MAP D2 ■ Via della Croce 35 ■ 06 678 0179 ■ www.hotelpanda.it ■ €

An affordable option in the Piazza di Spagna area. Rooms are simple but clean and the staff are very friendly. The hotel has a breakfast deal with the bar downstairs.

Orsa Maggiore for Women Only

MAP C4 ■ Via S Francesco di Sales 1/a ■ 06 689 3753 ■ www.foresteriaorsa.altervista.org ■ No air conditioning ■ €

Run by the International Women's House in a 17th-century convent, this Trastevere hostel offers 13 rooms for women only. The rooms are single, double and multiple-occupancy, and all are spacious, bright and quiet, overlooking either the garden, cloister or city rooftops. There's also an organic café.

Blue Hostel

MAP F3 ■ Via Carlo Alberto 13 ■ 340 925 8503 ■ www.bluehostel.it ■ No credit cards ■ €€

A high-level hostel with fantastic double or triple rooms in the Esquiline. Each room has wooden floors and ceilings, and offers en suite bathroom and Wi-Fi. Perfect for families or small groups.

Residences and Apartments

Apartment Rentals

AT@HOME: Via del Corso 300 ▪ 06 3212 0102 ▪ www.at-home-italy.com ▪ Rome Sweet Home ▪ 06 6992 4091 ▪ www.romesweethome.it ▪ Cross-Pollinate ▪ 06 9028 8130 ▪ www.cross-pollinate.com ▪ €
Numerous services offer more unconventional apartment rentals. Prices vary depending on type of apartment, length of stay and number of people.

Aurelia Residence

Via Aurelia 145 ▪ 06 393 8648 ▪ www.aurelia residence.it ▪ €
This residence-style accommodation near the Vatican is perfect for families. The rooms are stylish and clean and the shopping area is just a few minutes' walk away. The roof garden offers views of St Peter's dome. Minimum two-night stay.

Residenza Bollo Apartments

MAP K4 ▪ Vicolo del Bollo 4 ▪ 06 320 7625 ▪ www.bolloapartments.com ▪ €
In a quiet pedestrian street an easy walk from Piazza Navona, this 17th-century palazzo has a range of apartment options, characterized by large windows, wood floors and beamed ceilings. At reception you can rent a bike and arrange guided tours.

Retrome

MAP E5 ▪ Via Marco Aurelio 47 ▪ 06 7049 5471 ▪ www.retrome.net ▪ €
Retrome manages one small hotel and 10 well-equipped apartments, all

in a contemporary style. They are in various locations throughout the city, including the Piazza Navona, Campo de' Fiori and Colosseum areas.

Trastevere

MAP K6 ▪ Via I. Manara 24A–25 ▪ 06 581 4713 ▪ www.hoteltrastevere.net ▪ €
Located just a block away from the main piazza, this unassuming, modest establishment captures the charm of Trastevere. The rooms have views of the local market. There are also small, clean apartments with kitchens.

Vatican Suites

MAP A3 ▪ Via Nicolò V 5 ▪ 06 633 306 ▪ www.vatican-suites.com ▪ €
Three historic mansions in Prati have been transformed into residence hotels offering studio apartments and one- and two-bedroom suites of varying sizes, all simply decorated and clean, with well-equipped kitchenettes.

Aldrovandi Residence

Via Aldrovandi 11 ▪ Tram No. 19 ▪ 06 322 1430 ▪ www.aldrovandi residence.it ▪ €€
This elegant residence is outside the frenetic city centre, just beyond Villa Borghese in the upmarket, peaceful Parioli district, full of greenery. The furnishings are handsome and the service deferential. Guests are welcome to use the pool of the Hotel Aldrovandi next door. There is a minimum one-week stay requirement.

Residence Palazzo al Velabro

MAP N4 ▪ Via del Velabro 16 ▪ 06 679 2758 ▪ www.velabro.it ▪ €€
An elegant establishment just around the corner from Piazza Venezia. The setting offers understated luxury, convenience and privacy. Apartments are named after a Roman emperor, god, king or poet. There is also a breakfast room, lounge and fitness area available to guests. Minimum three-day stay.

Residenza Farnese

MAP K4 ▪ Via del Mascherone 59 ▪ 06 6821 0980 ▪ www.residenza farneseroma.it ▪ €€
Housed in a restructured 15th-century palazzo in an area loaded with history, Residenza Farnese offers space and comfort just a stone's throw from the lovely Piazza Farnese and the river.

Santa Chiara

MAP M3 ▪ Via S Chiara 21 ▪ 06 687 2979 ▪ www.albergosantachiara.com ▪ €€
Santa Chiara is situated just behind the Pantheon in three historic buildings and has been run by the same family for 200 years. Rooms as well as three apartments for two to five people are available. The topmost has beamed ceilings, a fireplace and a terrace with an unforgettable view of the huge ancient dome. All rooms are spacious and full of character. Design features include oak headboards, marble-topped desks and travertine bathrooms.

For a key to hotel price categories see p170

General Index

Acknowledgments

Author

Reid Bramblett is an American writer who has lived in Rome, on and off, since childhood. He has contributed to more than half a dozen guidebooks on Italy, and is also the author of *DK Eyewitness Top 10 Travel Guide to Tuscany*.

Jeffrey Kennedy is American by birth, but has lived in Rome for almost 20 years. A graduate of Stanford University, he divides his time between producing, writing and acting. Most recently he has been scripting and producing museum guides in Italy and has featured on the Discovery Channel's *Must See Rome*.

Additional contributor
Ros Belford

Publishing Director Georgina Dee
Publisher Vivien Antwi
Design Director Phil Ormerod
Editorial Ankita Awasthi-Tröger, Michelle Crane, Rachel Fox, Fíodhna Ní Ghríofa, Freddie Marriage, Sally Schafer, Jackie Staddon, Anna Streiffert, Christine Stroyan
Design Richard Czapnik, Marisa Renzullo
Picture Research Phoebe Lowndes, Susie Peachey, Ellen Root, Oran Tarjan
Cartography Simonetta Giori, Mohammad Hassan, Suresh Kumar, Casper Morris
DTP Jason Little, George Nimmo, Azeem Siddiqui, Joanna Stenlake
Production Olivia Jeffries
Factchecker Solveig Steinhardt, Arianna Vatteroni
Proofreader Helena Smith
Indexer Kathryn O'Donoghue
Illustrator Chris Orr & Associates
Revisions Hansa Babra, Parnika Bagla, Alice Fewery, Sumita Khatwani, Daniel Mosseri, Rada Radojicic, Ankita Sharma, Payal Sharotri, Anupama Shukla, Rituraj Singh, Akanksha Siwach, Jackie Staddon, Priyanka Thakur, Vinita Venugopal.

First edition produced by Sargasso Media Ltd, London

Commissioned Photography Demetrio Carrasco, Mike Dunning, John Heseltine, Mockford and Bonetti, Kim Sayer, Stuart West, Rough Guides/Chris Hutty, Rough Guides/James McConnachie, Rough Guides/Roger d'Olivere Mapp, Rough Guides/Natascha Sturny, Kim Sayer, Deborah Soria.

Picture Credits

The publisher would like to thank the following for their kind permission to reproduce their photographs:
[Key: Key: a-above; b-below/bottom; c-centre; f-far; l-left; r-right; t-top]

4Corners: SIME/Luigi Vaccarella 3tr, 160–61; SIME/Giovanni Simeone 4t.

Acqua Madre Hammam: 111tr.

Alamy Images: Agencja Fotograficzna Caro 110bl; Vito Arcomano 43cr, 99cla, 126bc, 131bl, 132bl; Stephen Bisgrove 85clb; CFimages 120tr; Tristan Deschamps 71cra; PE Forsberg 69b; Francesco Gustincich 84tr; Hemis 147cl; imageBROKER 78t; Kadri Kalda 70t; John Kellerman 98tl; Gunter Kirsch 61cl; Lautaro 118br; Elio Lombardo 138ca; Marcin Łukaszewicz 74tr; nagelestock.com 11tl; B. O'Kane 52br; Stefano Paterna 64t; Realy Easy Star/Tullio Valente 79clb; Ed Rooney 152b; Riccardo Sala 66tl; Kumar Sriskandan 109clb; Fabrizio Troiani 69cra; Martyn Vickery 120bl; Steve Vidler 108t; Alvaro German Vilela 113cl; Tim E White 83tr; Zumapress.com/Nurphoto/Luigi Orru 151clb.

Alamy Stock Photo: Hemis 80b

Caffe Sant'Eustachio: 78bl.

Casina Valadier: 123cra.

Cinecitta si Mostra: 67bc.

Corbis: 35crb; Elena Aquila 127tl; C.E. Bolles 64cb; Demotix/eidon photographers 63cl, 85tr; Design Pics/Peter M. Wilson 4cr; dpa/Lars Halbauer 102cla; Chris Hellier 23tl; Duncan James 74bc; Andrea Jemolo 82tl; Bob Krist 58br; Leemage 4clb, 34clb, 37clb, 37b, 46tr; Massimo Listri 29tr; R. Ian Lloyd 89br; Araldo de Luca 29cla, 31t; Mauro Magliani 24cla, 24clb, 25cra; Masterfile/Siephoto 156t; Mario Matassa 74cl; National Geographic Society/Tino Soriano 2tl, 8–9, 28cla; 136t, Vittoriano Rastelli 47tr; Reuters/Max Rossi 67cl; Paul Seheult 31bc; Sylvain Sonnet 51tr; Vatican Museu /Alessandra Benedetti 57t; Roger Wood 65br; Marco Zeppetella 84bl.

Dorling Kindersley: Courtesy of the Capitoline Museum, Rome (Musei Capitolini)/Mike Dunning 30tl, 30cr; Galleria Borghese, Roma, Courtesy of the Ministero della Pubblica Instruzione/John Heseltine 6crb, 10crb; Courtesy of MAXXI/Mockford and Bonetti 5b, 55b, 83bl; Courtesy of Basilica San Clemente/Mockford and Bonetti 62tl; Courtesy of Villa Medici/Mockford and Bonetti 116cra.

Dreamstime.com: 36189341 20–21, 32–3; Adisa 131tr; Ajafoto 79tc; Alexirina27000 24br; Leonid Andronov 51cla; Anitasstudio 4cla, 10tr, 15crb; Azurita 75cl; Yehuda Bernstein 146t; Maurizio Biso 137b; Goran Bogicevic/Boggy 26tl; Ciolca 42–3c, 130cla; Dennis Dolkens 155tr; Donyanedomam 144b; Emicristea 26clb; Nataliya Hora 7tr, 10bl; Ilfede 14t; Inkwelldodo 117clb; Mariusz Jurgielewicz 137tr, 139tl; Marcovarro 68clb; Maurodp75 104–105; Salvatore Micillo 88cla; Monkey Business Images 75tr; Luciano Mortula 1, 7cr; Juan Moyano 89tl; Roland Nagy 115tr; Nicknickko 48t; Thomas

Perkins 79tl; William Perry 11bl, 16bl; Perseomedusa 91bl; Phant 38–9; Photka 143t; Janusz Pieńkowski 133bl; Olimpiu Alexa-pop 92bl; Marek Poplawski 27cr, 125bl; Preisler 10cla, 116bl; Sborisov 18cl, 61tl; Scaliger 17bl, 49clb, 124cra, 148–9; Jozef Sedmak 52cla, 53tl, 97bl, 132t; Olga Shtytlkova 2tr, 44–5; Sjankauskas 82bc; Krzysztof Slusarczyk 48bc; Flavia Soprani 55tl; Dariusz Szwangruber 6cla, 19tc; Tasstock 100tl; Tinamou 34br, 35cl; Tomas1111 97t; Daniel Vincek 135cl; Zerbor 73cr.

Fiaschetteria Beltramme da Cesaretto: 123tl.

Freni e Frizioni: 150cla.

Getty Images: Gonzalo Azumendi 36bl; Bloomberg 134bl; Paolo Cordelli 93cl; Giorgio Cosulich 138br; DEA /G. Nimatallah 56cl; Heritage Images 15bc; Don Klein 82tc; Digitaler Lumpensammler 12–13c; Mondadori 47clb; Alberto Pizzoli 73crb; Stock Montage 65clb; Slow Images 4crb; Universal Images Group/Hulton Fine Art 49tr; UniversalImagesGroup 156br; Guy Vanderelst 4cl; Visions Of Our Land 3tl, 86–7.

Ginger Roma: 122b. **Glasshostaria:** 73t.

Il Pagliaccio: 72bl.

Open Colonna: 141cr.

Peretti Communications: Dorchester Collection/Niall Clutton 140cl.

Polvere di Tempo: 147br.

Rashomon: 128cr.

Ristorante Andrea: 141bl.

Ristorante Antico Arco: 153cla.

Ristorante Da Pancrazio: 67tr.

Ristorante l'Archeologia: 159cl.

Roscioli: 76clb.

Photo Scala, Florence: 11ca, 17tc, 42bl; DeAgostini Picture Library 23cb, 36tr; Fondo Edifici di Culto – Min. dell'Interno 38br; Ministero Beni e Att. Culturali 11cb, 34cra, 40crb, 40bl, 41tr, 41cl, 42cla; White Images 40cla.

ColosseumSuperStock: 38cla; DeAgostini 12cl; Universal Images Group 29bl.

Too Much: 93br.

Volpetti: 129bl.

Cover

Front and spine: **4Corners:** Susanne Kremer
Back: **Getty Images:** Slow Image

Pull out map cover

Map cover: **4Corners:** Susanne Kremer

All other images are: © Dorling Kindersley. For further information see www.dkimages.com.

*As a guide to abbreviations in visitor information blocks: **Adm** = admission charge; **D** = dinner; **L** = lunch.*

Printed and bound in China

First American Edition, 2002
Published in the United States by
DK Publishing, 345 Hudson Street,
New York, New York 10014

Copyright 2002, 2018 © Dorling Kindersley Limited

A Penguin Random House Company

18 19 20 21 10 9 8 7 6 5 4 3 2 1

Reprinted with revisions 2003, 2004, 2006, 2007, 2008, 2010, 2011, 2012, 2013, 2014, 2016 (twice), 2017, 2018

Published in Great Britain by Dorling Kindersley Limited.

A catalog record for this book is available from the Library of Congress.

ISSN 1479-344X
ISBN 978-1-4654-7150-5

SPECIAL EDITIONS OF DK TRAVEL GUIDES

Phrase Book

In an Emergency

Help!	Aiuto!	eye-yoo-toh
Stop!	Ferma!	fair-mah
Call a doctor.	Chiama un medico.	kee-ah-mah oon meh-deekoh
Call an ambulance.	Chiama un' ambulanza.	kee-ah-mah oon am-boo-lan-tsa
Call the police.	Chiama la polizia.	kee-ah-mah lah pol-ee-tsee-ah
Call the fire brigade.	Chiama i pompieri.	kee-ah-mah ee pom-pee-air-ee

Communication Essentials

Yes/No	Sì/No	see/noh
Please	Per favore	pair fah-vor-eh
Thank you	Grazie	grah-tsee-eh
Excuse me	Mi scusi	mee skoo-zee
Hello	Buongiorno	bwon jor-noh
Goodbye	Arrivederci	ah-ree-veh-dair-chee
Good evening	Buona sera	bwon-ah sair-ah
What?	Che?	keh
When?	Quando?	kwan-doh
Why?	Perchè?	pair-keh
Where?	Dove?	doh-veh

Useful Phrases

How are you?	Come sta?	koh-meh stah
Very well, thank you.	Molto bene, grazie.	moll-toh beh-neh grah-tsee-eh
Pleased to meet you.	Piacere di conoscerla.	pee-ah-chair-eh dee coh-noh-shair-lah
That's fine.	Va bene.	va beh-neh
Where is/are...?	Dov'è/ Dove sono...?	dov-eh/ doveh soh-noh
How do I get to...?	Come faccio per arrivare a...?	koh-meh fah-cho pair arri-var-eh a
Do you speak English?	Parla inglese?	par-lah een-gleh-zeh
I don't understand.	Non capisco.	non ka-pee-skoh
I'm sorry.	Mi dispiace.	mee dee-spee-ah-cheh

Shopping

How much does this cost?	Quant'è, per favore?	kwan-teh pair fah-vor-eh
I would like...	Vorrei...	vor-ray
Do you have...?	Avete...?	ah-veh-teh
Do you take credit cards?	Accettate carte di credito?	ah-chet-tah-teh kar-teh dee creh-dee-toh
What time do you open/close?	A che ora apre/ chiude?	a keh ora a-preh/ kee-oo-deh
this one	questo	kweh-stoh
that one	quello	kwell-oh
expensive	caro	kar-oh
cheap	a buon prezzo	ah bwon pret-soh
size (clothes)	la taglia	lah tah-lee-ah
size (shoes)	il numero	eel noo-mair-oh
white	bianco	bee-ang-koh
black	nero	neh-roh
red	rosso	ross-oh
yellow	giallo	jal-loh
green	verde	vair-deh
blue	blu	bloo

Types of Shop

bakery	il forno/ panificio	eel forn-oh/ panee-fee-cho
bank	la banca	lah bang-kah
bookshop	la libreria	lah lee-breh-ree-ah
cake shop	la pasticceria	lah pas-tee-chair-ee-ah
chemist	la farmacia	lah far-mah-chee-ah
delicatessen	la salumeria	lah sah-loo-meh-ree-ah
department store	il grande magazzino	eel gran-deh ma-gad-zeenoh
grocery	alimentari	ah-lee-men-tah-ree
hairdresser	il parrucchiere	eel par-oo-kee-air-eh
ice-cream parlour	la gelateria	lah jel-lah-tair-ree-ah
market	il mercato	eel mair-kah-toh
newsstand	l'edicola	leh-dee-koh-lah
post office	l'ufficio postale	loo-fee-choh pos-tah-leh
supermarket	il supermercato	eel su-pair-mair-kah-toh
tobacconist	il tabaccaio	eel tah-bak-eye-oh
travel agency	l'agenzia di viaggi	lah-jen-tsee-ah dee vee-ad-jee

Sightseeing

art gallery	la pinacoteca	lah peena-koh-teh-kah
bus stop	la fermata dell'autobus	lah fair-mah-tah dell-ow-toh-booss
church	la chiesa/ basilica	lah kee-eh-zah bah-seel-ee-kah
closed for holidays	chiuso per ferie	kee-oo-zoh pair fair-ee-eh
garden	il giardino	eel jar-dee-no
museum	il museo	eel moo-zeh-oh
railway station	la stazione	lah stah-tsee-oh-neh
tourist information	l'ufficio del turismo	loo-fee-choh del too-ree-smoh

Staying in a Hotel

Do you have any vacant rooms?	Avete camere libere?	ah-veh-teh kah-mair-eh lee-bair-eh
double room	una camera doppia	oona kah-mairah doh-pee-ah
with double bed	con letto matrimoniale	kon let-toh mah-tree-moh-nee-ah-leh
a room with bath/ shower	una camera con bagno/ doccia	oona ka-mair-ah kon ban-yoh/ dot-chah
twin room	una camera con due letti	oona kah-mairah kon doo-eh let-tee

| single room | una camera singola | oona kah-mairah sing-goh-lah |
| I have a reservation. | Ho fatto una prenotazione. | oh fat-toh oona preh-noh-tah-tsee-oh-neh |

Eating Out

Have you got a table for…?	Avete un tavolo per…?	ah-veh-teh oon tah-voh-loh pair
I'd like to reserve a table.	Vorrei prenotare un tavolo.	vor-ray pre-noh-ta-reh oon tah-voh-loh
breakfast	colazione	koh-lah-tsee-oh-neh
lunch	pranzo	pran-tsoh
dinner	cena	cheh-nah
the bill	il conto	eel kon-toh
waitress	cameriera	kah-mair-ee-air-ah
waiter	cameriere	kah-mair-ee-air-eh
fixed-price menu	il menù a prezzo fisso	eel meh-noo ah pret-soh fee-soh
dish of the day	piatto del giorno	pee-ah-toh dell jor-no
starter	l'antipasto	lan-tee-pass-toh
first course	il primo	eel pree-moh
main course	il secondo	eel seh-kon-doh
vegetables	i contorni	ee kon-tor-noh
dessert	il dolce	eel doll-cheh
wine list	la lista dei vini	lah lee-stah day vee-nee
glass	il bicchiere	eel bee-kee-air ch
bottle	la bottiglia	lah bot-teel-yah
knife	il coltello	eel kol-tell-oh
fork	la forchetta	lah for-ket-tah
spoon	il cucchiaio	eel koo-kee-eye-oh

Menu Decoder

l'acqua minerale	lah-kwah meenair-ah-leh	mineral water
gassata/ naturale	gah-zah-tah/ nah-too-rah-leh	fizzy/ still
agnello	ah-niell-oh	lamb
aglio	al-ee-oh	garlic
al forno	al for-noh	baked
alla griglia	ah-lah greel-yah	grilled
la birra	lah beer-rah	beer
la bistecca	lah bee-stek-ah	steak
il burro	eel boor-oh	butter
il caffè	eel kah-feh	coffee
la carne	la kar-neh	meat
carne di maiale	kar-neh dee mah-yah-leh	pork
la cipolla	la chip-oh-lah	onion
il formaggio	eel for-mad-joh	cheese
le fragole	leh frah-goh-leh	strawberries
il fritto misto	eel free-toh mees-toh	mixed fried seafood
la frutta	la froot-tah	fruit
frutti di mare	froo-tee dee mah-reh	seafood
i funghi	ee foon-ghee	mushrooms
i gamberi	ee gam-bair-ee	prawns
il gelato	eel jel-lah-toh	ice cream

l'insalata	leen-sah-lah-tah	salad
il latte	eel laht-teh	milk
il manzo	eel man-tsoh	beef
l'olio	loh-lee-oh	oil
il pane	eel pah-neh	bread
le patate	leh pah-tah-teh	potatoes
le patatine fritte	leh pah-tah-teen-eh free-teh	chips
il pepe	eel peh-peh	pepper
il pesce	eel pesh-eh	fish
il pollo	eel poll-oh	chicken
il pomodoro	eel poh-moh-dor-oh	tomato
il prosciutto cotto/ crudo	eel pro-shoo-toh kot-toh/ kroo-doh	ham cooked/ cured
il riso	eel ree-zoh	rice
il sale	eel sah-leh	salt
la salsiccia	lah sal-see-chah	sausage
il succo d'arancia	eel soo-koh dah-ran-chah	orange juice
il tè	eel teh	tea
la torta	lah tor-tah	cake/tart
l'uovo	loo-oh-voh	egg
vino bianco	vee-noh bee-ang-koh	white wine
vino rosso	vee-noh ross-oh	red wine
lo zucchero	loh zoo-kair-oh	sugar
la zuppa	lah tsoo-pah	soup

Time

one minute	un minuto	oon mee-noo-toh
one hour	un'ora	oon or-ah
a day	un giorno	oon jor-noh
Monday	lunedì	loo-neh-dee
Tuesday	martedì	mar-teh-dee
Wednesday	mercoledì	mair-koh-leh-dee
Thursday	giovedì	joh-veh-dee
Friday	venerdì	ven-air-dee
Saturday	sabato	sah-bah-toh
Sunday	domenica	doh-meh-nee-ka

Numbers

1	uno	oo-noh
2	due	doo-eh
3	tre	treh
4	quattro	kwat-roh
5	cinque	ching-kweh
6	sei	say-ee
7	sette	set-teh
8	otto	ot-toh
9	nove	noh-veh
10	dieci	dee-eh-chee
11	undici	oon-dee-chee
17	diciassette	dee-chah-set-teh
18	diciotto	dee-chot-toh
19	diciannove	dee-cha-noh-veh
20	venti	ven-tee
30	trenta	tren-tah
40	quaranta	kwah-ran-tah
50	cinquanta	ching-kwan-tah
60	sessanta	sess-an-tah
70	settanta	set-tan-tah
80	ottanta	ot-tan-tah
90	novanta	noh-van-tah
100	cento	chen-toh
1,000	mille	mee-leh

Street Index